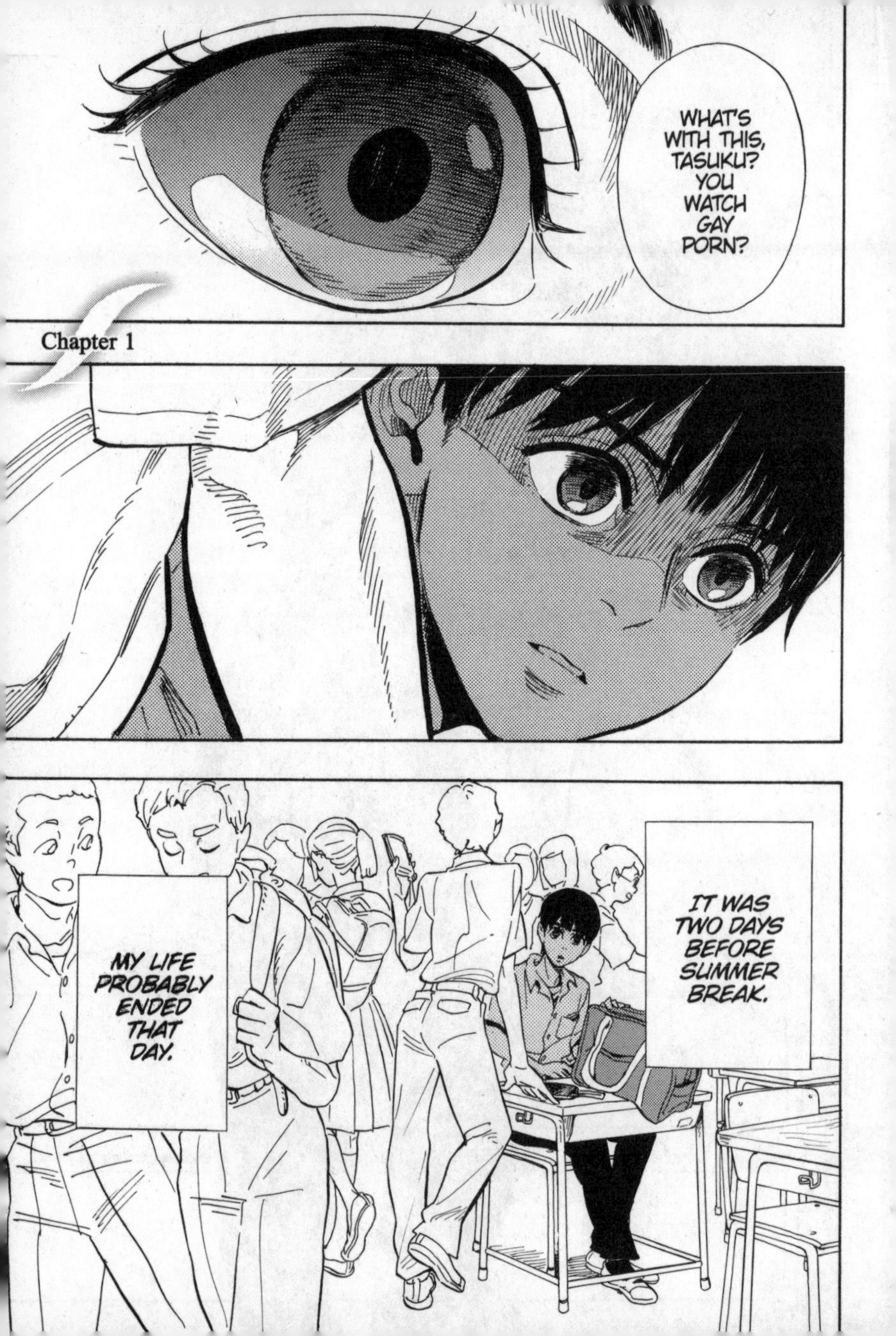
WHAT'S WITH THIS, TASUKU? YOU WATCH GAY PORN?
Chapter 1
IT WAS TWO DAYS BEFORE SUMMER BREAK.
MY LIFE PROBABLY ENDED THAT DAY.

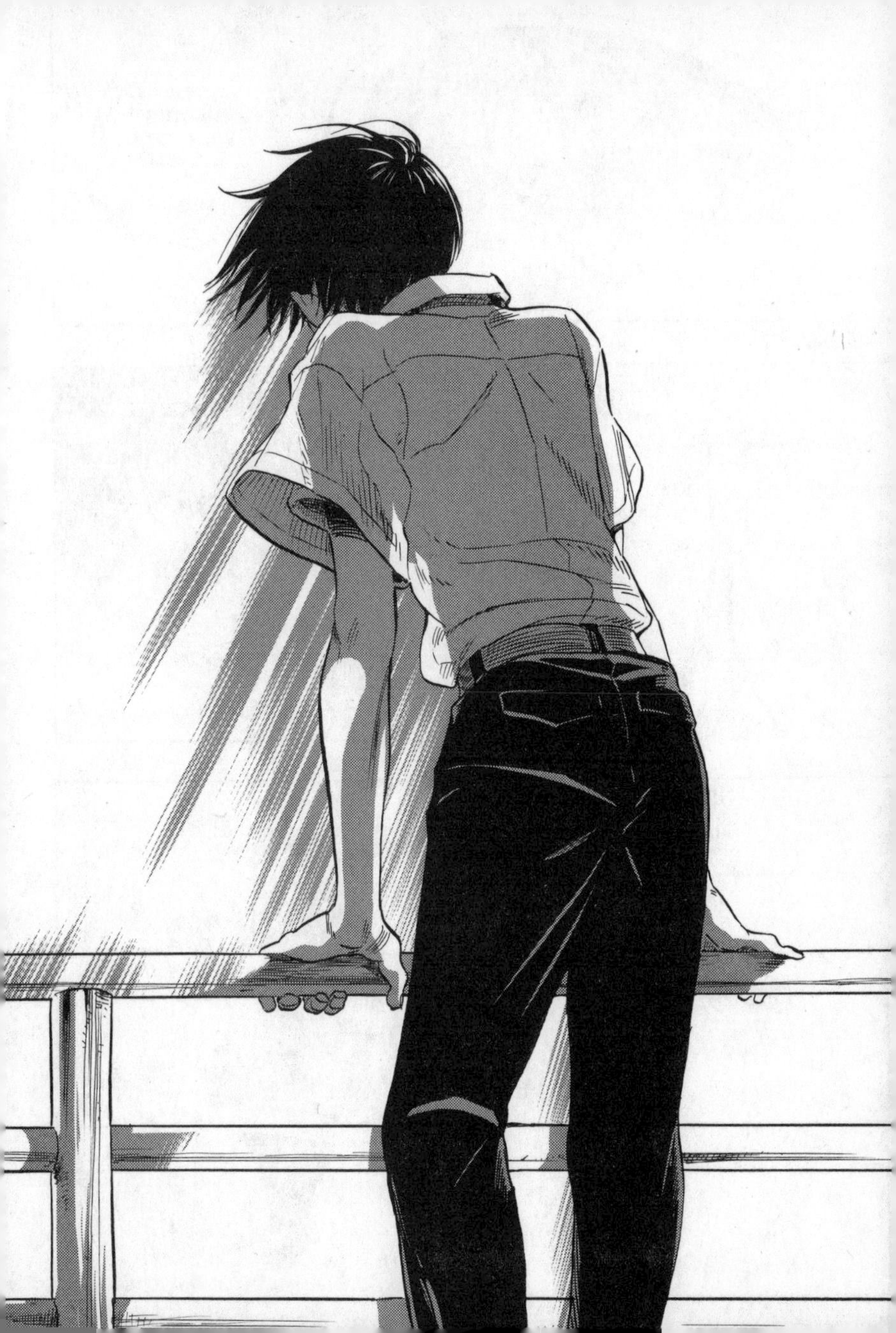

Chapter 1

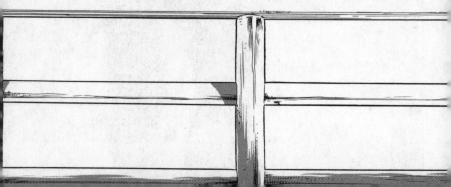

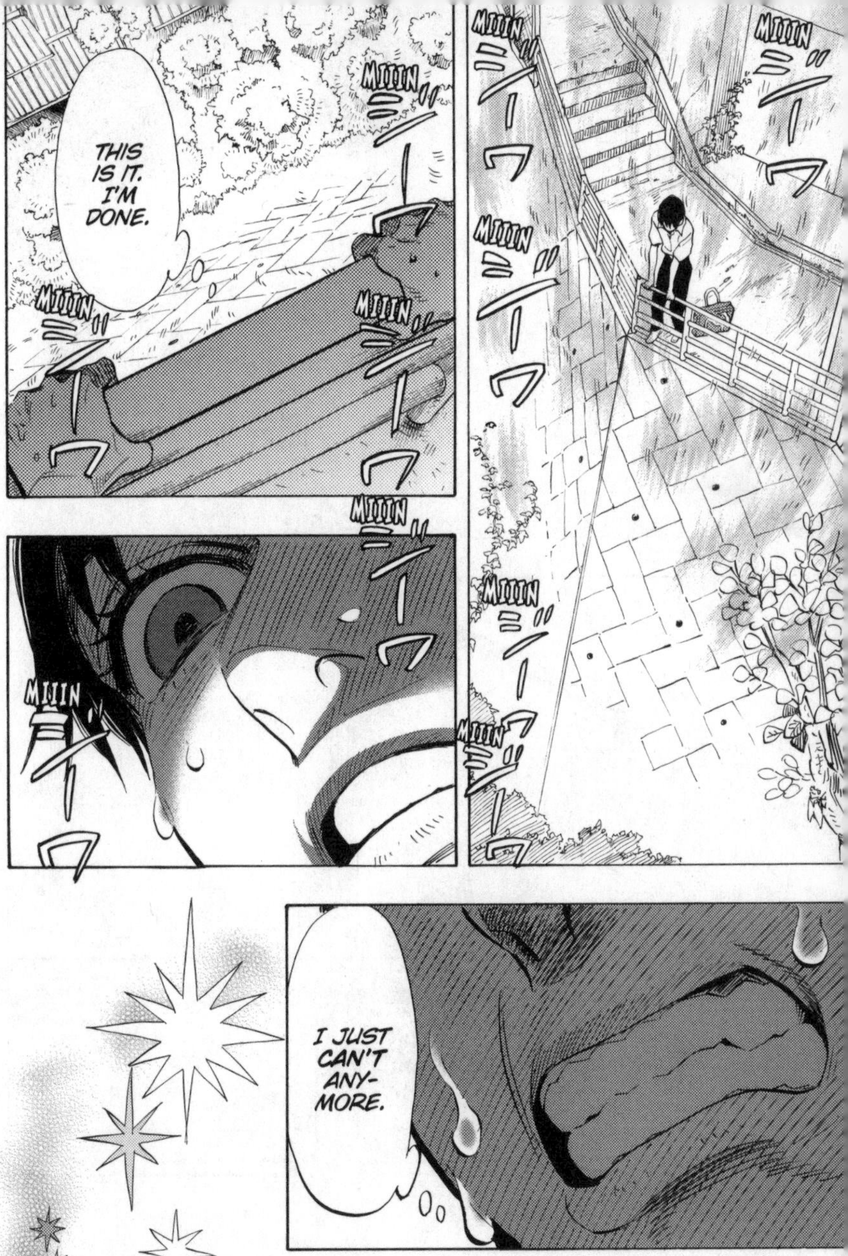
MIIIN
MIIIN
MIIIN
MIIIN
MIIIN
MIIIN
THIS IS IT. I'M DONE.
MIIIN
MIIIN
MIIIN
MIIIN
I JUST CAN'T ANYMORE.

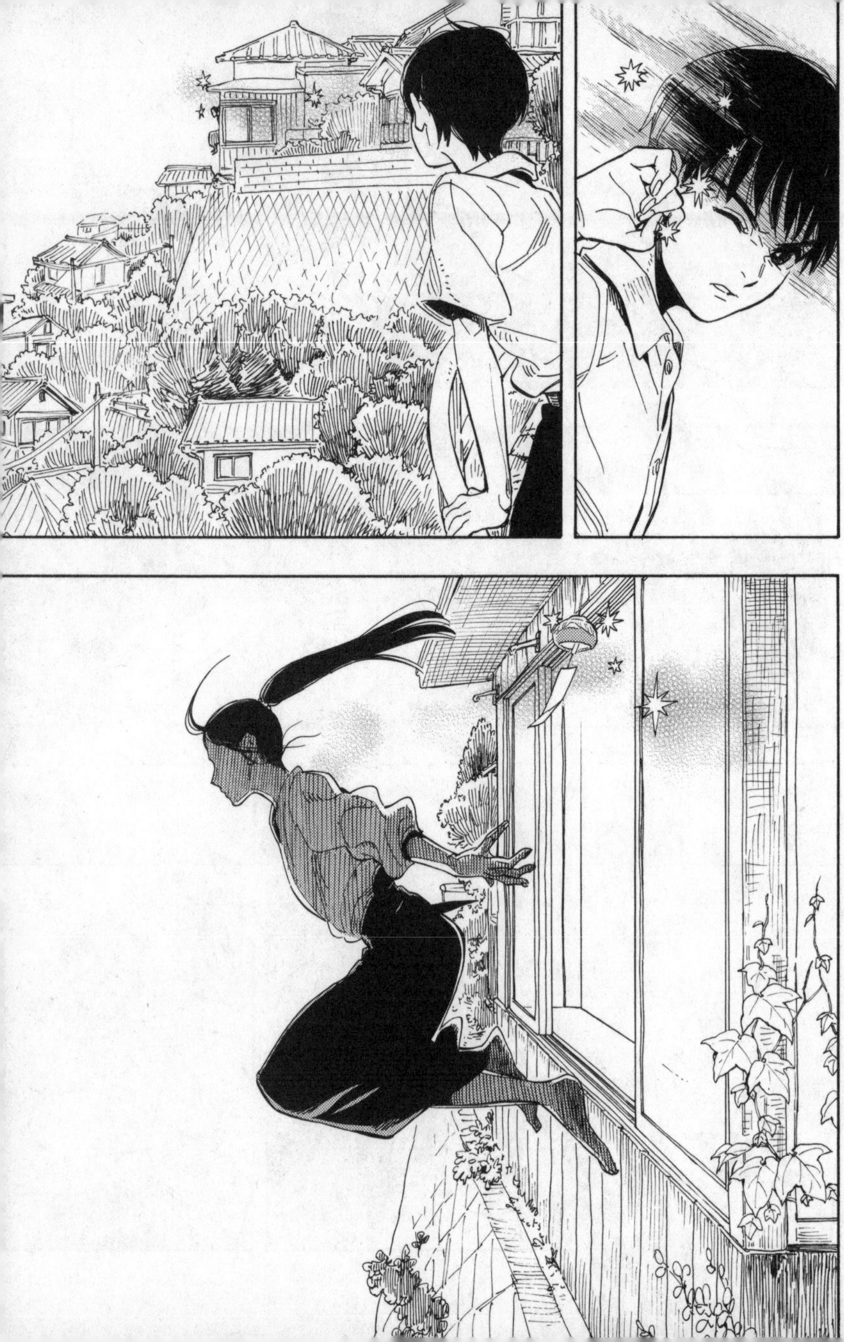

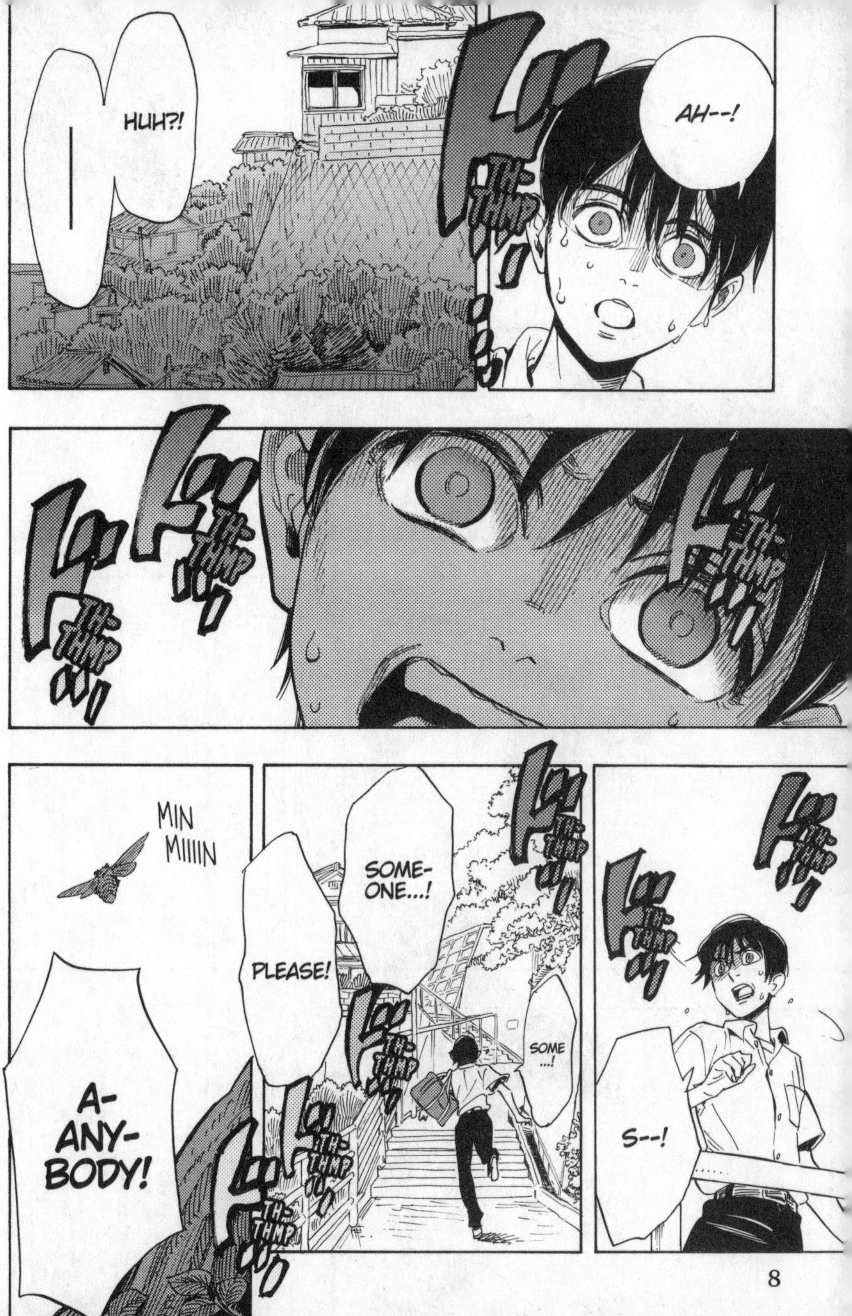
AH--!
TH-THMP
HUH?!
TH-THMP
TH-THMP
TH-THMP
TH-THMP
S--!
TH-THMP
SOME-ONE...!
PLEASE!
SOME...!
TH-THMP
MIN MIIIIN
A-ANY-BODY!

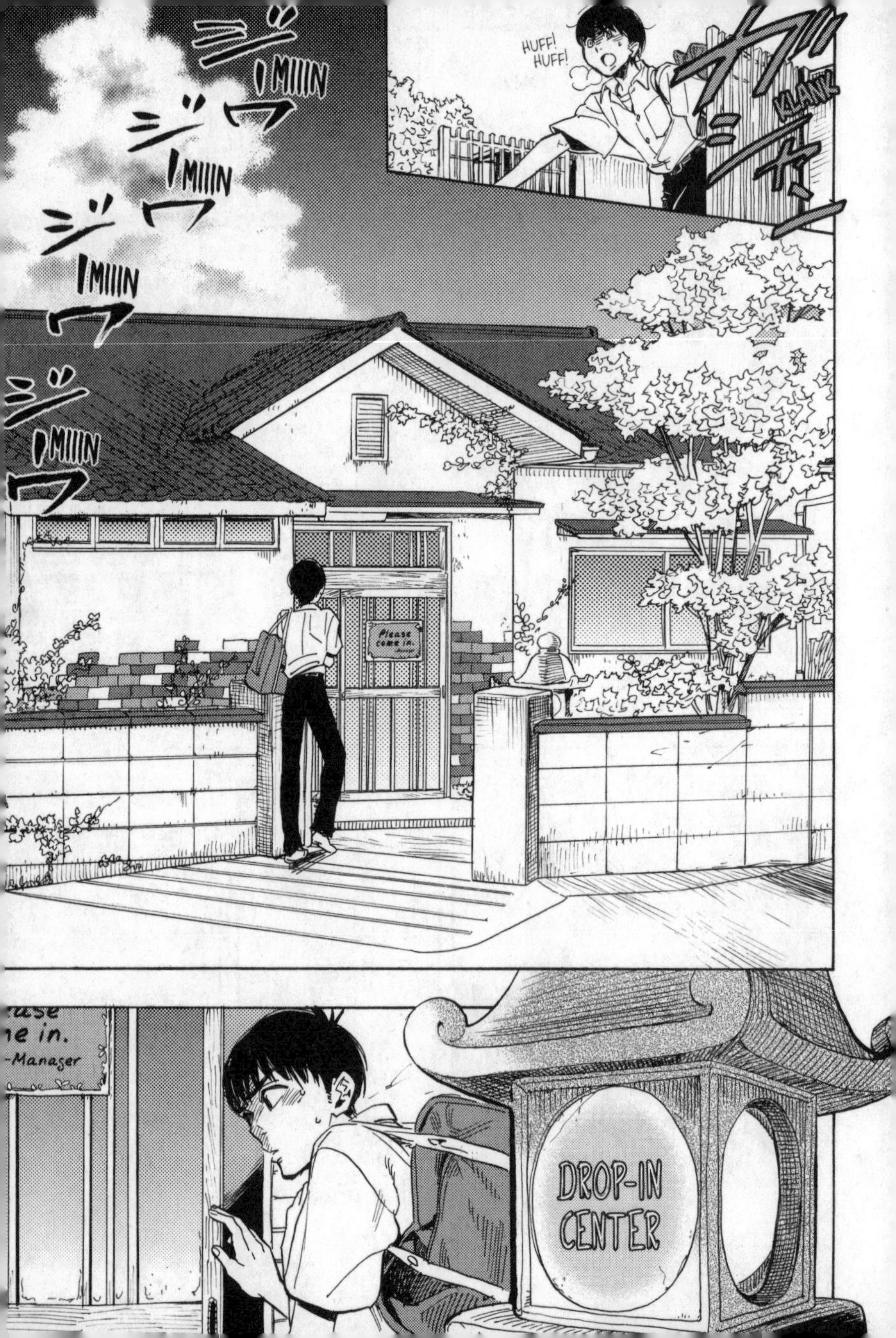
HUFF! HUFF!
KLANK
MIIIN
MIIIN
MIIIN
MIIIN
Please come in. -Manager
DROP-IN CENTER

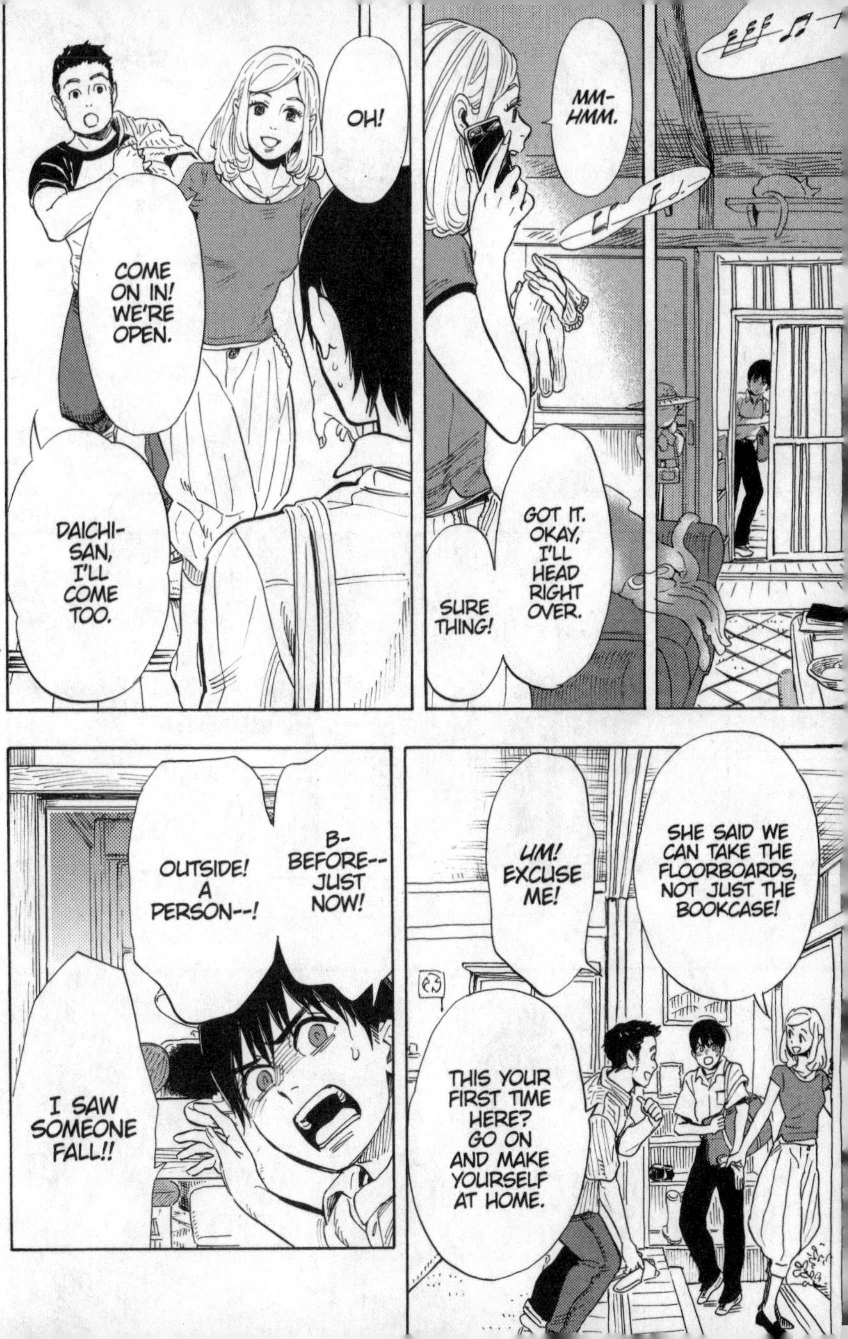
MM-HMM.
GOT IT. OKAY, I'LL HEAD RIGHT OVER.
SURE THING!
OH!
COME ON IN! WE'RE OPEN.
DAICHI-SAN, I'LL COME TOO.
SHE SAID WE CAN TAKE THE FLOORBOARDS, NOT JUST THE BOOKCASE!
UM! EXCUSE ME!
THIS YOUR FIRST TIME HERE? GO ON AND MAKE YOURSELF AT HOME.
B- BEFORE-- JUST NOW!
OUTSIDE! A PERSON--!
I SAW SOMEONE FALL!!

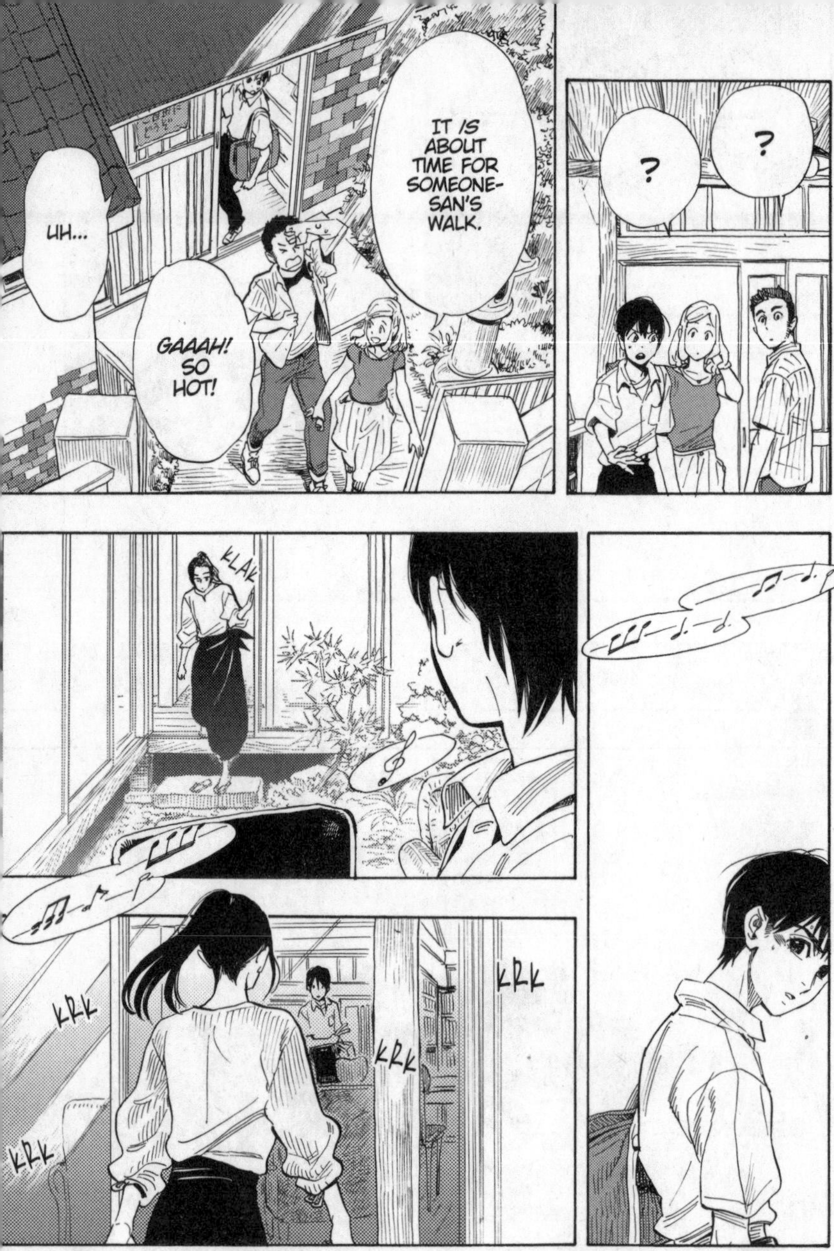
?
?
IT IS ABOUT TIME FOR SOMEONE-SAN'S WALK.
GAAAH! SO HOT!
UH...
KLAK
KRK
KRK
KRK
KRK

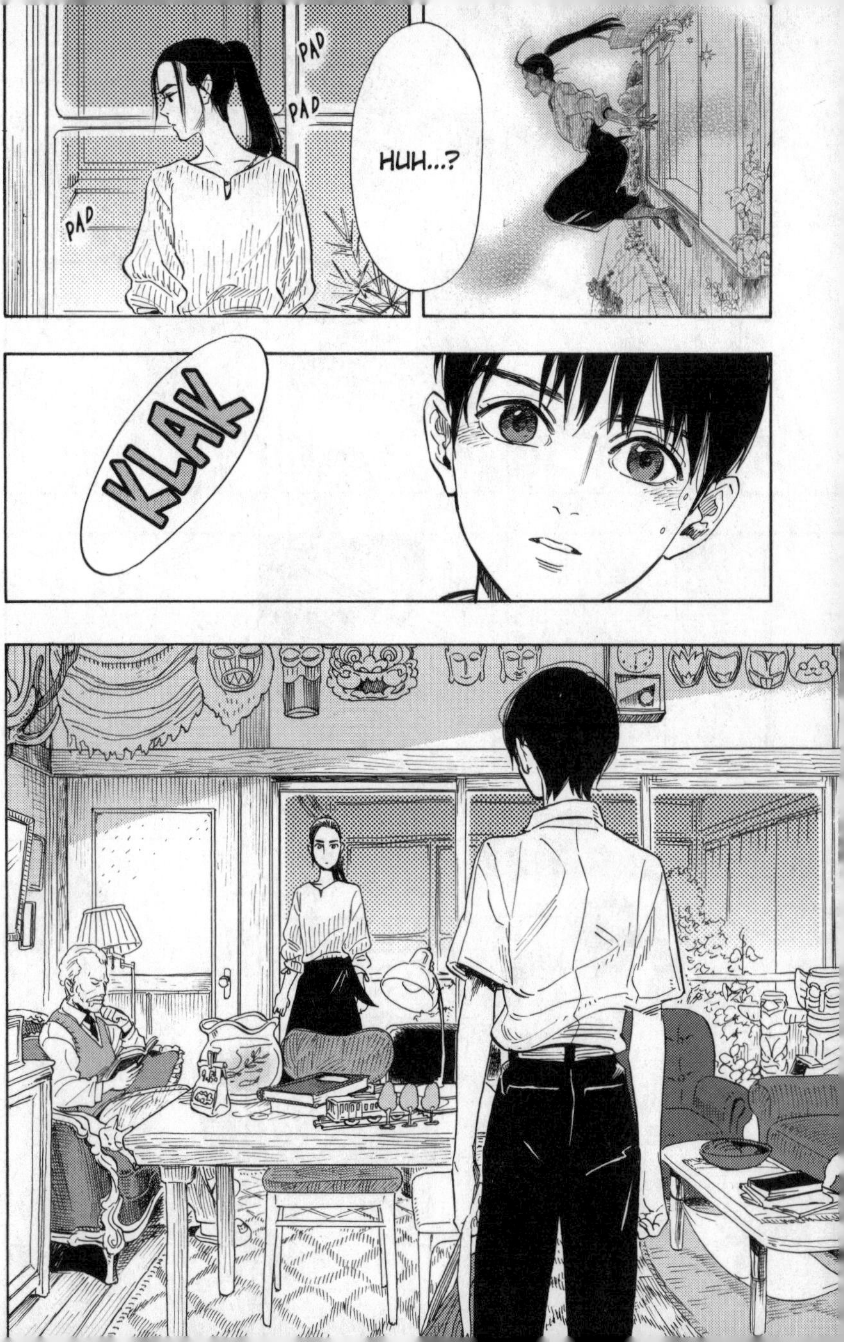
HUH...?
PAD
PAD
PAD
KLAK

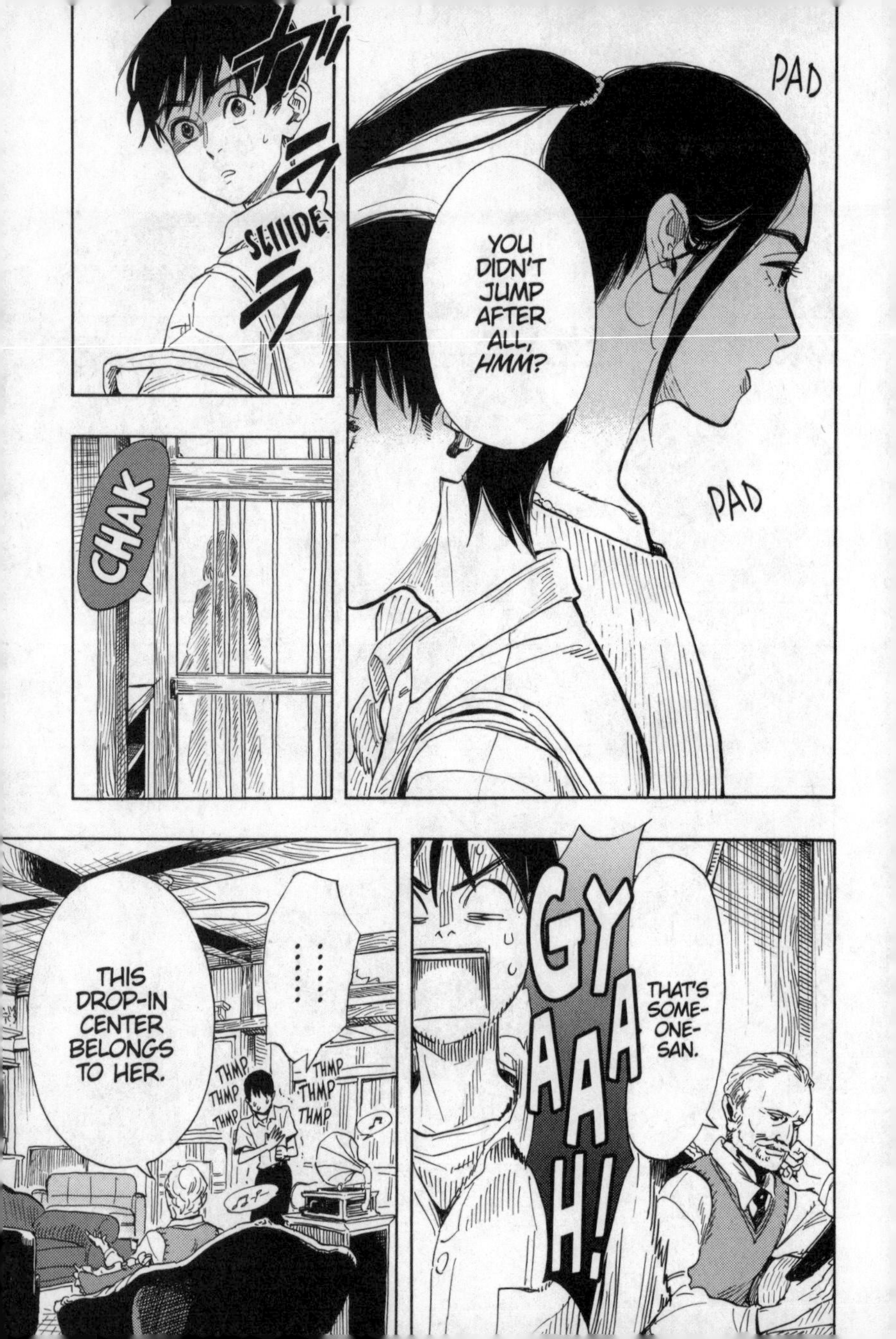
PAD
YOU DIDN'T JUMP AFTER ALL, HMM?
PAD
SLIIIDE
CHAK
GYAAAH!
THAT'S SOME-ONE-SAN.
......
THIS DROP-IN CENTER BELONGS TO HER.
THMP THMP THMP
THMP THMP THMP

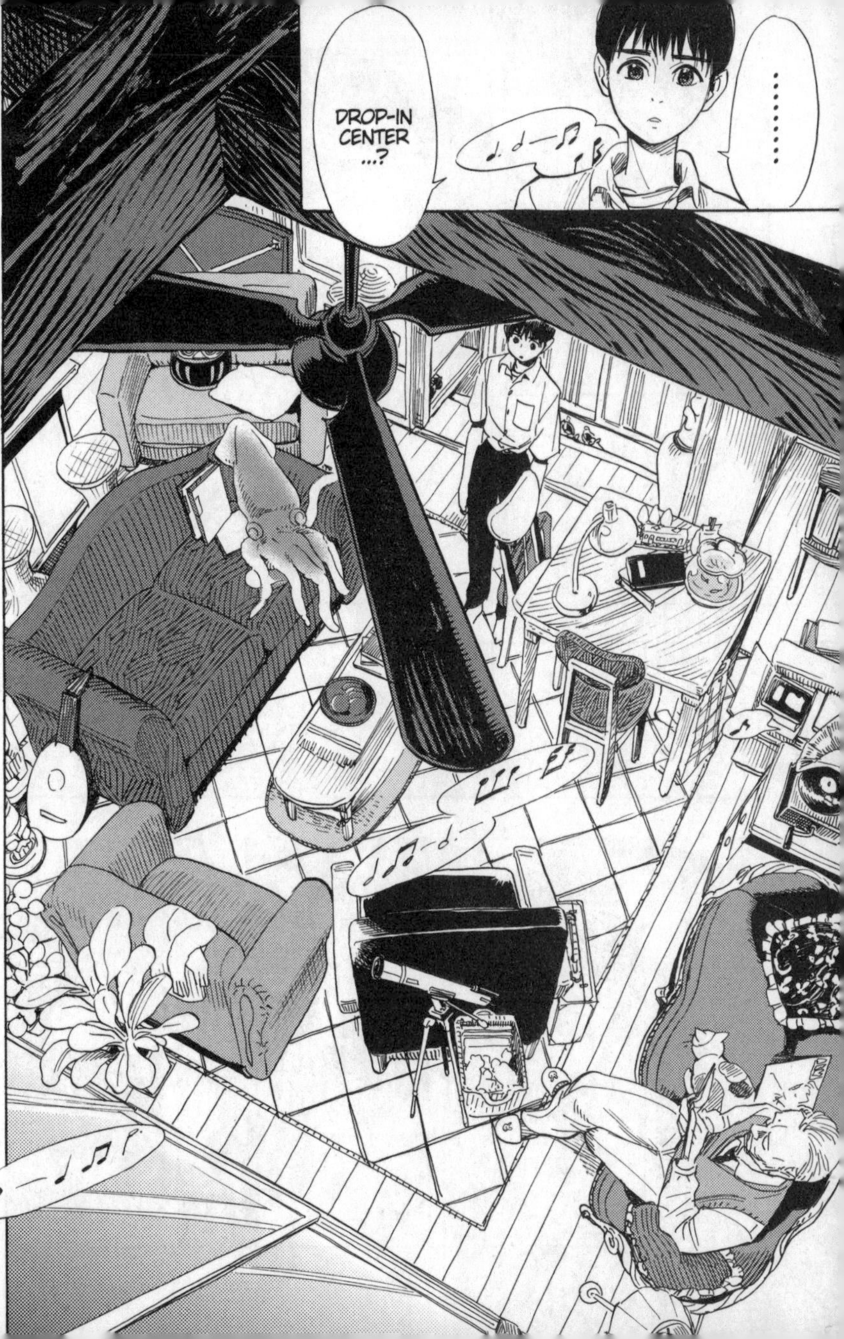
……
DROP-IN CENTER …?

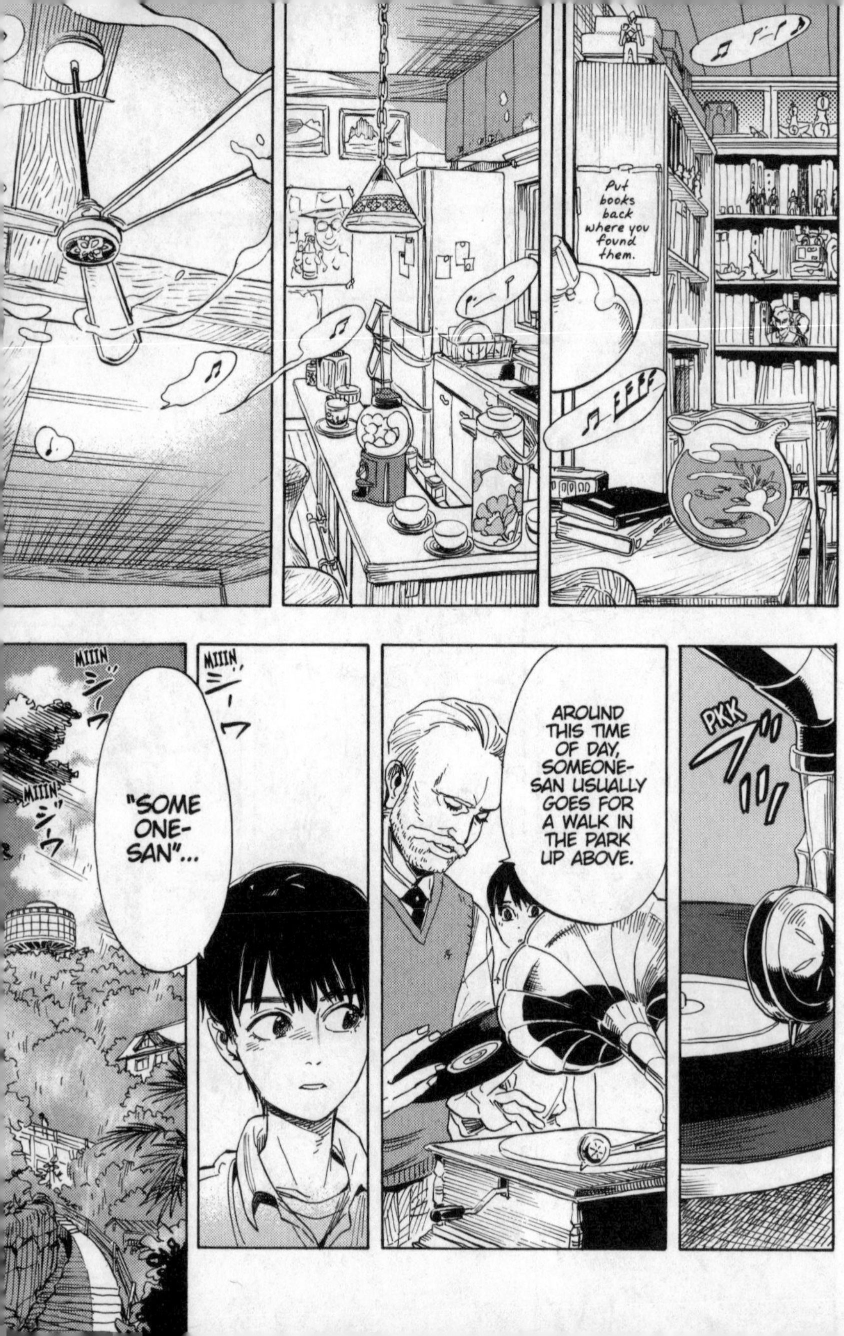

Put books back where you found them.
PKK
AROUND THIS TIME OF DAY, SOMEONE-SAN USUALLY GOES FOR A WALK IN THE PARK UP ABOVE.
MIIIN
"SOME ONE-SAN"...
MIIIN
MIIIN

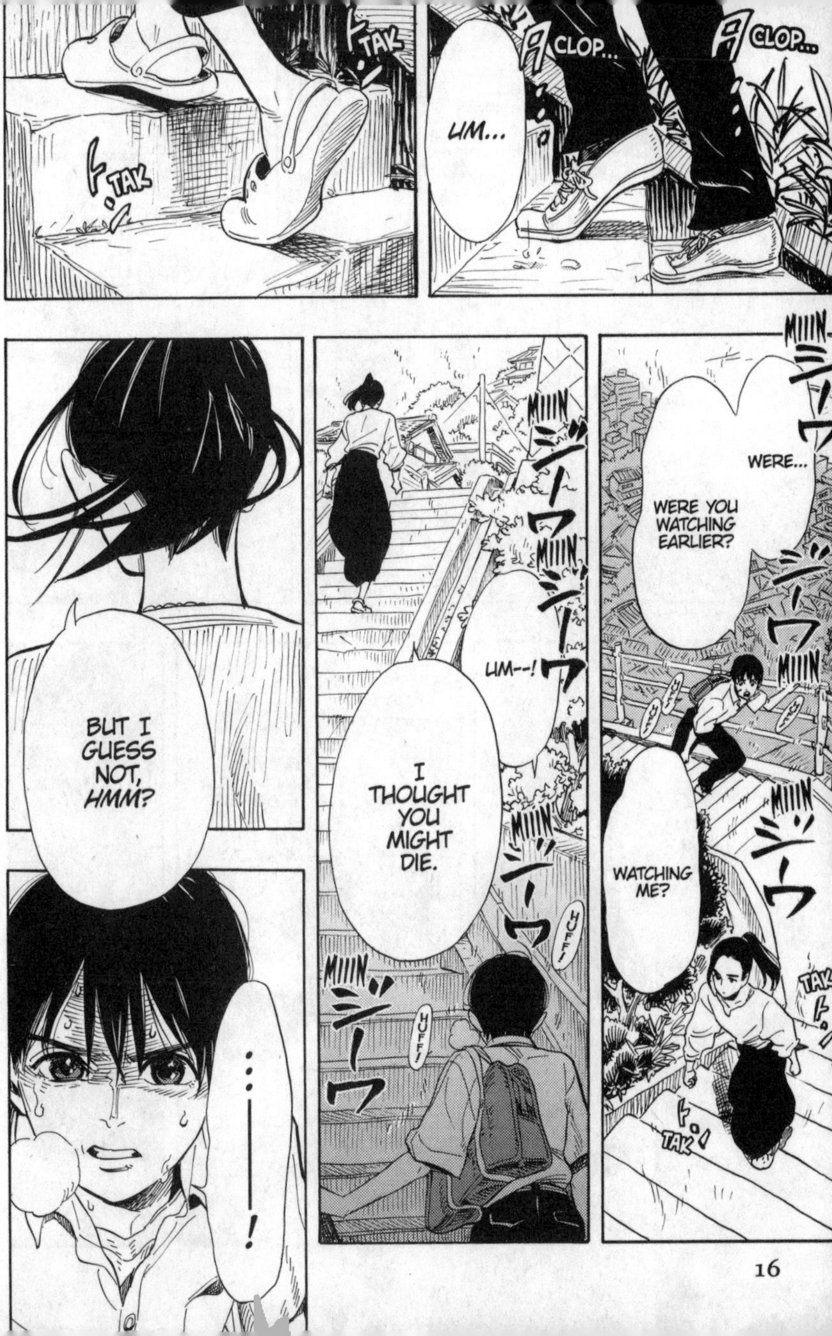
CLOP...
CLOP...
UM...
TAK
TAK
MIIIN
WERE...
WERE YOU WATCHING EARLIER?
WATCHING ME?
TAK
TAK
UM--!
I THOUGHT YOU MIGHT DIE.
HUFF!
HUFF!
BUT I GUESS NOT, HMM?
...——!

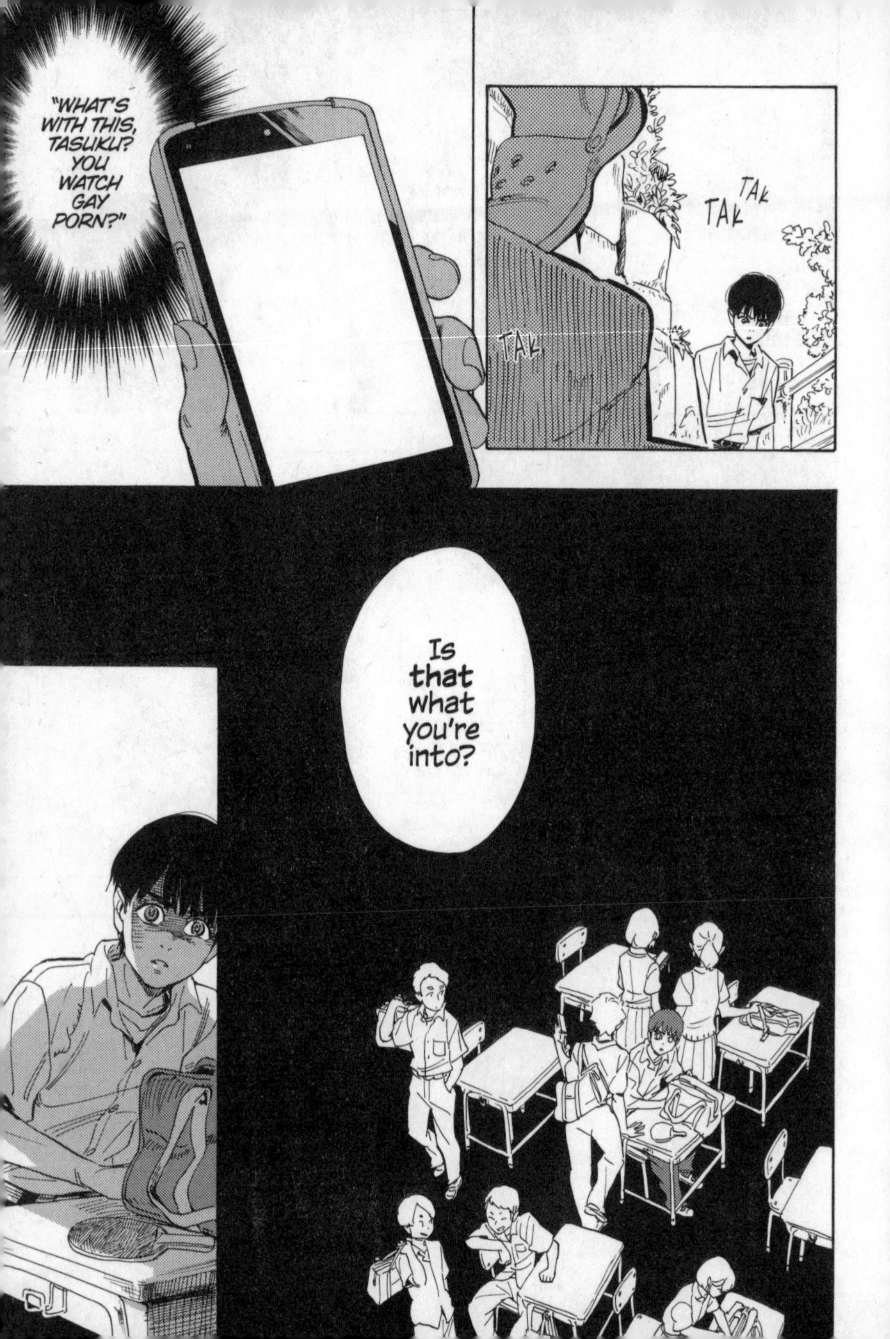
TAK TAK
TAK
"WHAT'S WITH THIS, TASUKU? YOU WATCH GAY PORN?"
Is that what you're into?

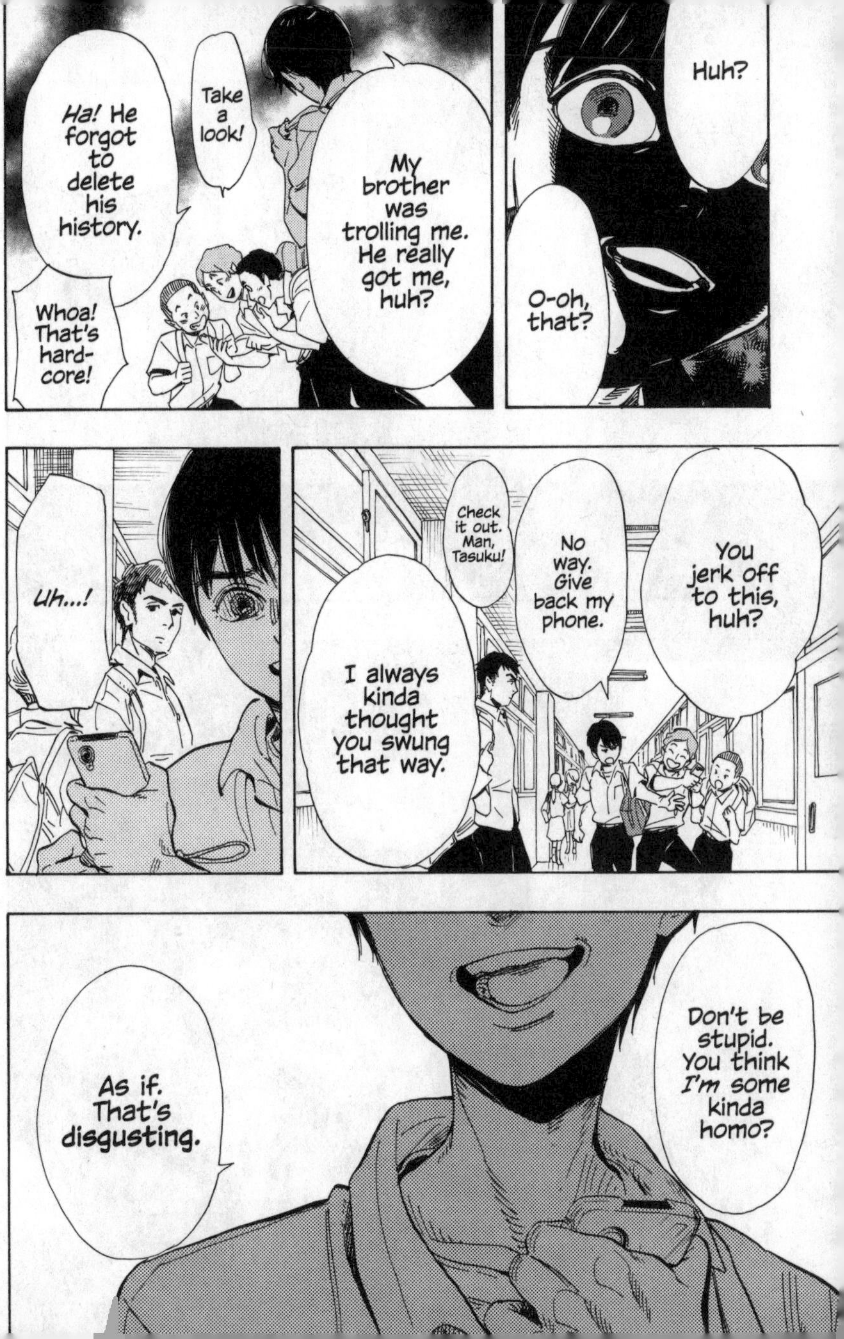
Huh?
O-oh, that?
My brother was trolling me. He really got me, huh?
Take a look!
Ha! He forgot to delete his history.
Whoa! That's hard-core!
You jerk off to this, huh?
No way. Give back my phone.
Check it out. Man, Tasuku!
I always kinda thought you swung that way.
Uh...!
Don't be stupid. You think *I'm* some kinda homo?
As if. That's disgusting.

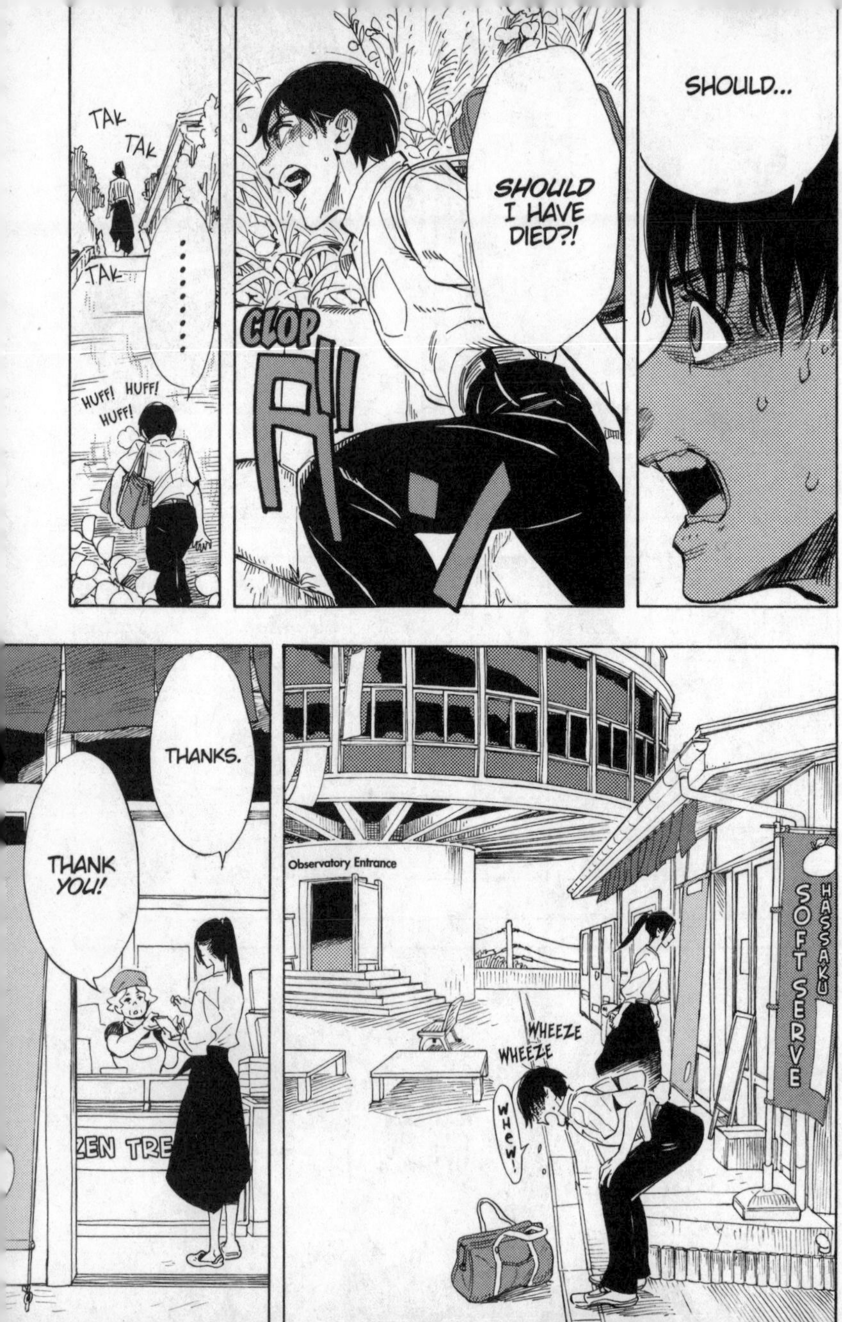
SHOULD...
SHOULD I HAVE DIED?!
CLOP
TAK
TAK
TAK
......
HUFF! HUFF!
HUFF!
Observatory Entrance
HASSAKU
SOFT SERVE
WHEEZE
WHEEZE
WHEW!
THANKS.
THANK YOU!
ZEN TRE

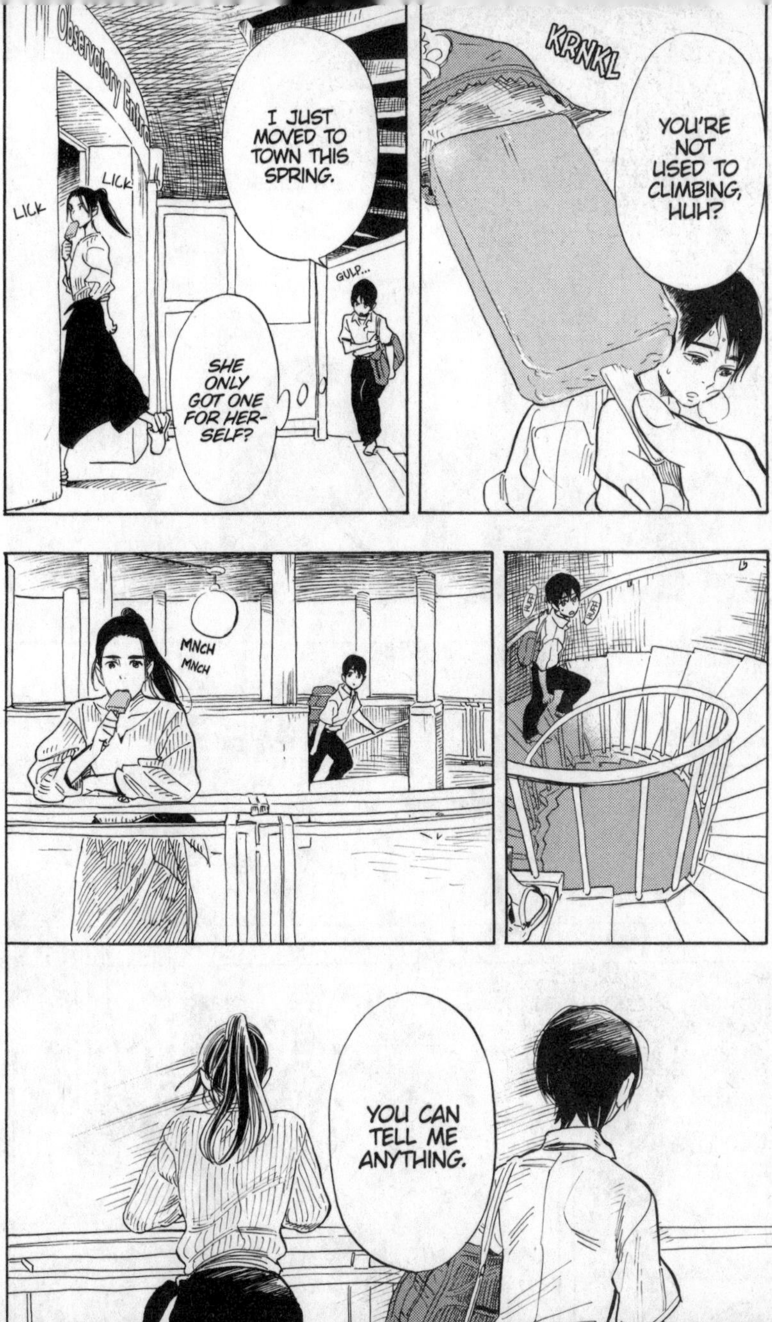
KRNKL
YOU'RE NOT USED TO CLIMBING, HUH?
I JUST MOVED TO TOWN THIS SPRING.
Observatory Entra
GULP...
SHE ONLY GOT ONE FOR HER-SELF?
LICK
LICK
MNCH MNCH
YOU CAN TELL ME ANYTHING.

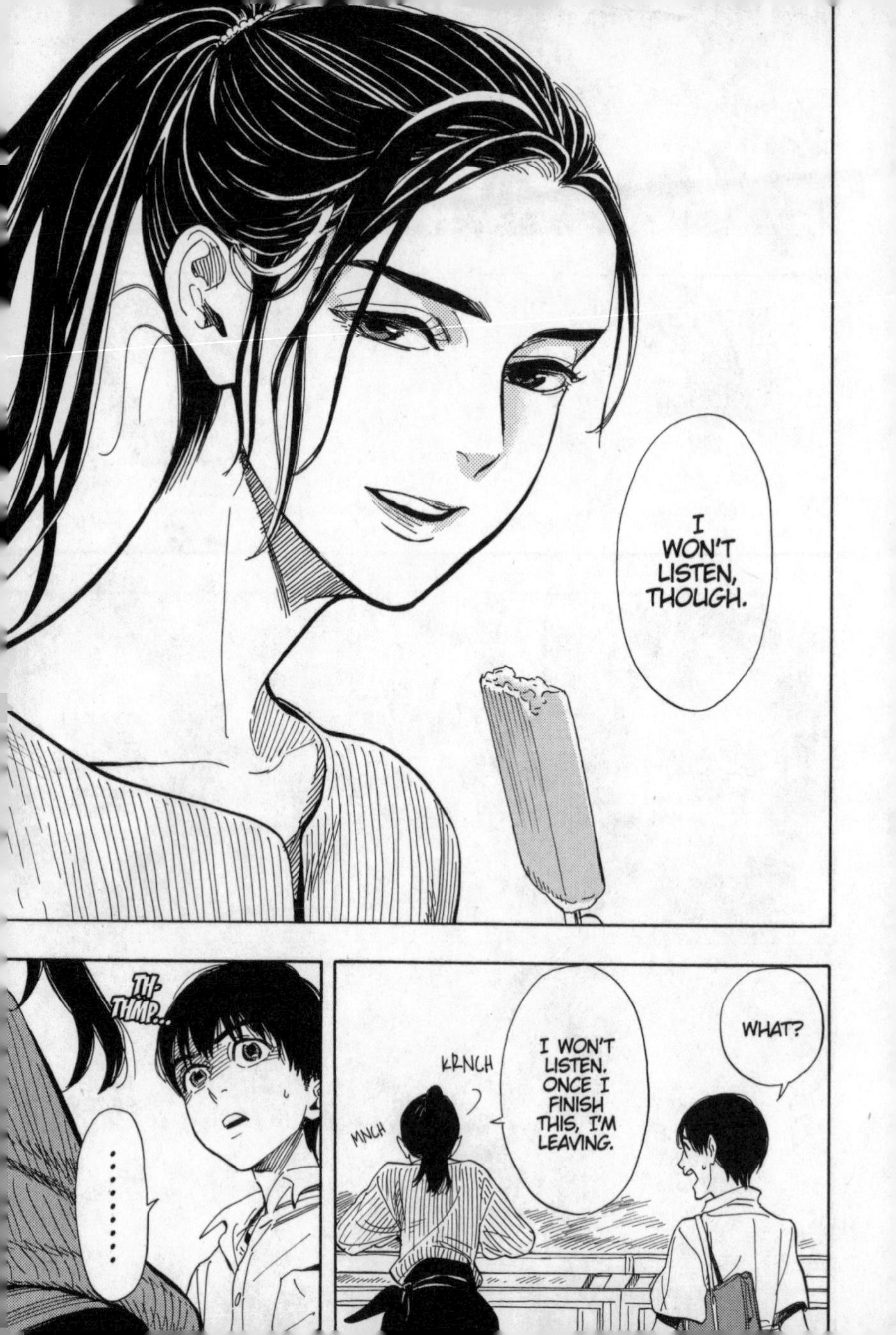
I WON'T LISTEN, THOUGH.
WHAT?
I WON'T LISTEN. ONCE I FINISH THIS, I'M LEAVING.
KRNCH
MNCH
TH-THMP...
......

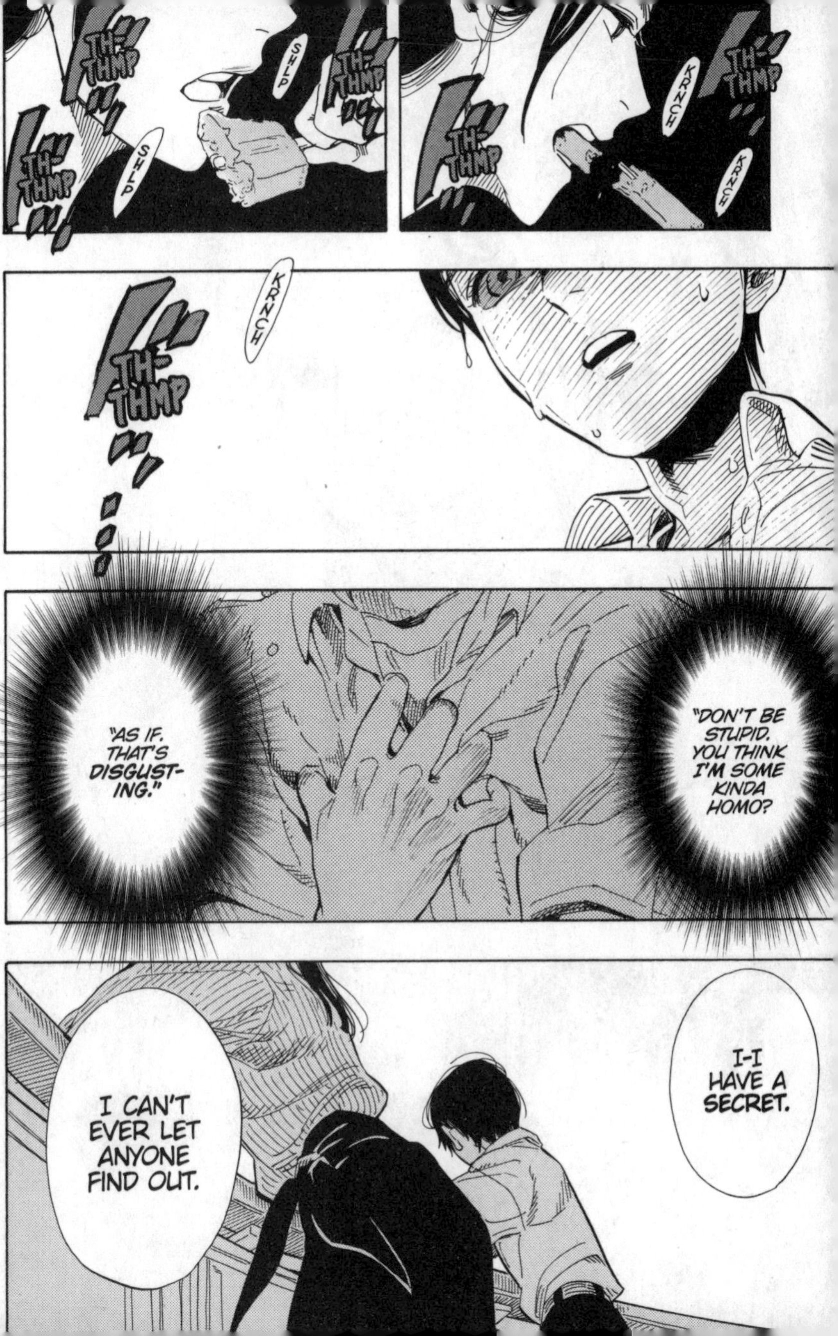
TH-THMP
KRNCH
KRNCH
TH-THMP
TH-THMP
SHLP
TH-THMP
SHLP
TH-THMP
KRNCH
TH-THMP
"DON'T BE STUPID. YOU THINK I'M SOME KINDA HOMO?
"AS IF. THAT'S DISGUSTING."
I-I HAVE A SECRET.
I CAN'T EVER LET ANYONE FIND OUT.

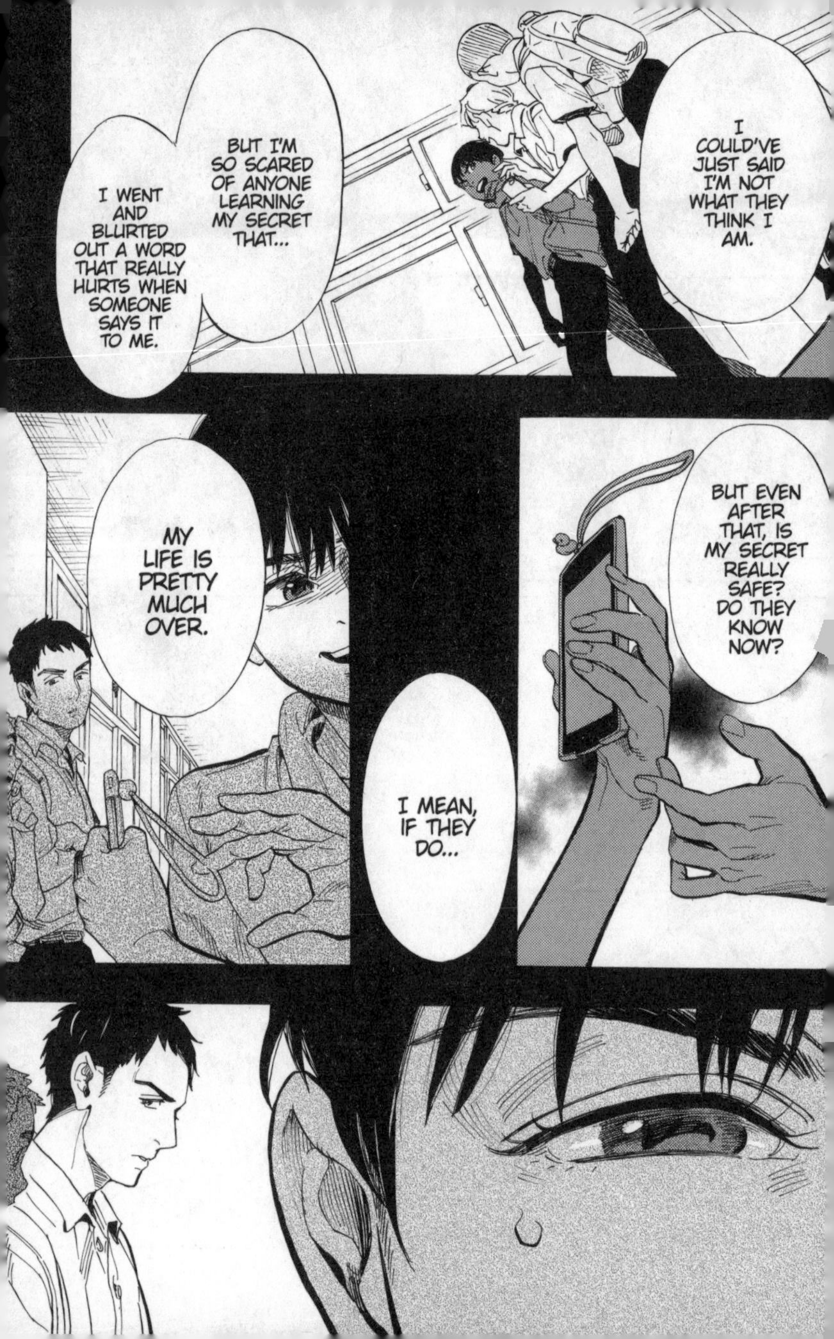
I COULD'VE JUST SAID I'M NOT WHAT THEY THINK I AM.
BUT I'M SO SCARED OF ANYONE LEARNING MY SECRET THAT...
I WENT AND BLURTED OUT A WORD THAT REALLY HURTS WHEN SOMEONE SAYS IT TO ME.
BUT EVEN AFTER THAT, IS MY SECRET REALLY SAFE? DO THEY KNOW NOW?
I MEAN, IF THEY DO...
MY LIFE IS PRETTY MUCH OVER.

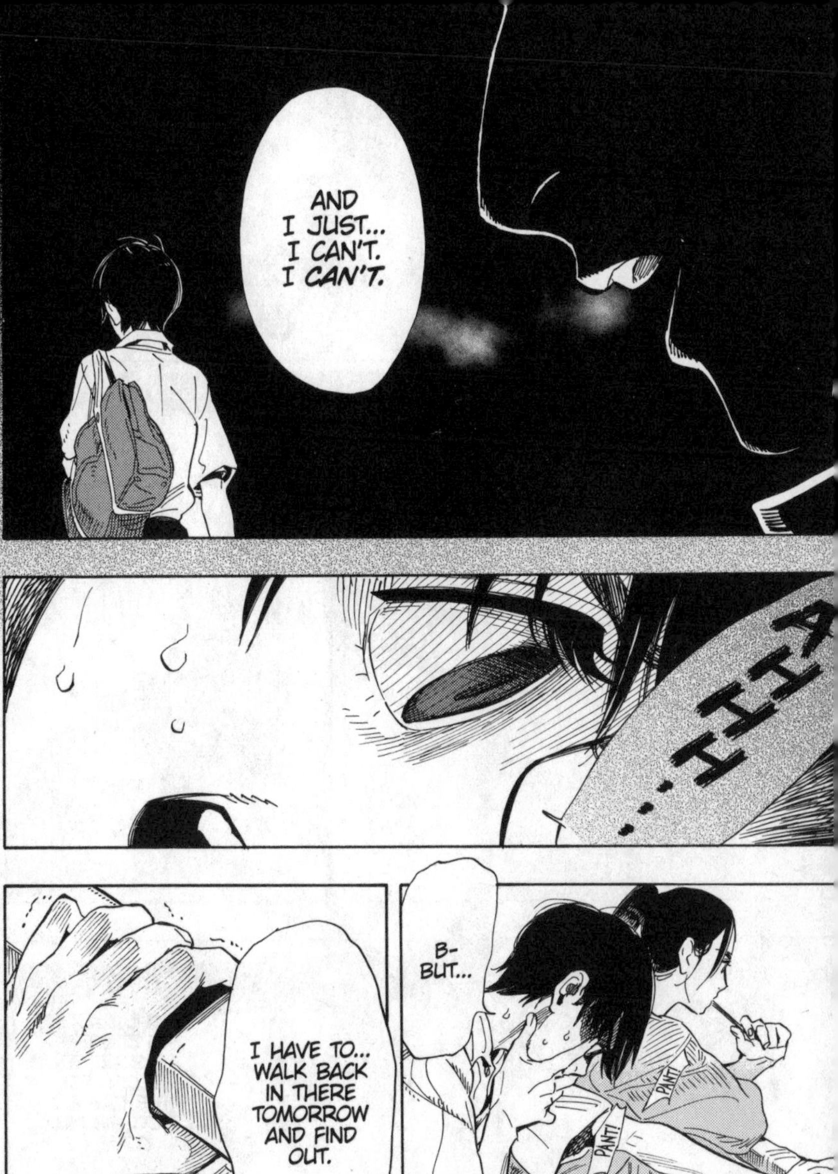
AND I JUST... I CAN'T. I CAN'T.
AHHH...
B-BUT...
PANT!
PANT!
I HAVE TO... WALK BACK IN THERE TOMORROW AND FIND OUT.

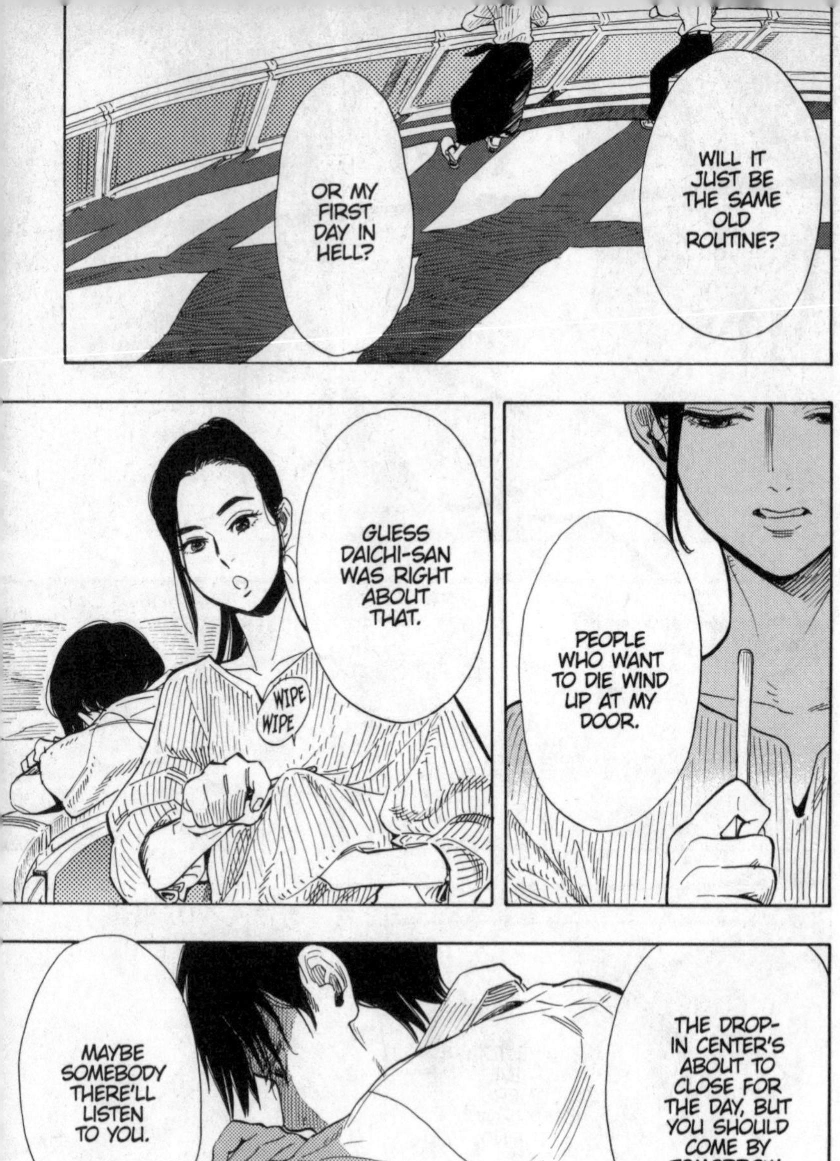
WILL IT JUST BE THE SAME OLD ROUTINE?
OR MY FIRST DAY IN HELL?
PEOPLE WHO WANT TO DIE WIND UP AT MY DOOR.
GUESS DAICHI-SAN WAS RIGHT ABOUT THAT.
WIPE WIPE
THE DROP-IN CENTER'S ABOUT TO CLOSE FOR THE DAY, BUT YOU SHOULD COME BY TOMORROW.
MAYBE SOMEBODY THERE'LL LISTEN TO YOU.

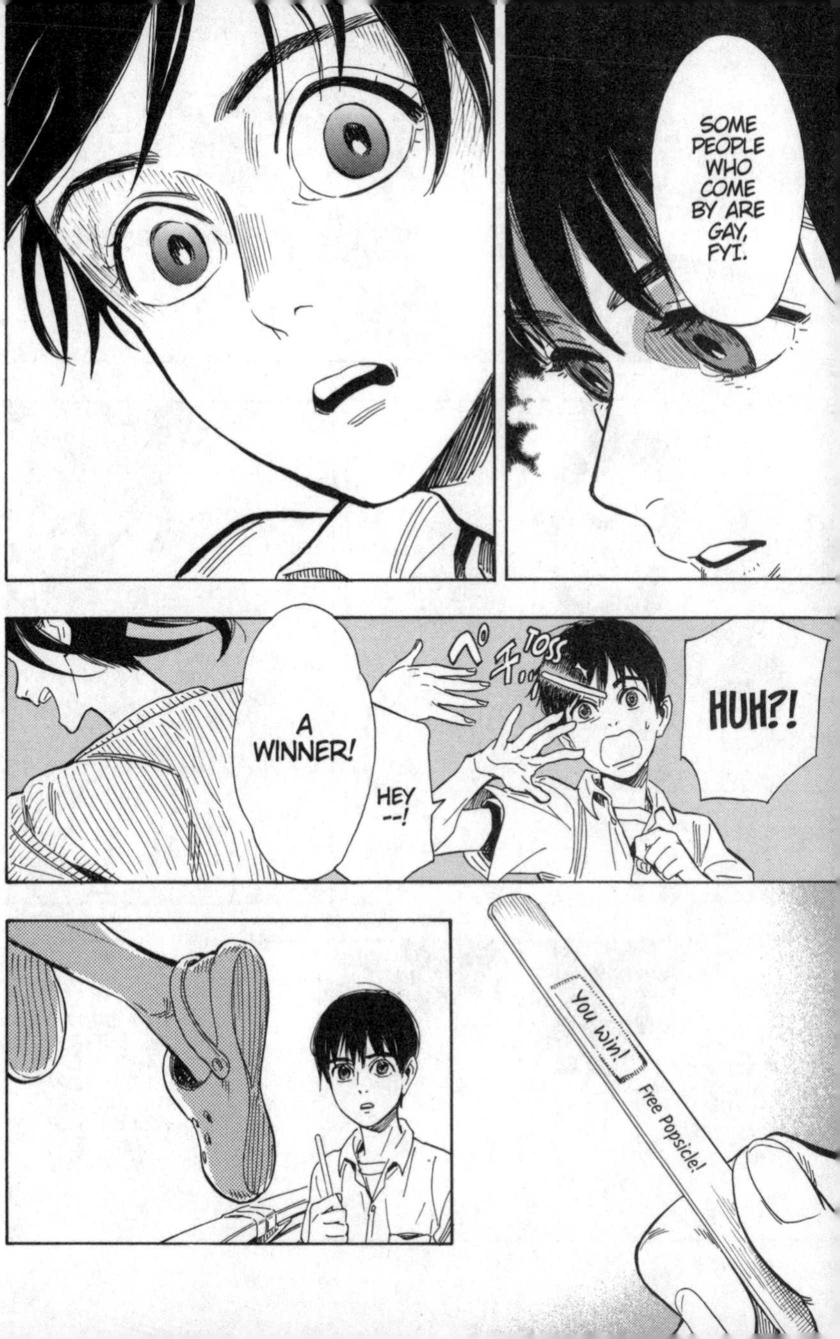
SOME PEOPLE WHO COME BY ARE GAY, FYI.
HUH?!
TOSS
HEY --!
A WINNER!
You win!
Free Popsicle!

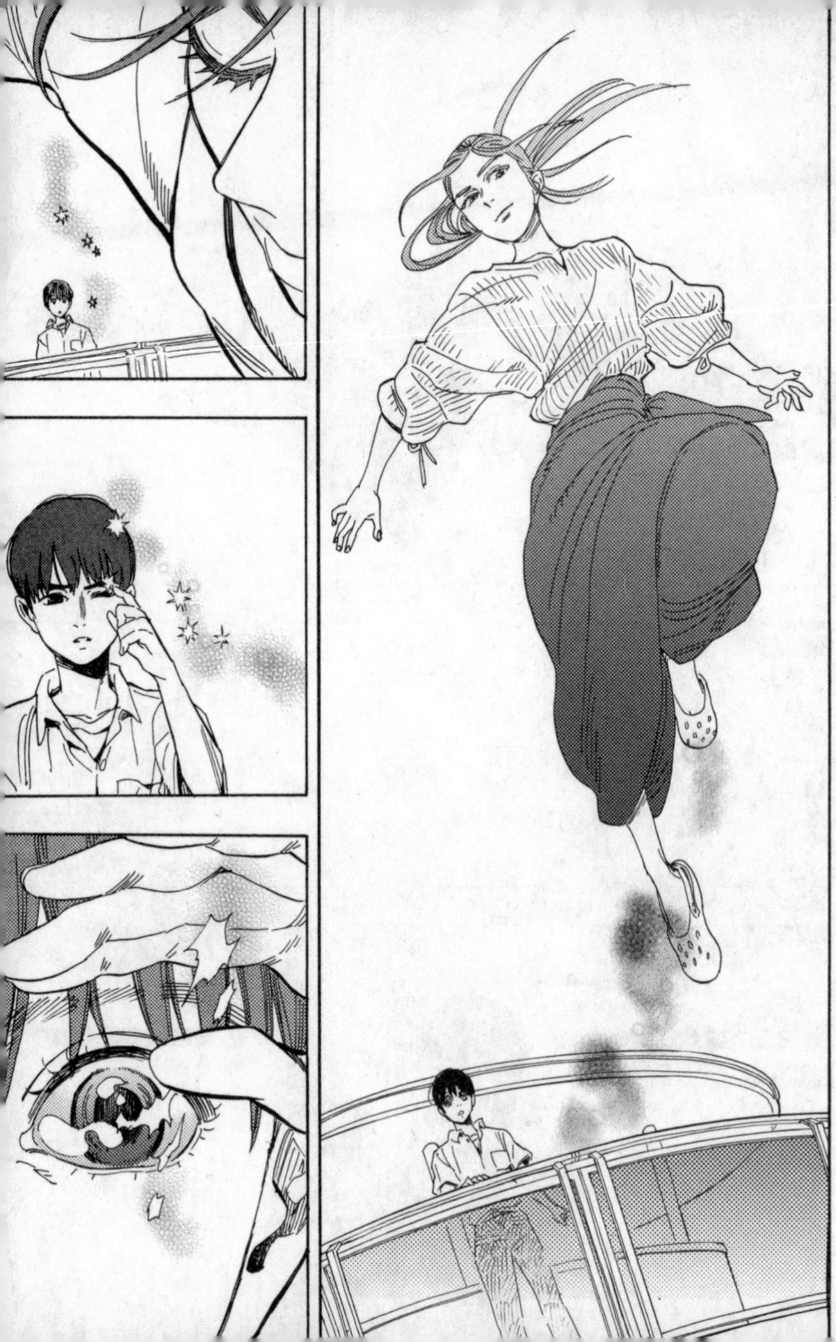

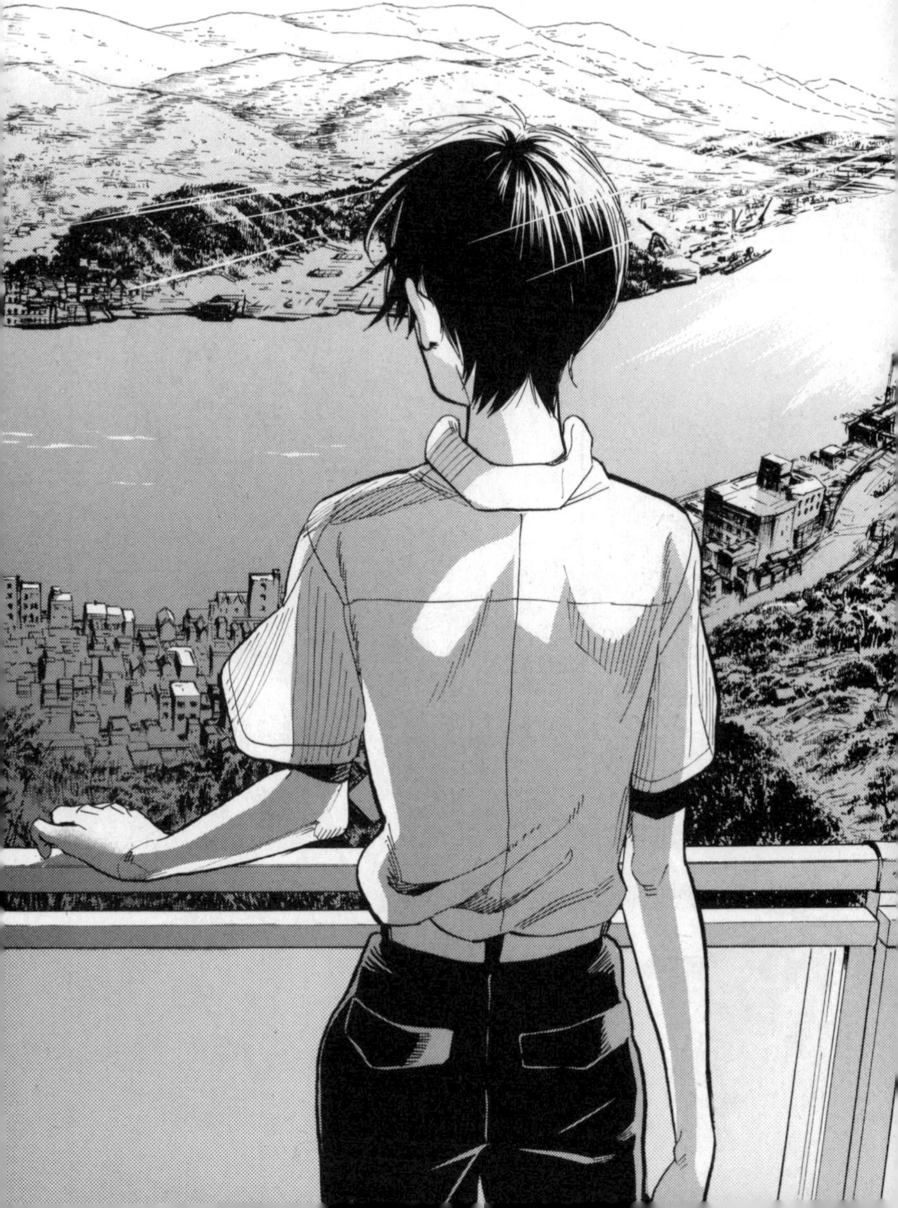

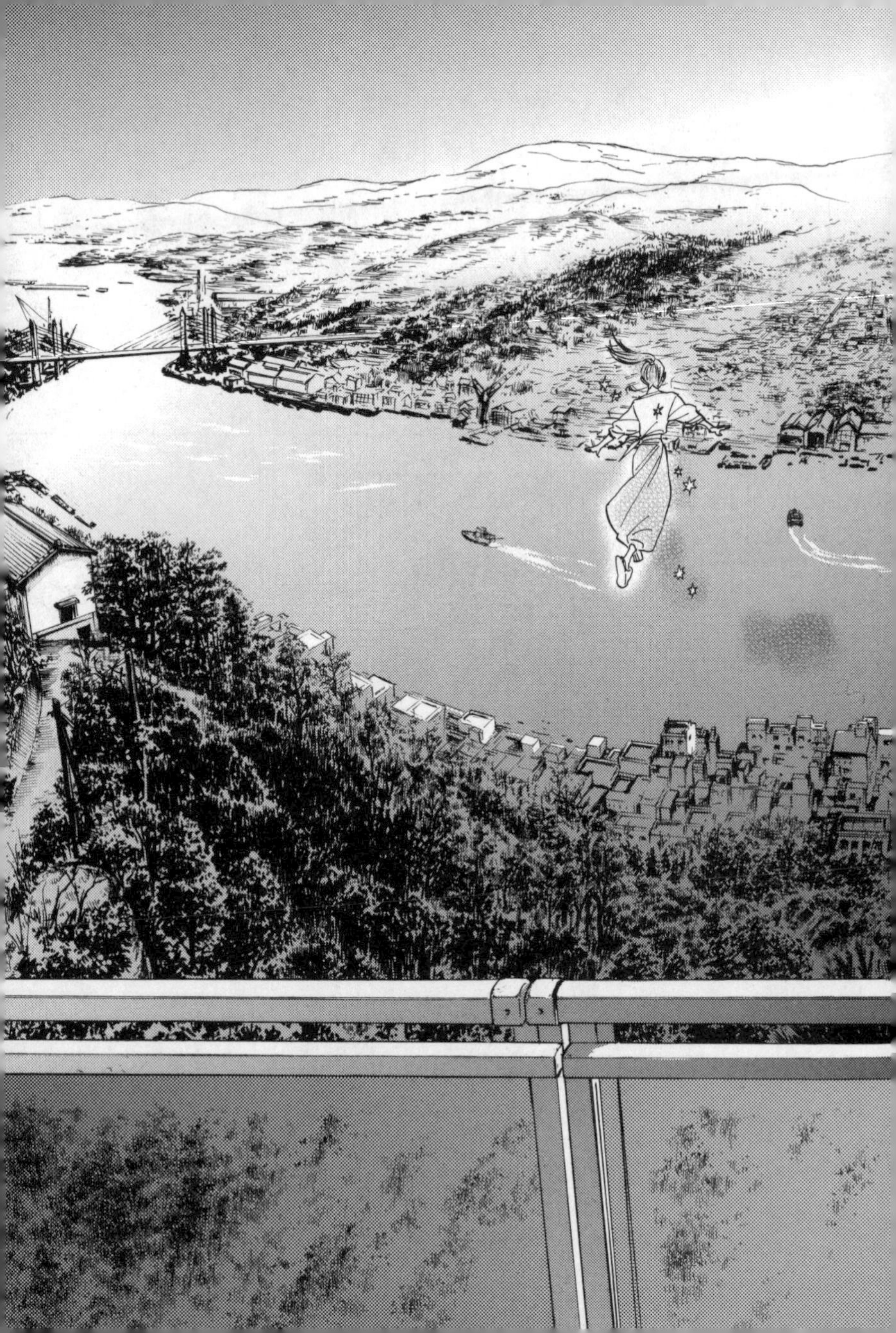

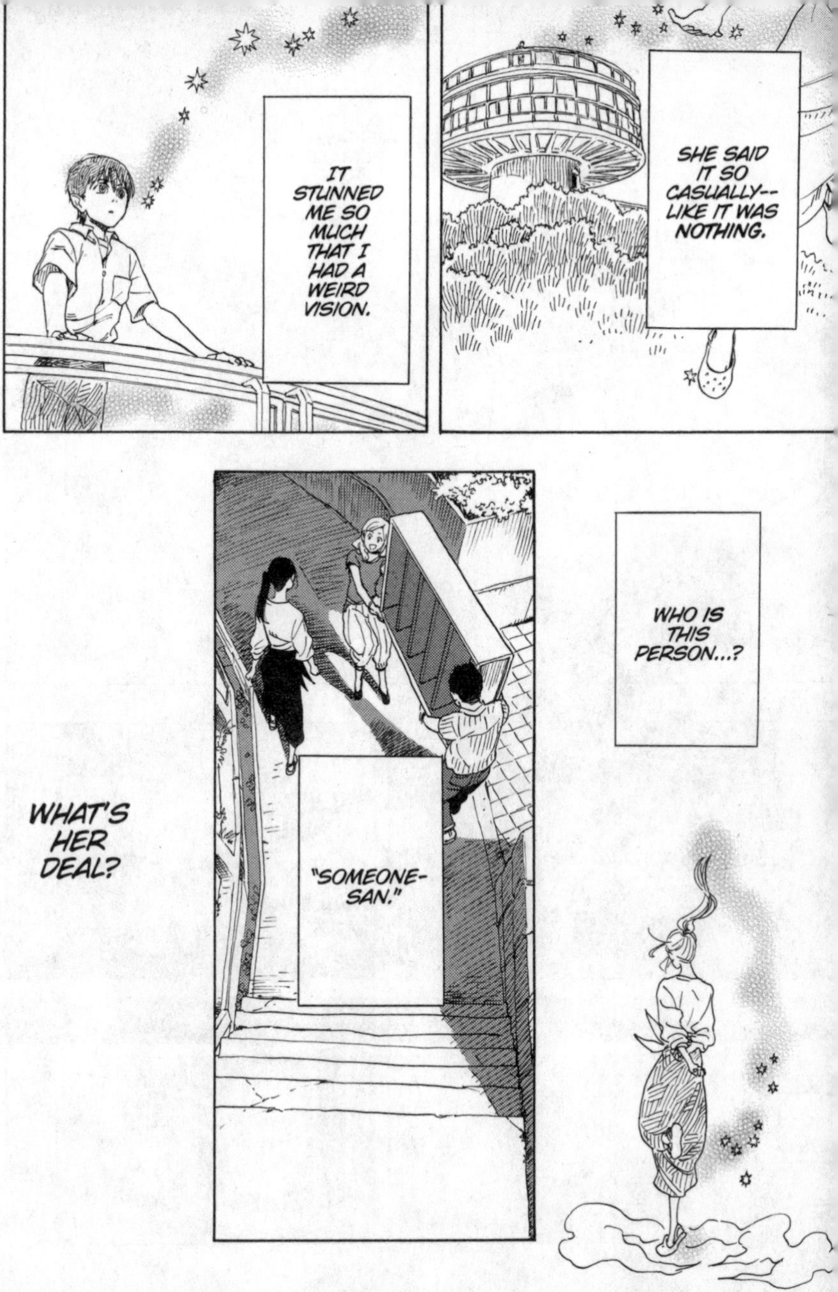
SHE SAID IT SO CASUALLY-- LIKE IT WAS NOTHING.
IT STUNNED ME SO MUCH THAT I HAD A WEIRD VISION.
WHO IS THIS PERSON...?
"SOMEONE-SAN."
WHAT'S HER DEAL?

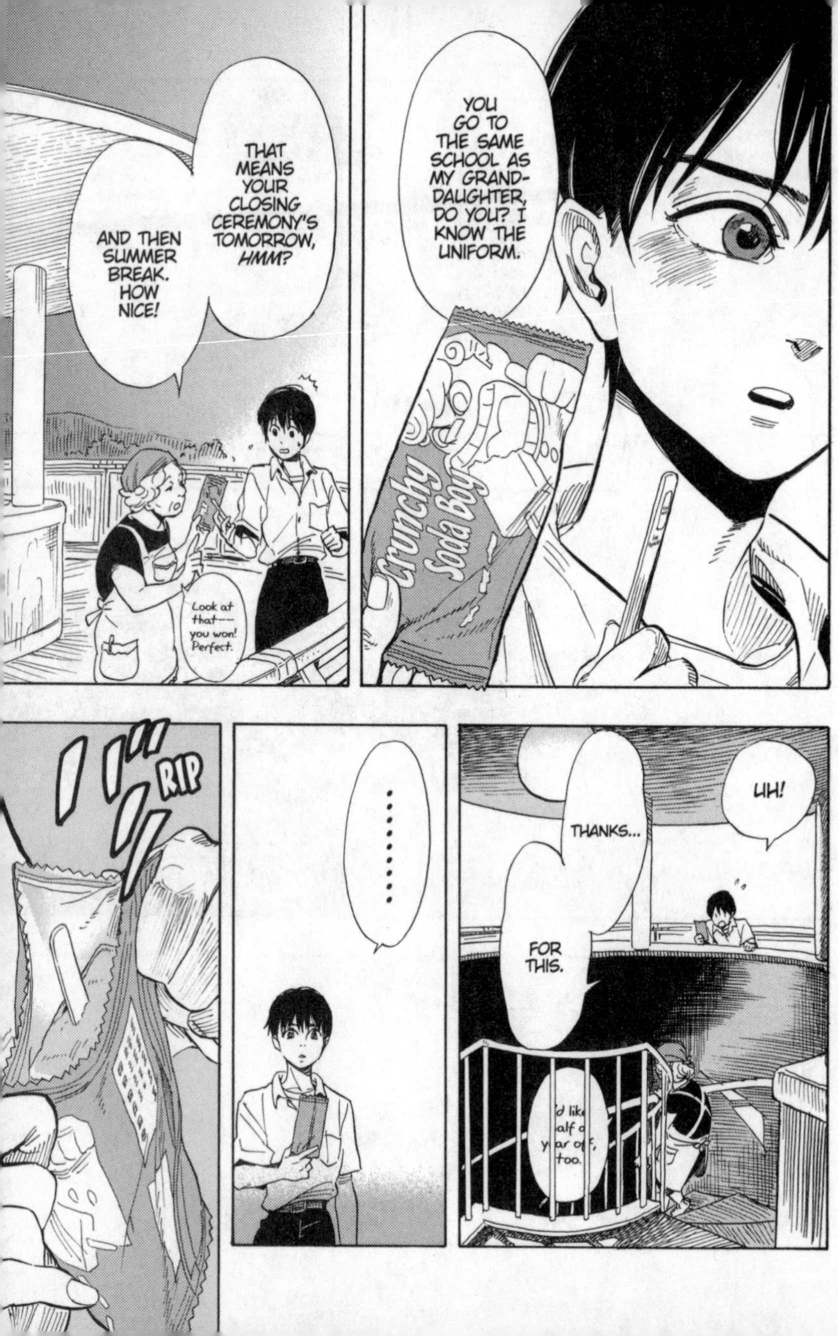
YOU GO TO THE SAME SCHOOL AS MY GRAND-DAUGHTER, DO YOU? I KNOW THE UNIFORM.
THAT MEANS YOUR CLOSING CEREMONY'S TOMORROW, *HMM?*
AND THEN SUMMER BREAK. HOW NICE!
Look at that—you won! Perfect.
Crunchy Soda Boy
UH!
THANKS...
FOR THIS.
'd like alf a year off, too.
......
RIP

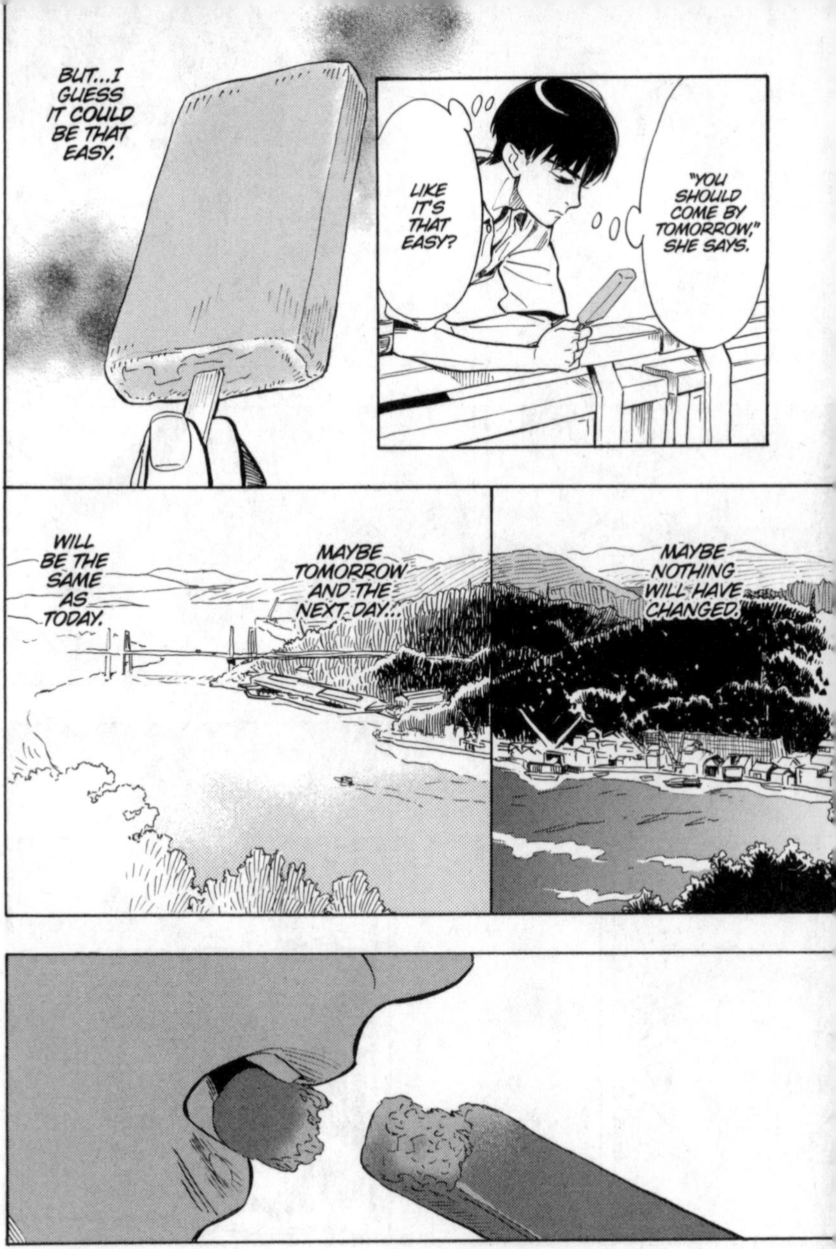
"YOU SHOULD COME BY TOMORROW," SHE SAYS.
LIKE IT'S THAT EASY?
BUT...I GUESS IT COULD BE THAT EASY.
MAYBE NOTHING WILL HAVE CHANGED.
MAYBE TOMORROW AND THE NEXT DAY...
WILL BE THE SAME AS TODAY.

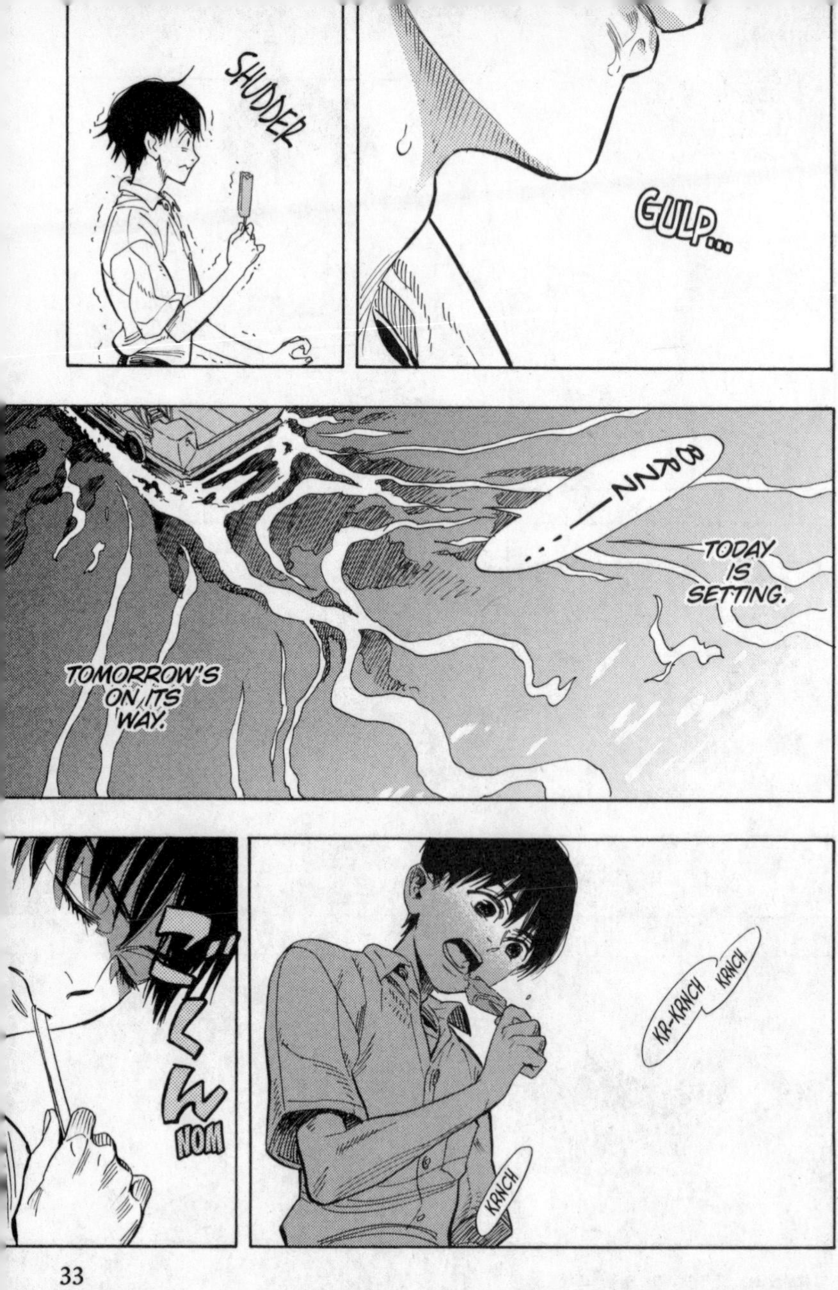
GULP...
SHUDDER
BRRNN—...
TODAY IS SETTING.
TOMORROW'S ON ITS WAY.
KR-KRNCH KRNCH
KRNCH
NOM

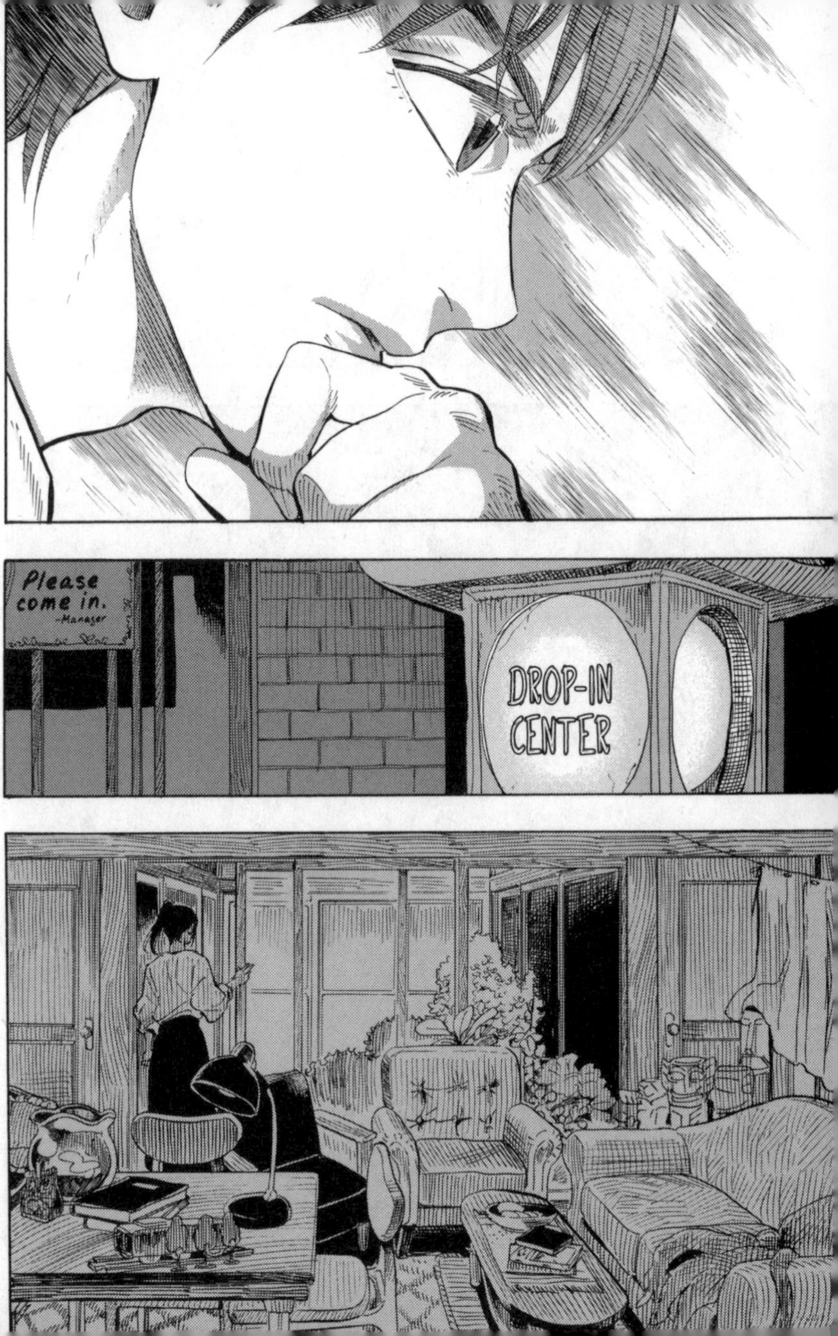
Please come in.
-Manager
DROP-IN CENTER

Our Dreams at Dusk

SHIMANAMI TASOGARE

This is where Shimanami Tasogare is set.
Chugoku Region
Tokyo
Hiroshima
Seto Inland Sea
Shikoku
Here.
Onomichi
Mihara
Mukai-shima

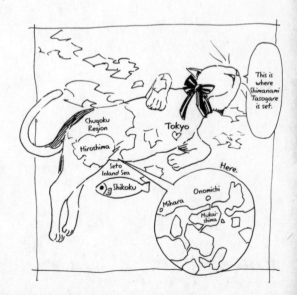

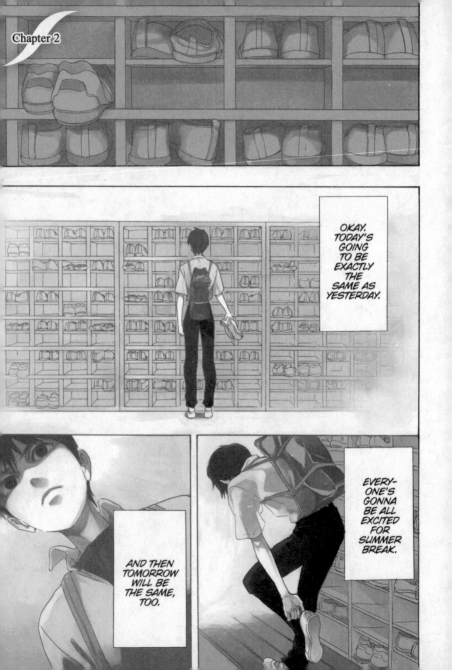

OKAY. TODAY'S GOING TO BE EXACTLY THE SAME AS YESTERDAY.

EVERY-ONE'S GONNA BE ALL EXCITED FOR SUMMER BREAK.

AND THEN TOMORROW WILL BE THE SAME, TOO.

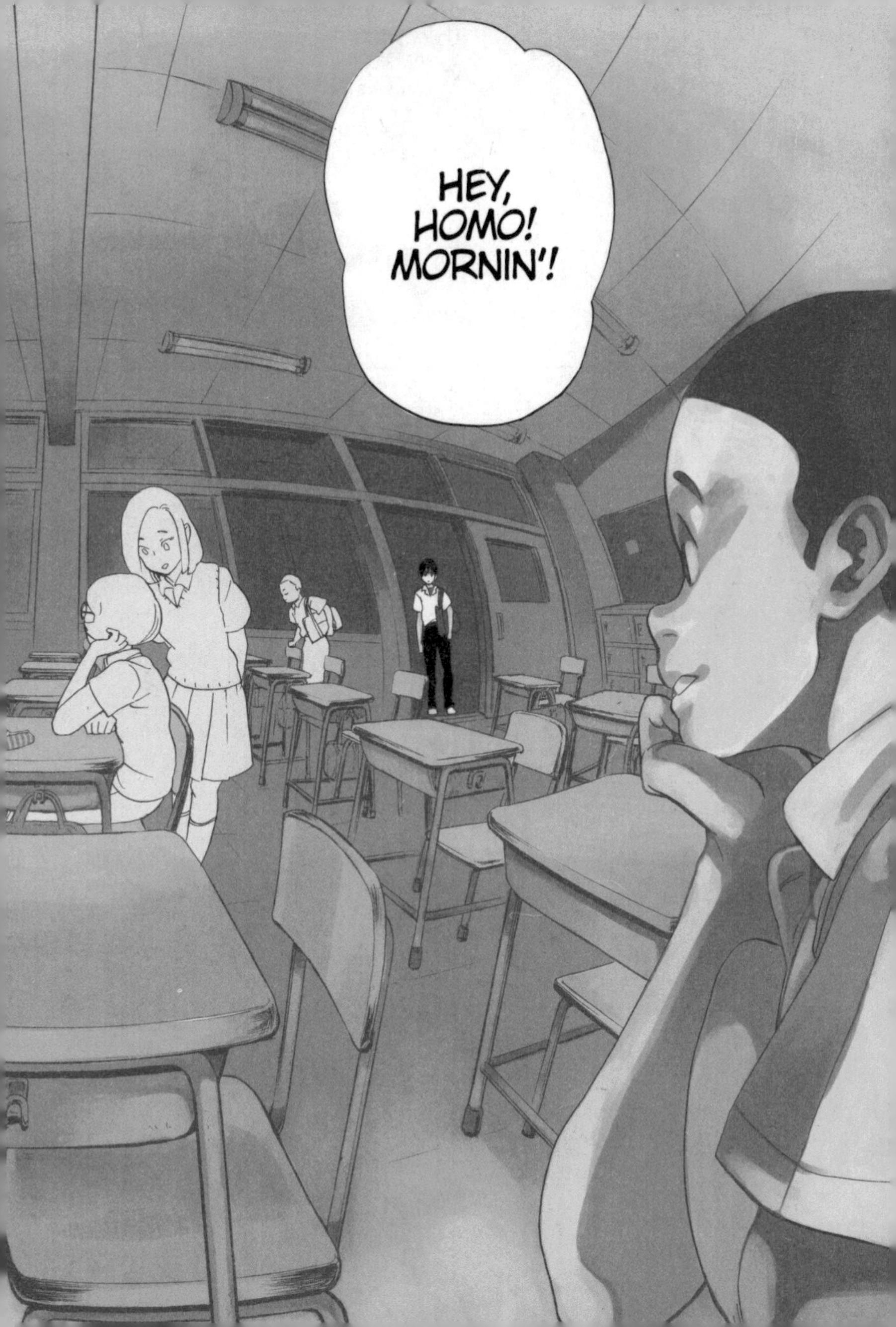
HEY, HOMO! MORNIN'!

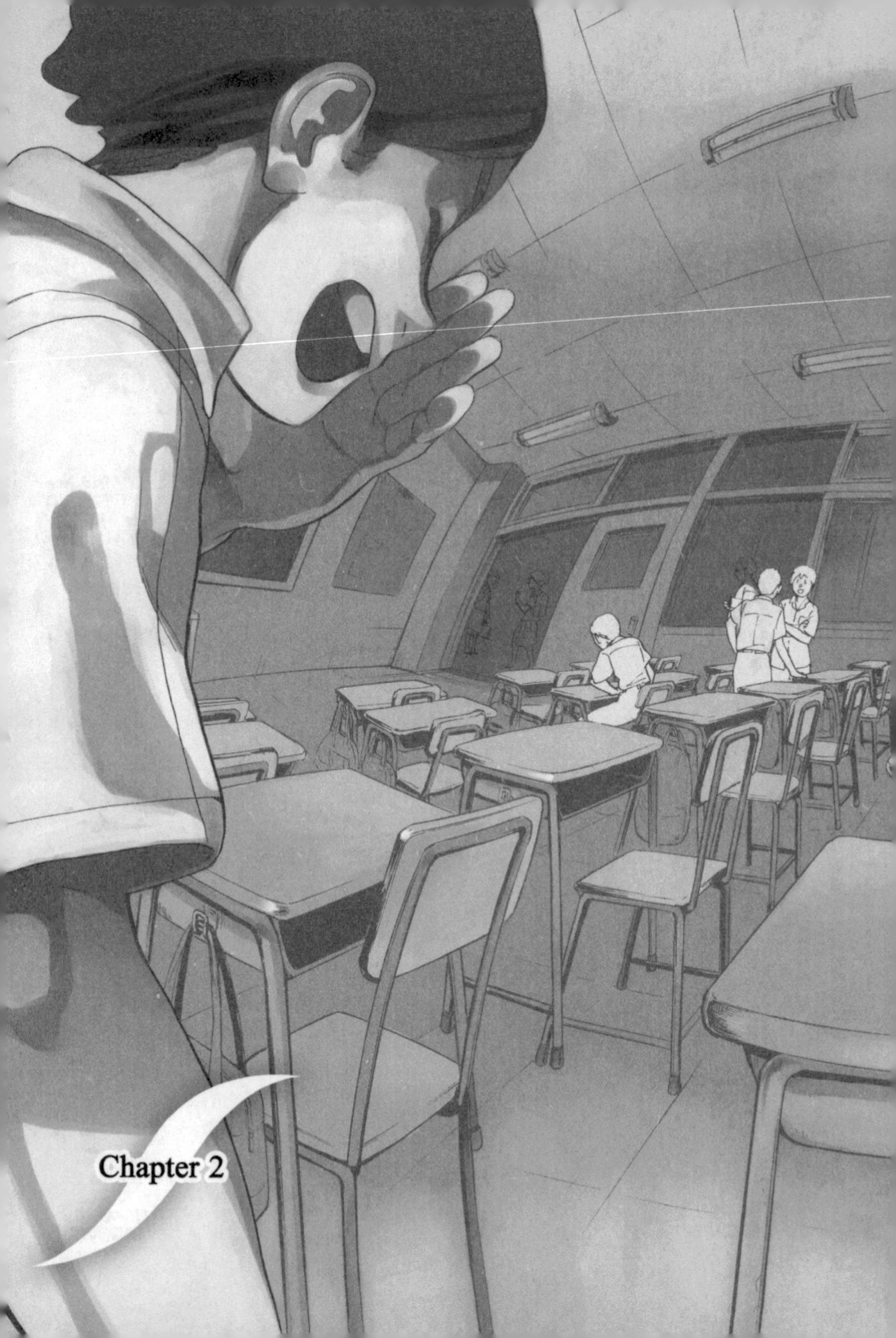
Chapter 2

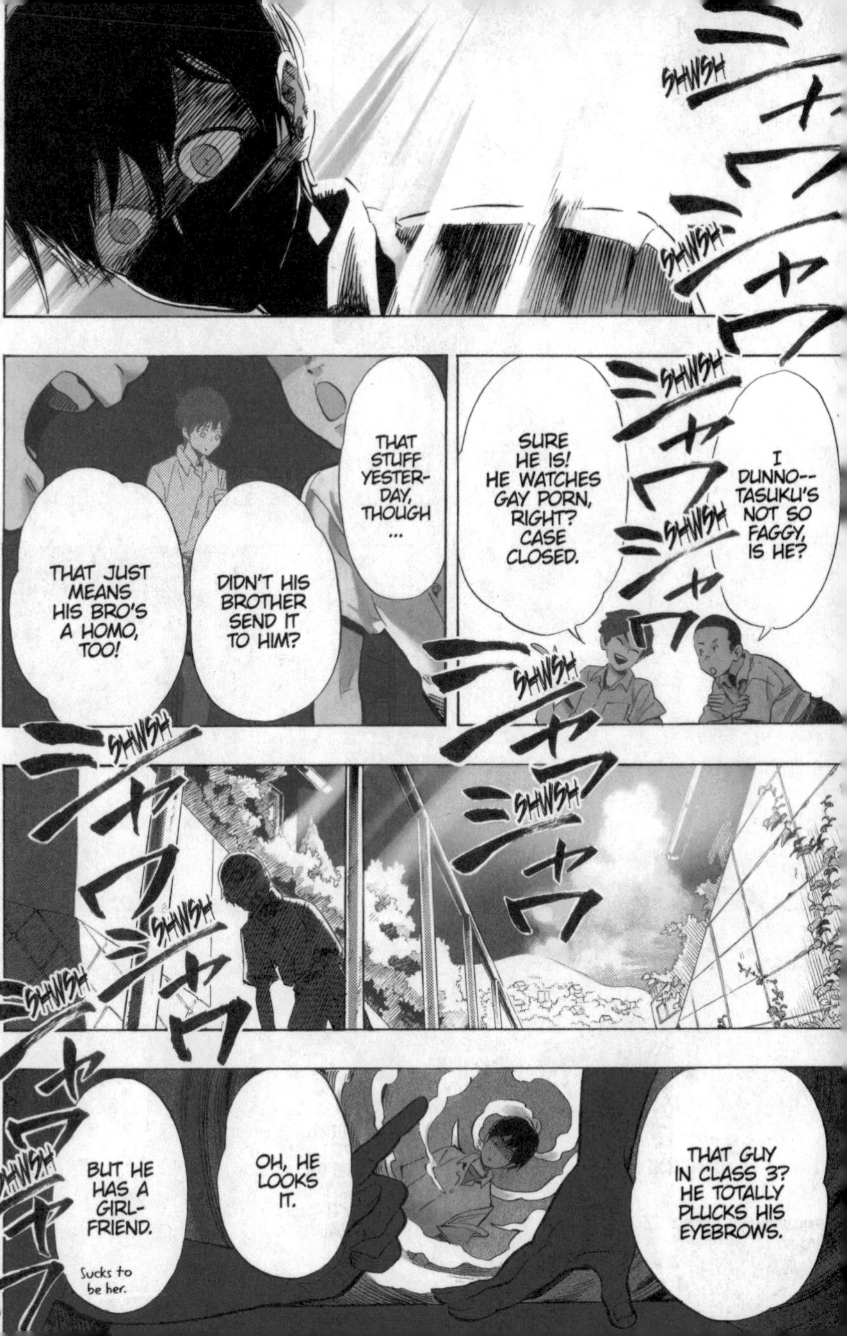
SHWSH
SHWSH
SHWSH
I DUNNO-- TASUKU'S NOT SO FAGGY, IS HE?
SHWSH
SURE HE IS! HE WATCHES GAY PORN, RIGHT? CASE CLOSED.
SHWSH
THAT STUFF YESTER-DAY, THOUGH...
DIDN'T HIS BROTHER SEND IT TO HIM?
THAT JUST MEANS HIS BRO'S A HOMO, TOO!
SHWSH
SHWSH
SHWSH
SHWSH
THAT GUY IN CLASS 3? HE TOTALLY PLUCKS HIS EYEBROWS.
OH, HE LOOKS IT.
BUT HE HAS A GIRL-FRIEND.
Sucks to be her.
SHWSH

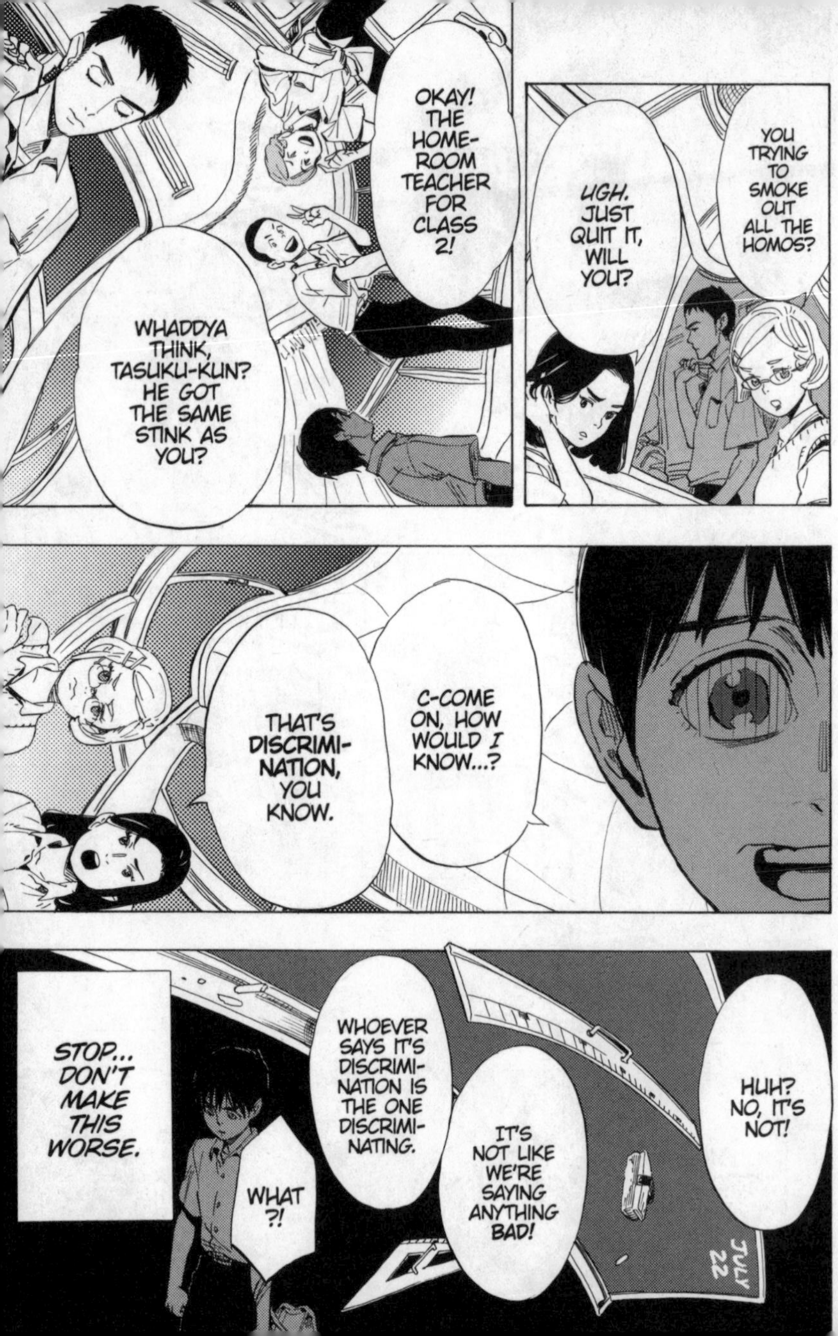
YOU TRYING TO SMOKE OUT ALL THE HOMOS?
UGH. JUST QUIT IT, WILL YOU?
OKAY! THE HOME-ROOM TEACHER FOR CLASS 2!
WHADDYA THINK, TASUKU-KUN? HE GOT THE SAME STINK AS YOU?
C-COME ON, HOW WOULD *I* KNOW...?
THAT'S DISCRIMI-NATION, YOU KNOW.
HUH? NO, IT'S NOT!
JULY 22
IT'S NOT LIKE WE'RE SAYING ANYTHING BAD!
WHOEVER SAYS IT'S DISCRIMI-NATION IS THE ONE DISCRIMI-NATING.
WHAT?!
STOP... DON'T MAKE THIS WORSE.

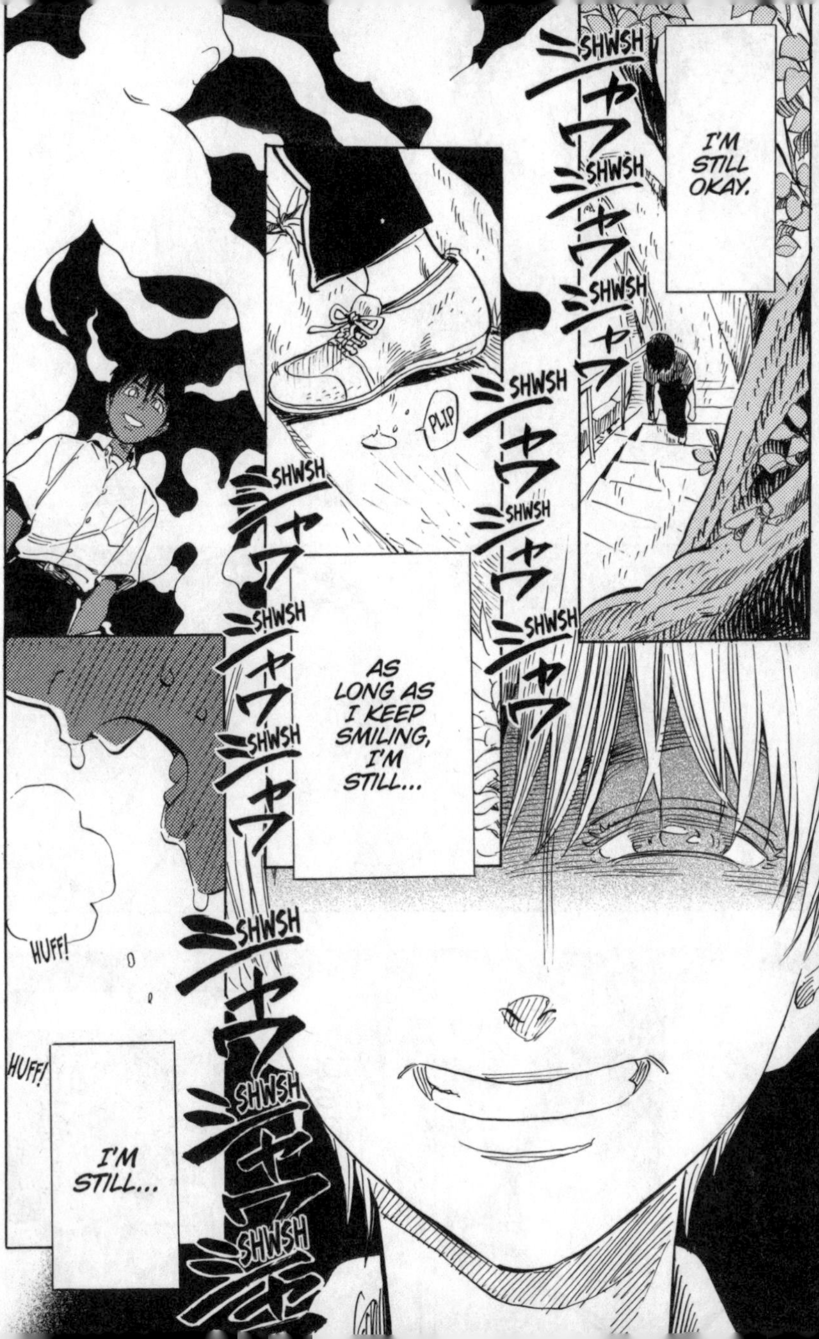
I'M STILL OKAY.
SHWSH
SHWSH
SHWSH
SHWSH
PLIP
SHWSH
SHWSH
SHWSH
AS LONG AS I KEEP SMILING, I'M STILL...
SHWSH
SHWSH
SHWSH
HUFF!
HUFF!
I'M STILL...

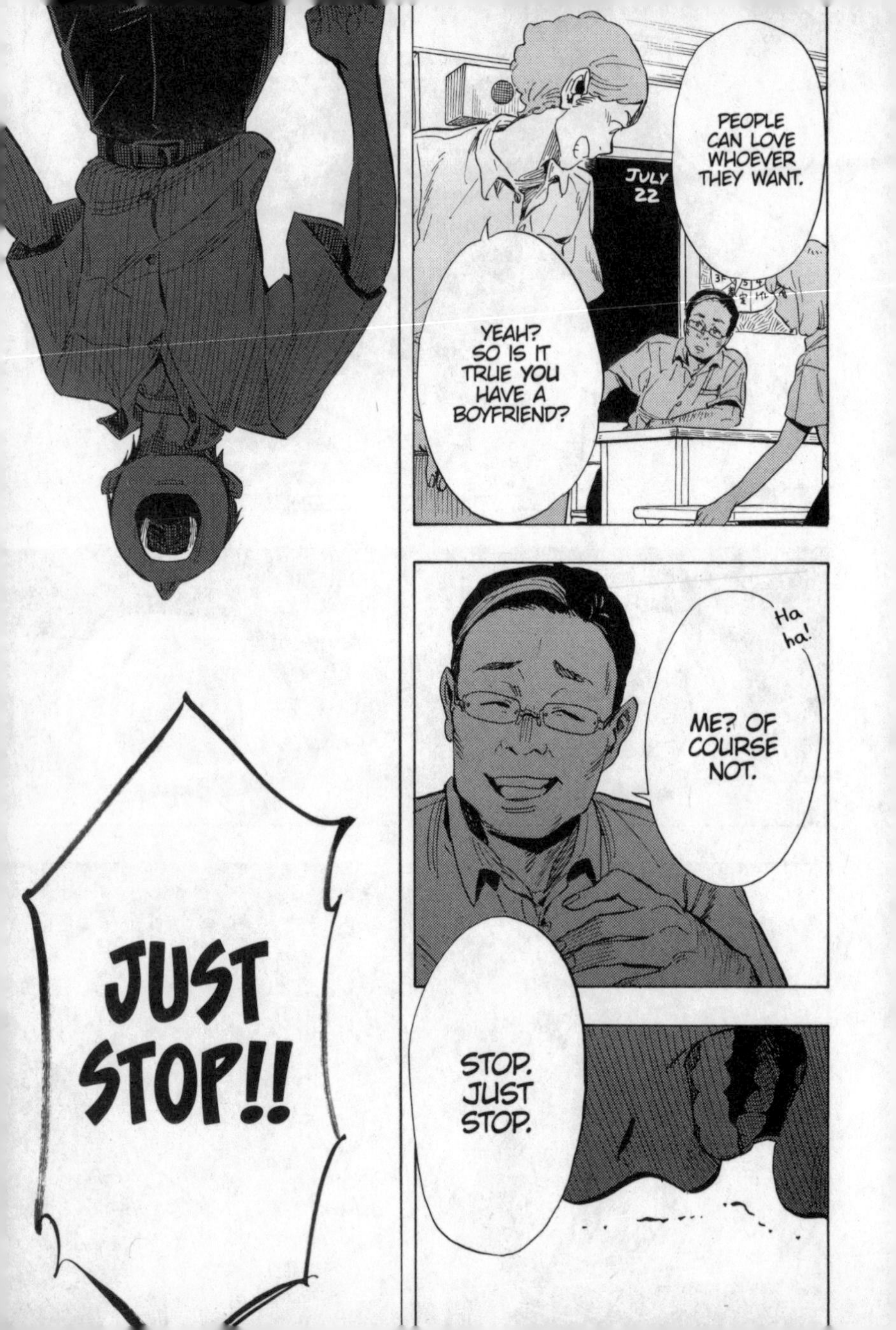
PEOPLE CAN LOVE WHOEVER THEY WANT.
JULY 22
YEAH? SO IS IT TRUE YOU HAVE A BOYFRIEND?
Ha ha!
ME? OF COURSE NOT.
STOP. JUST STOP.
JUST STOP!!

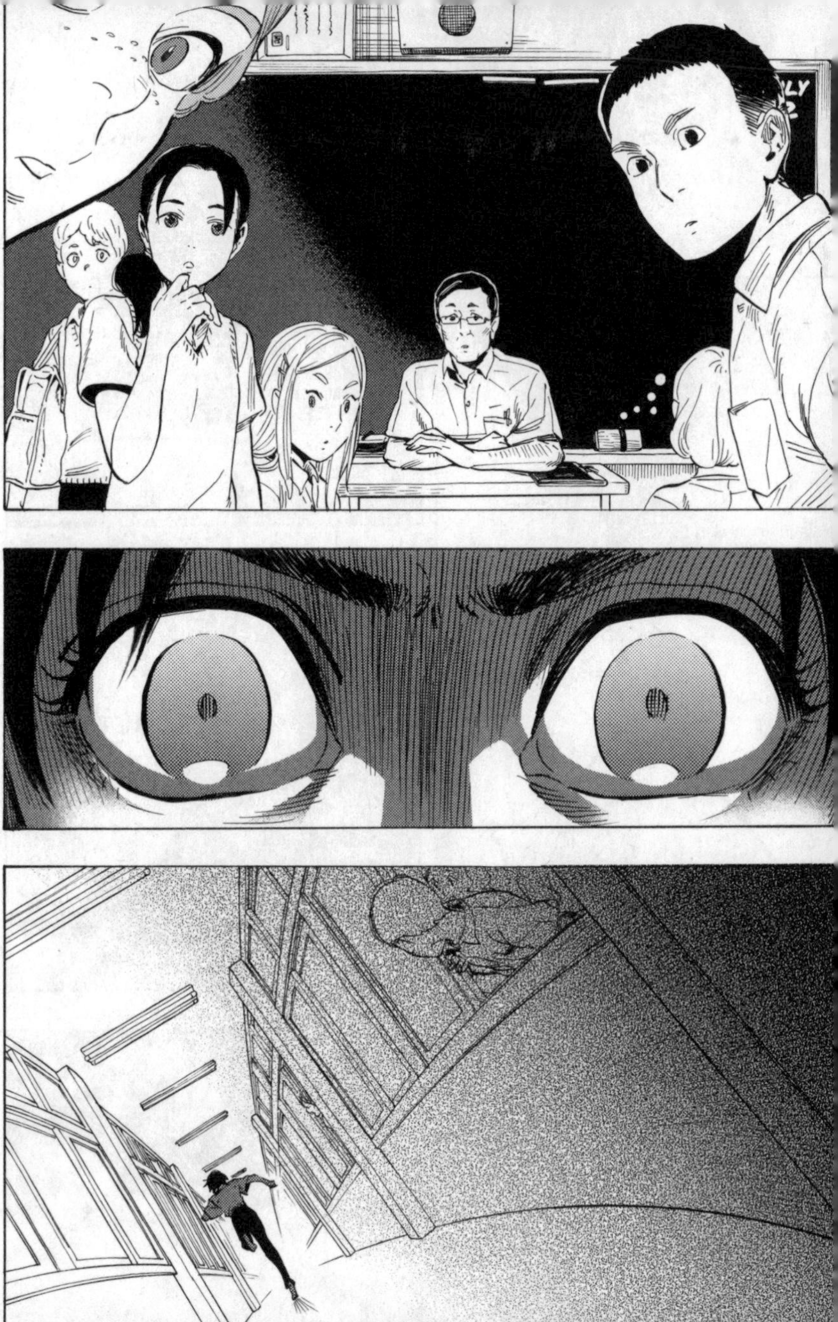

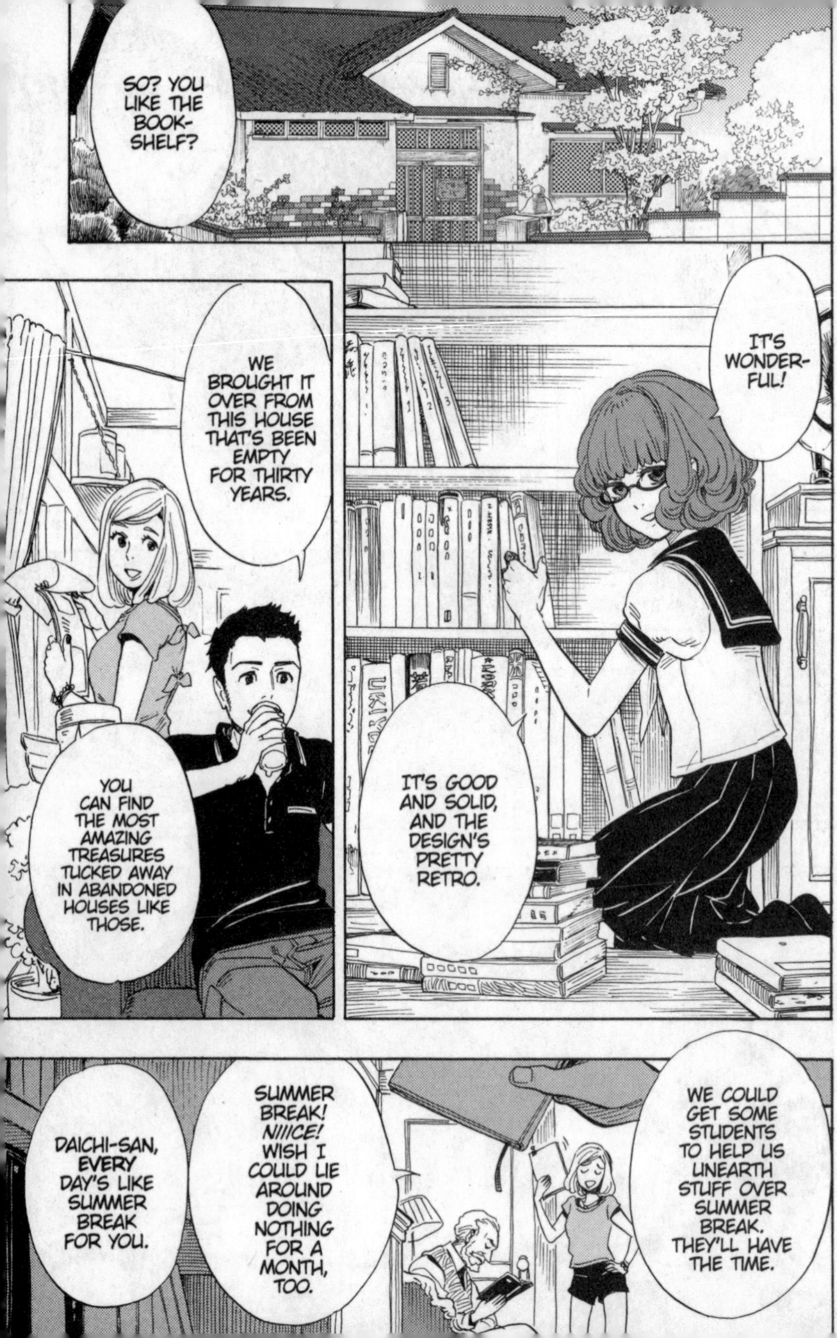
SO? YOU LIKE THE BOOKSHELF?
IT'S WONDERFUL!
IT'S GOOD AND SOLID, AND THE DESIGN'S PRETTY RETRO.
WE BROUGHT IT OVER FROM THIS HOUSE THAT'S BEEN EMPTY FOR THIRTY YEARS.
YOU CAN FIND THE MOST AMAZING TREASURES TUCKED AWAY IN ABANDONED HOUSES LIKE THOSE.
WE COULD GET SOME STUDENTS TO HELP US UNEARTH STUFF OVER SUMMER BREAK. THEY'LL HAVE THE TIME.
SUMMER BREAK! *NIIICE!* WISH I COULD LIE AROUND DOING NOTHING FOR A MONTH, TOO.
DAICHI-SAN, EVERY DAY'S LIKE SUMMER BREAK FOR YOU.

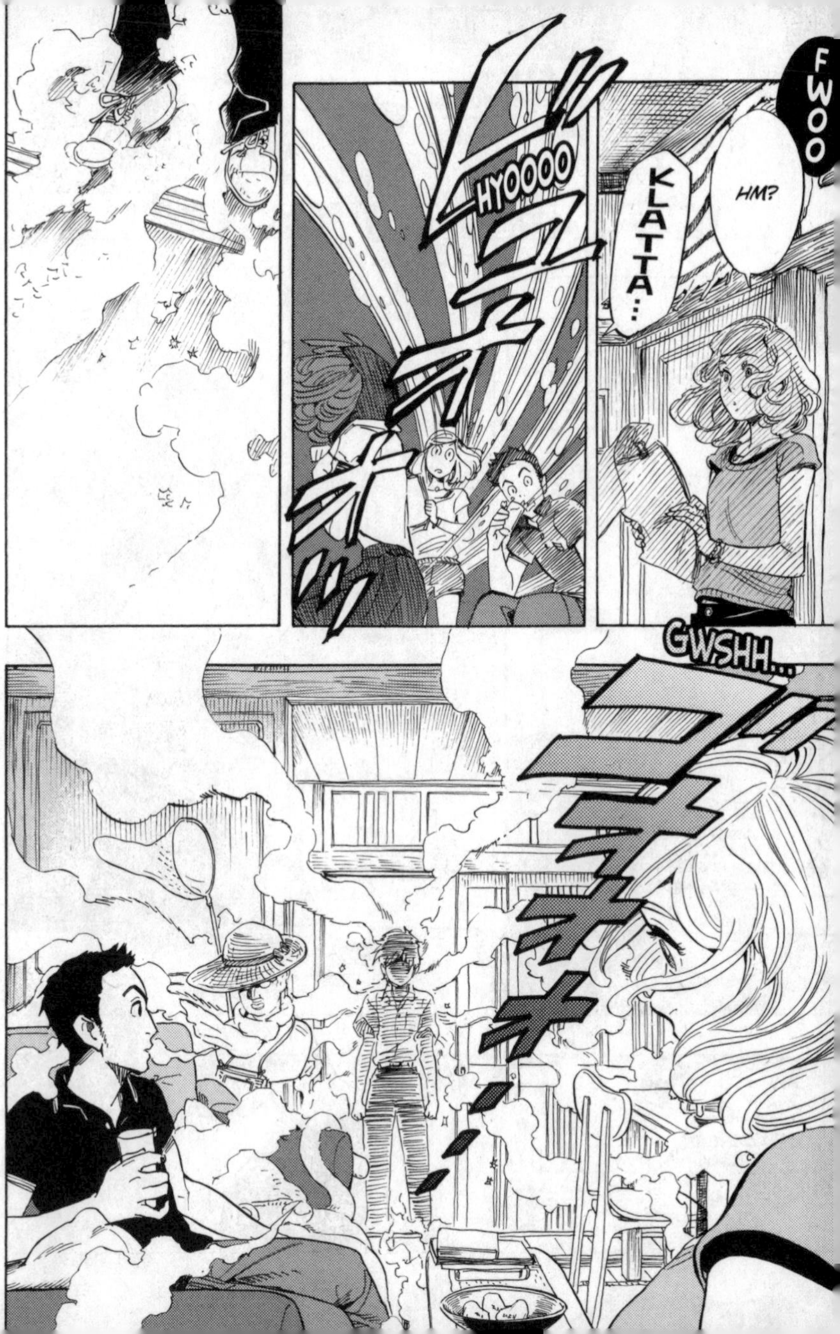
FWOO
HM?
KLATTA...
HYOOOO
GWSHH...

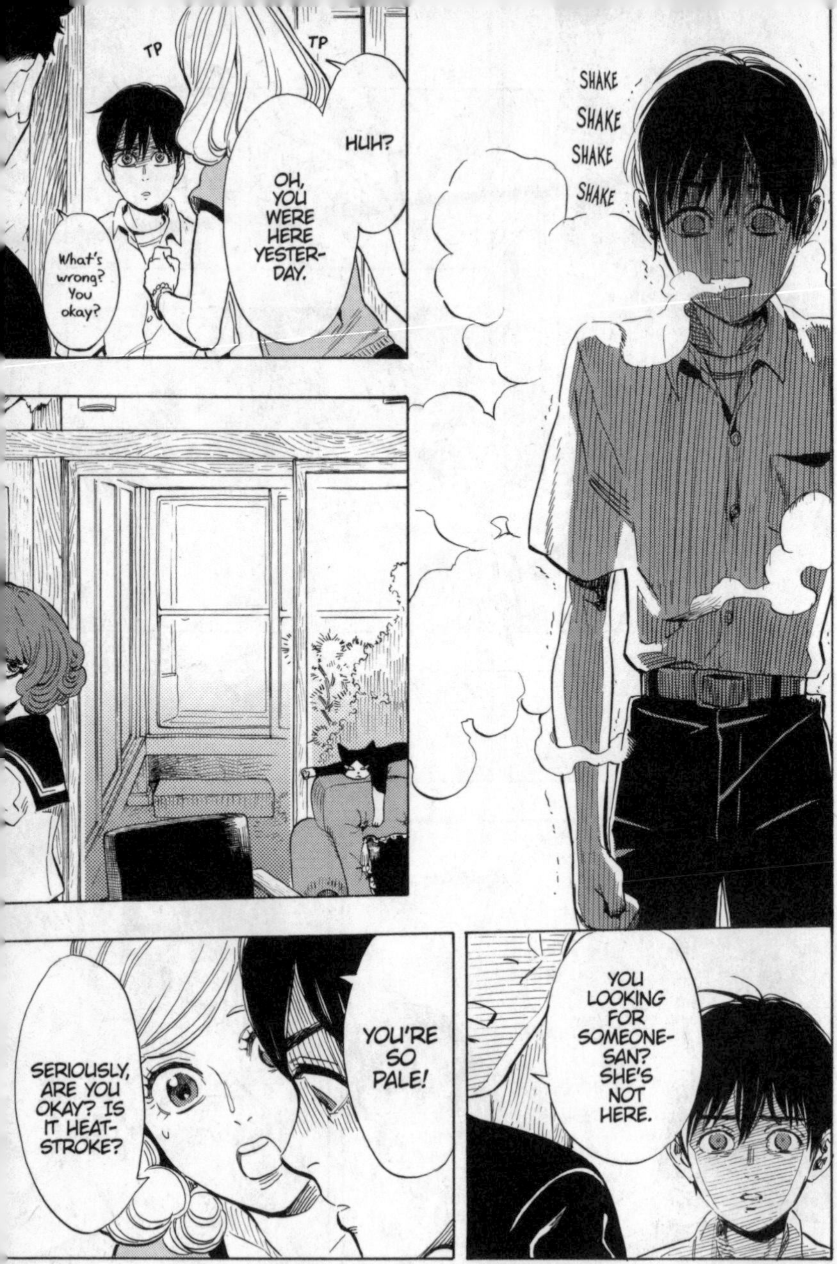
SHAKE SHAKE SHAKE SHAKE
TP
TP
HUH?
OH, YOU WERE HERE YESTER-DAY.
What's wrong? You okay?
YOU LOOKING FOR SOMEONE-SAN? SHE'S NOT HERE.
YOU'RE SO PALE!
SERIOUSLY, ARE YOU OKAY? IS IT HEAT-STROKE?

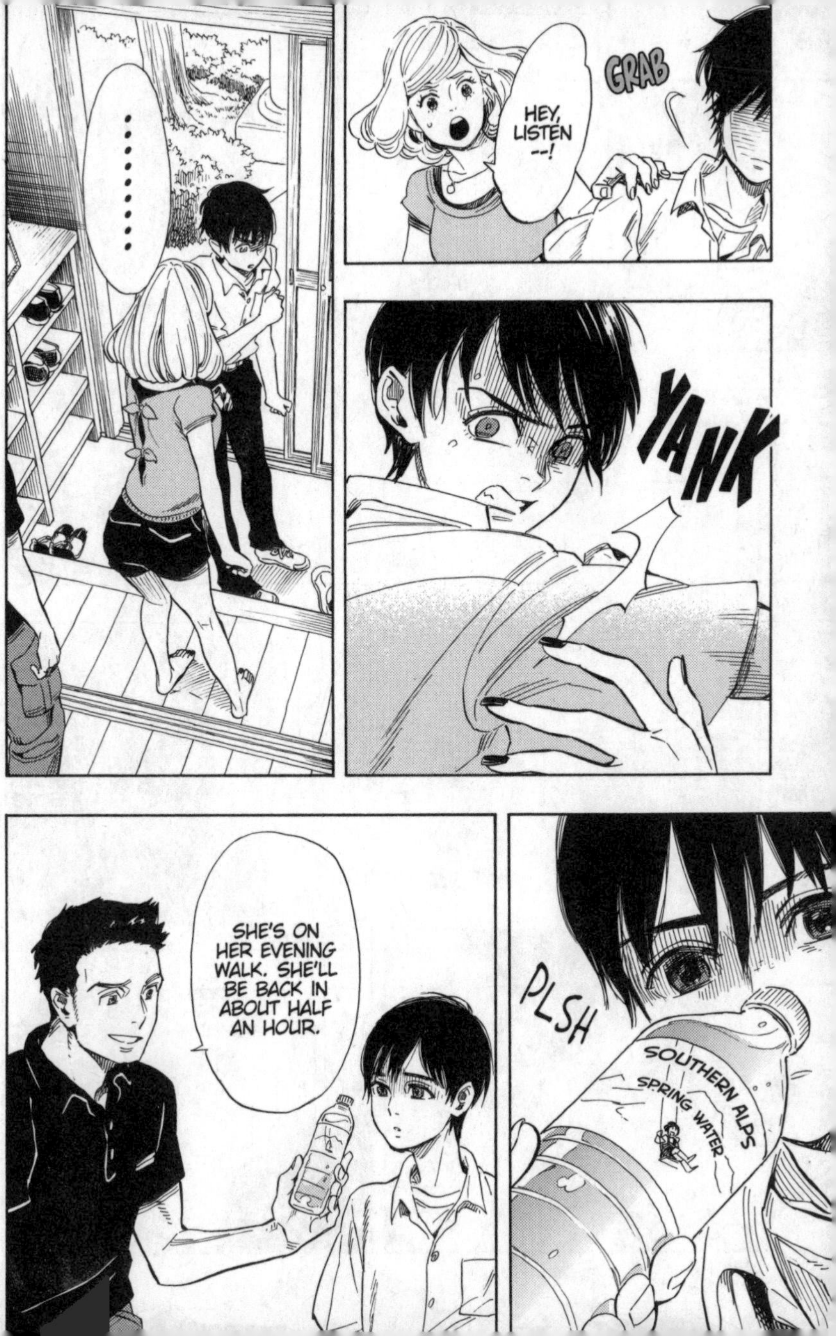
GRAB
HEY, LISTEN --!
YANK
......
PLSH
SOUTHERN ALPS SPRING WATER
SHE'S ON HER EVENING WALK. SHE'LL BE BACK IN ABOUT HALF AN HOUR.

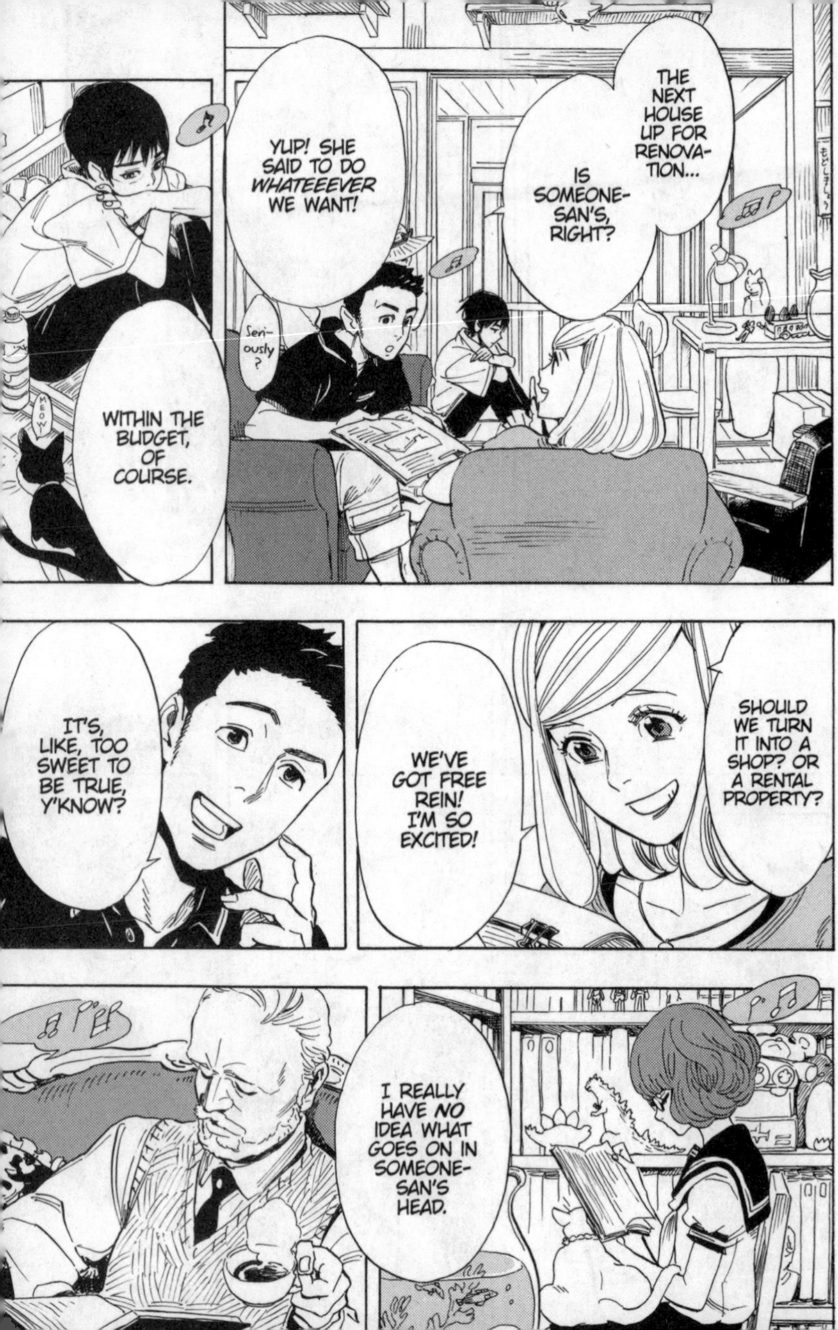
THE NEXT HOUSE UP FOR RENOVATION...
IS SOMEONE-SAN'S, RIGHT?
YUP! SHE SAID TO DO *WHATEEEVER* WE WANT!
Seri-ously?
WITHIN THE BUDGET, OF COURSE.
MEOW
SHOULD WE TURN IT INTO A SHOP? OR A RENTAL PROPERTY?
WE'VE GOT FREE REIN! I'M SO EXCITED!
IT'S, LIKE, TOO SWEET TO BE TRUE, Y'KNOW?
I REALLY HAVE *NO* IDEA WHAT GOES ON IN SOMEONE-SAN'S HEAD.

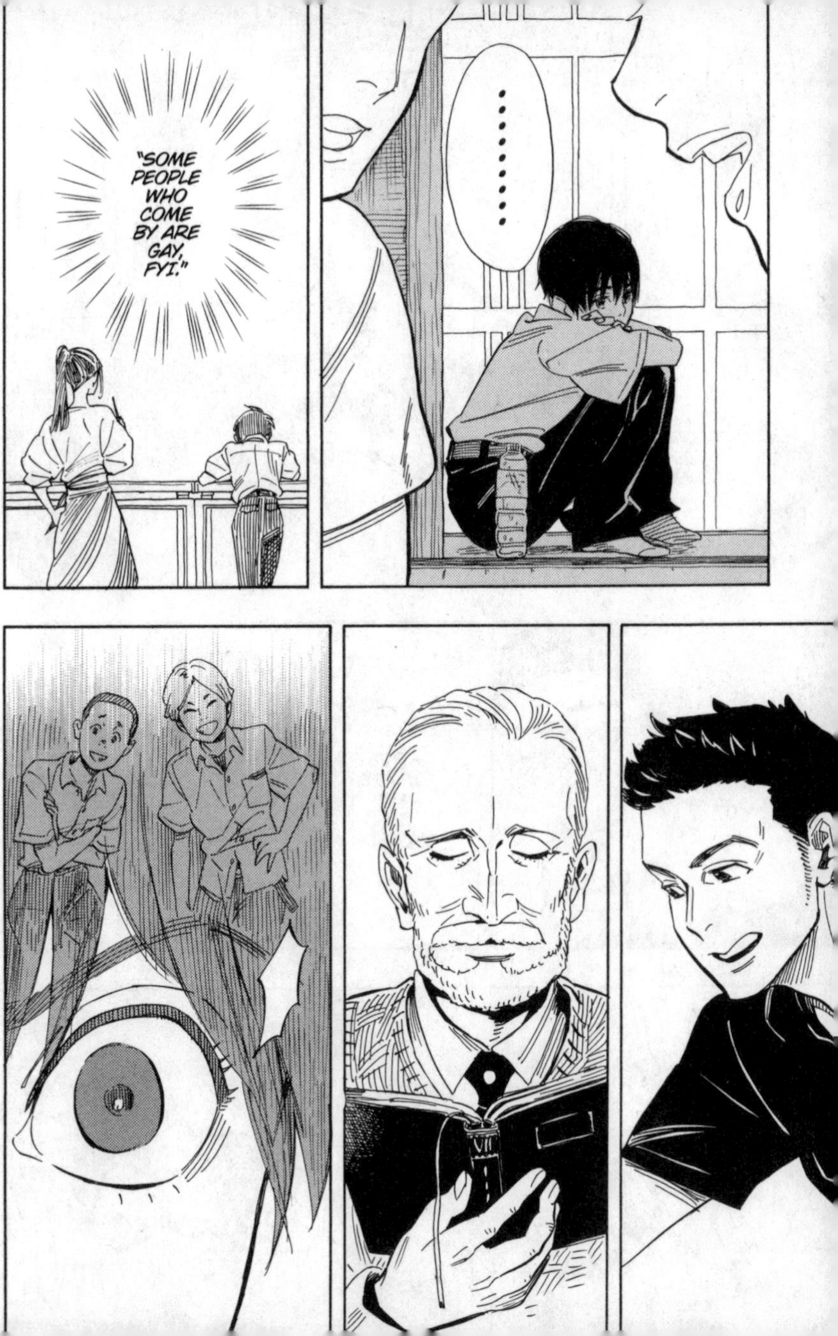
......
"SOME PEOPLE WHO COME BY ARE GAY, FYI."

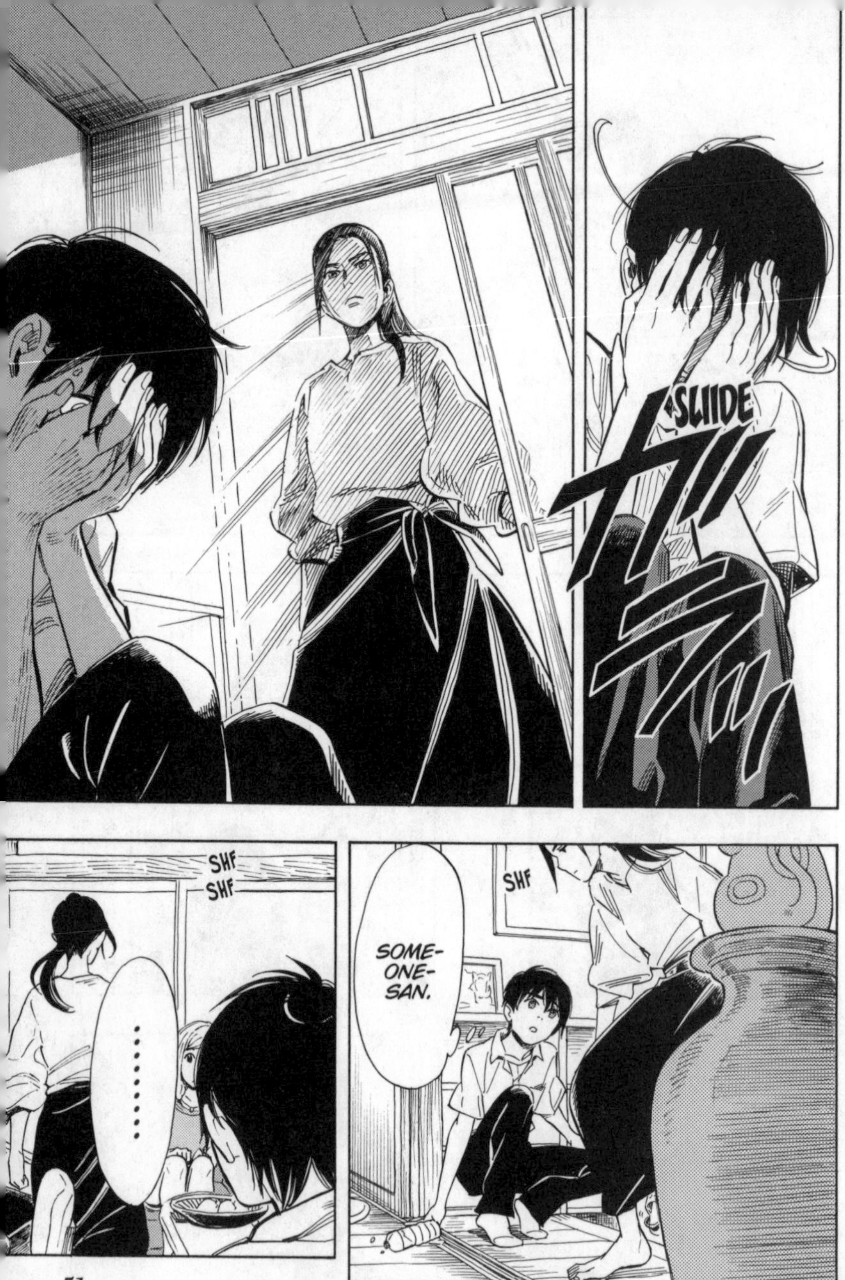
SLIIDE
SHF
SOME-ONE-SAN.
SHF
SHF
......

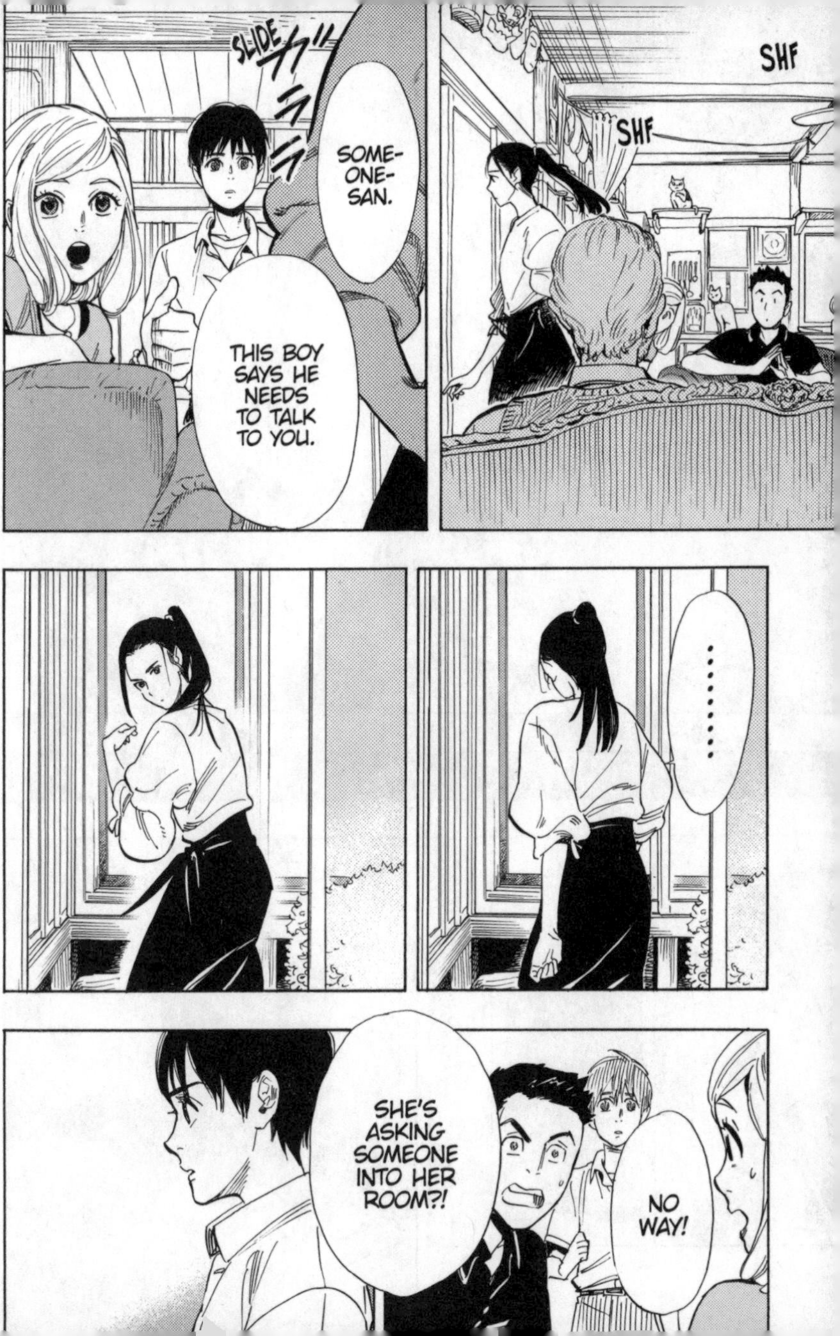
SHF
SHF
SLIDE
SOME-ONE-SAN.
THIS BOY SAYS HE NEEDS TO TALK TO YOU.
……
SHE'S ASKING SOMEONE INTO HER ROOM?!
NO WAY!

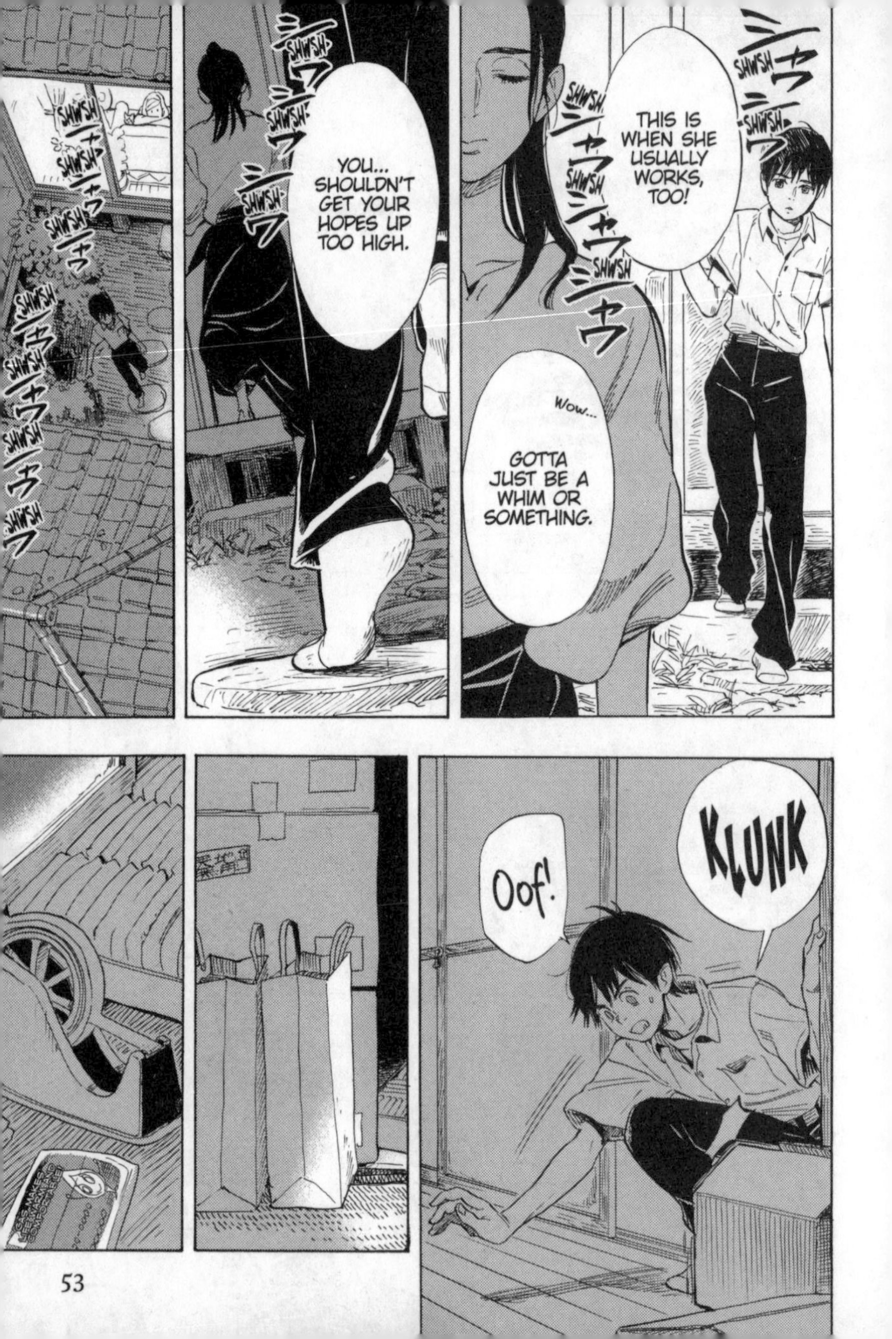
SHWSH
THIS IS WHEN SHE USUALLY WORKS, TOO!
Wow...
GOTTA JUST BE A WHIM OR SOMETHING.
SHWSH
YOU... SHOULDN'T GET YOUR HOPES UP TOO HIGH.
SHWSH
KLUNK
Oof!

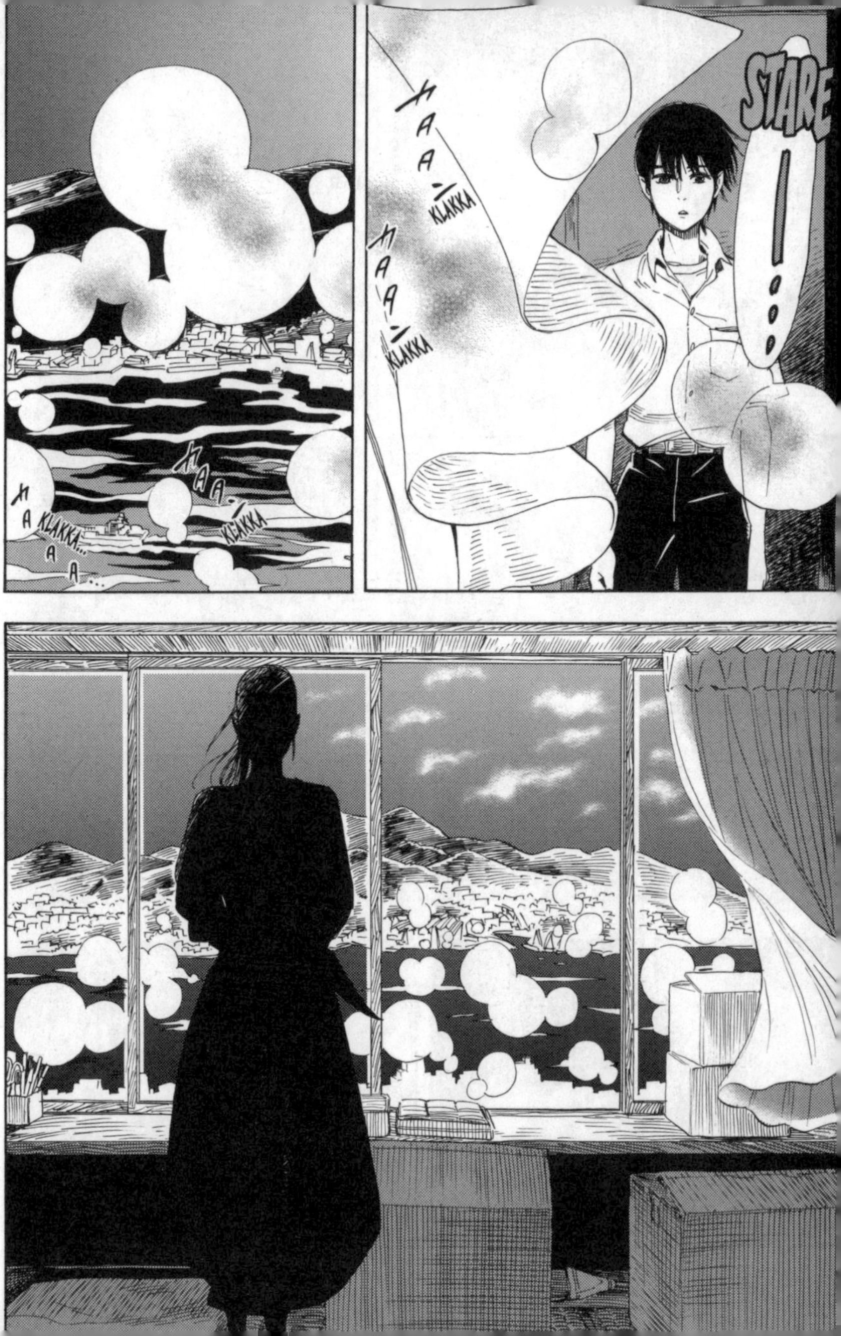

STARE
!...
HAA~ KLAKKA
HAAA~ KLAKKA
HAA~ KLAKKA
HA A KLAKKA... A A...

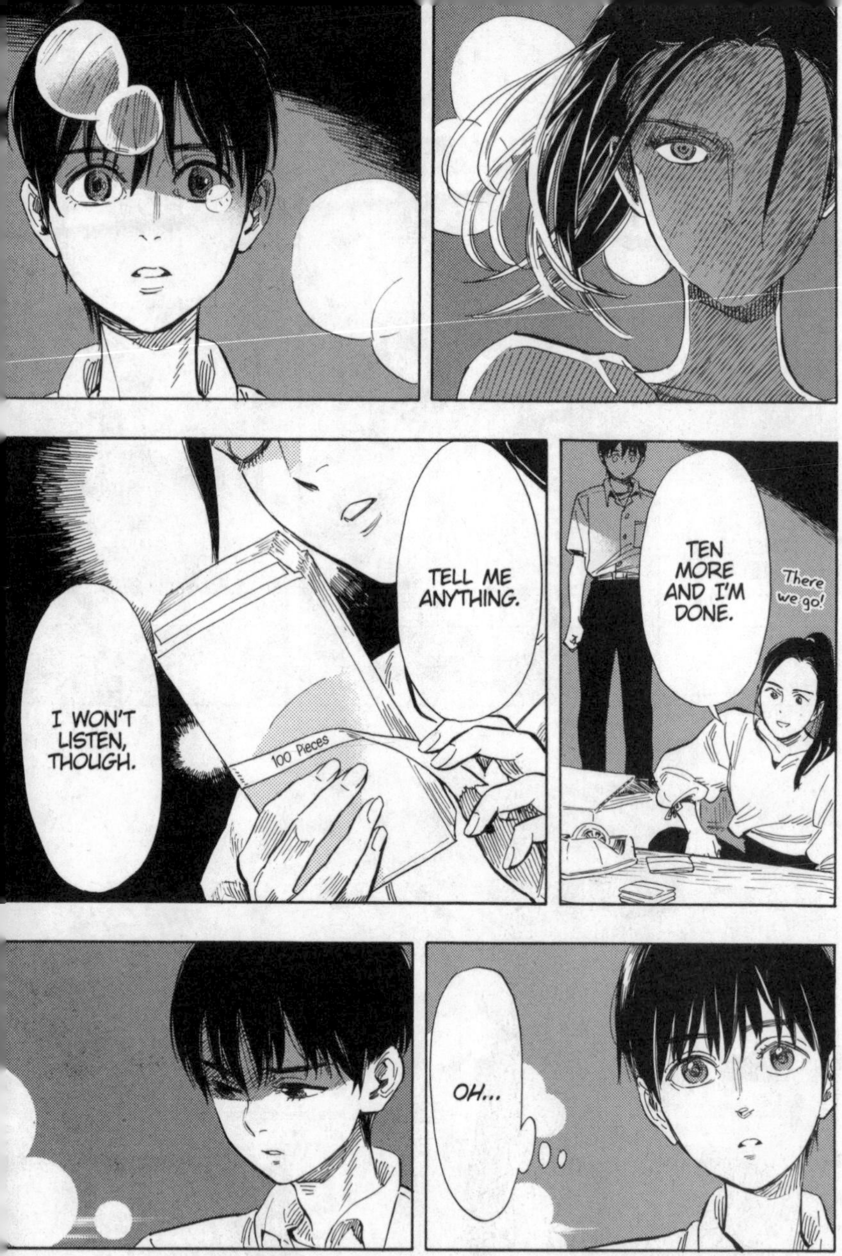
TEN MORE AND I'M DONE.
There we go!
TELL ME ANYTHING.
I WON'T LISTEN, THOUGH.
OH...

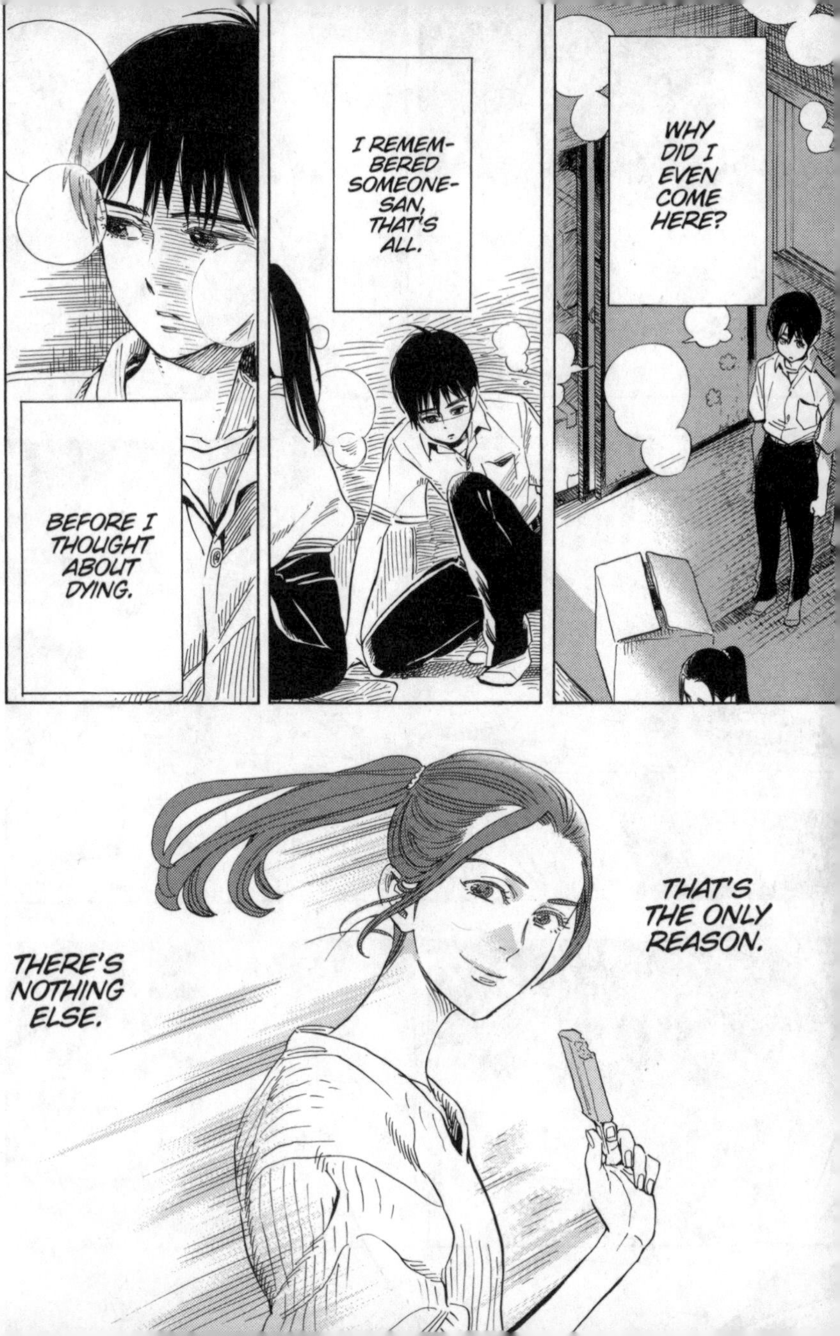
WHY DID I EVEN COME HERE?
I REMEMBERED SOMEONE-SAN, THAT'S ALL.
BEFORE I THOUGHT ABOUT DYING.
THAT'S THE ONLY REASON.
THERE'S NOTHING ELSE.

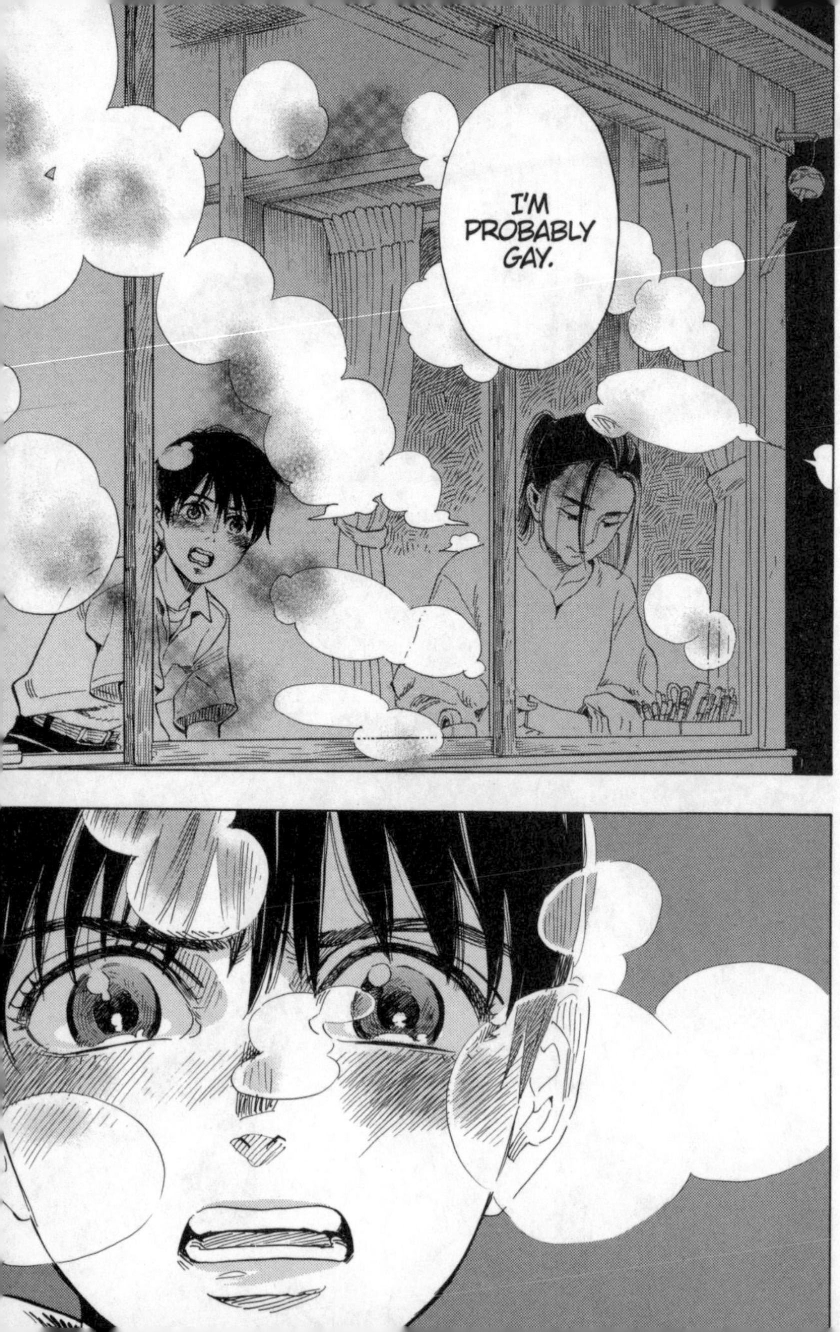
I'M PROBABLY GAY.

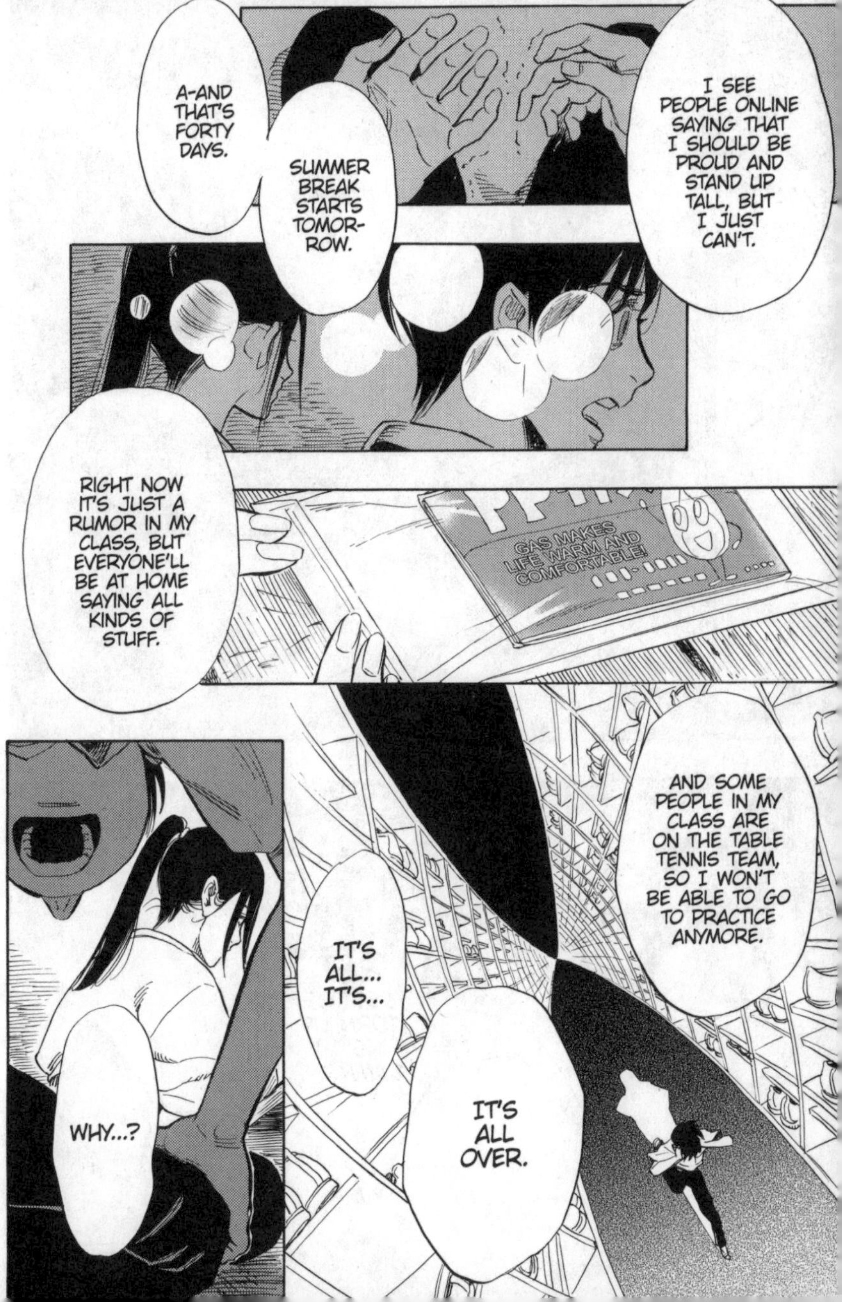
I SEE PEOPLE ONLINE SAYING THAT I SHOULD BE PROUD AND STAND UP TALL, BUT I JUST CAN'T.
SUMMER BREAK STARTS TOMOR-ROW.
A-AND THAT'S FORTY DAYS.
RIGHT NOW IT'S JUST A RUMOR IN MY CLASS, BUT EVERYONE'LL BE AT HOME SAYING ALL KINDS OF STUFF.
GAS MAKES LIFE WARM AND COMFORTABLE!
AND SOME PEOPLE IN MY CLASS ARE ON THE TABLE TENNIS TEAM, SO I WON'T BE ABLE TO GO TO PRACTICE ANYMORE.
IT'S ALL... IT'S...
IT'S ALL OVER.
WHY...?

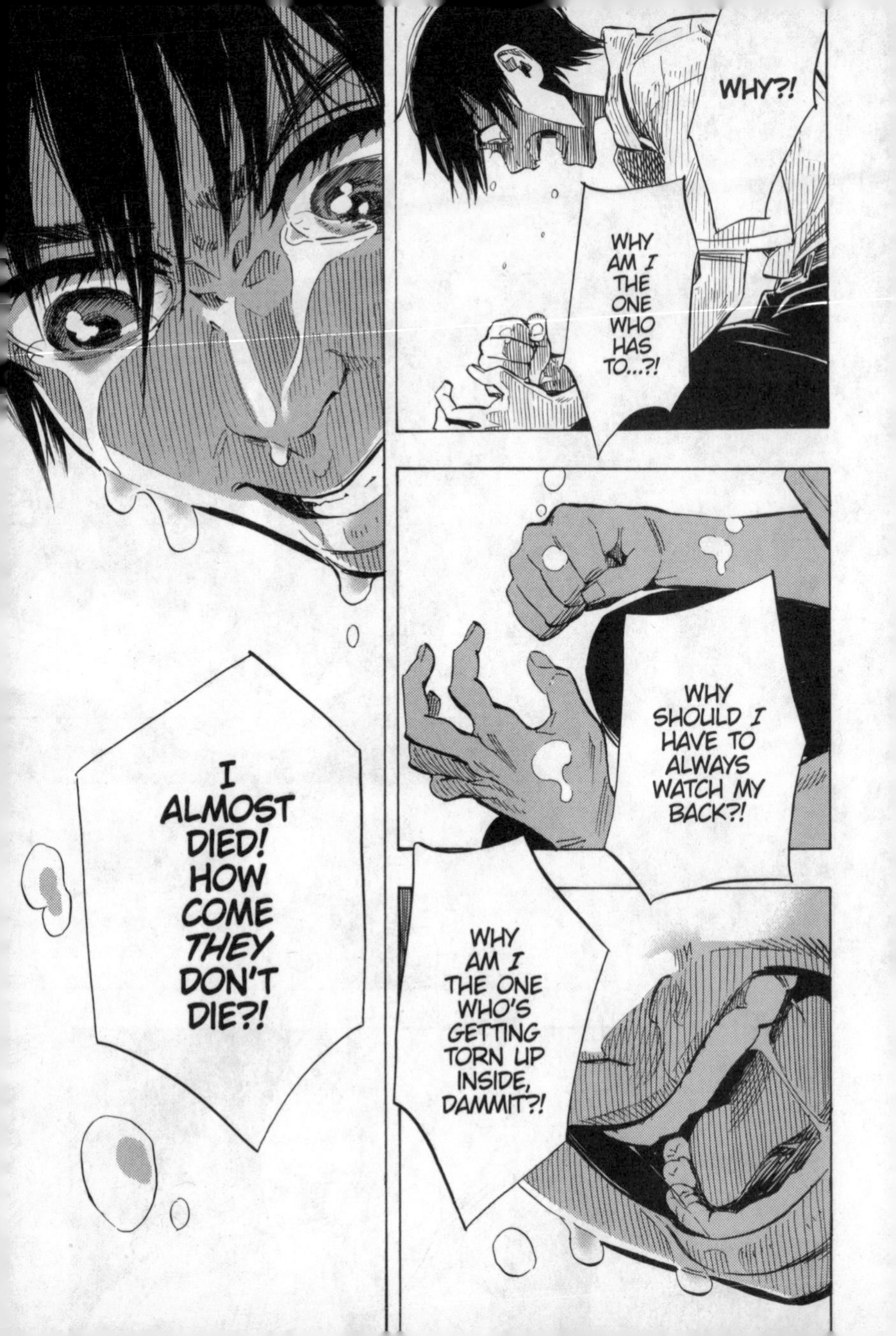
WHY?!
WHY AM I THE ONE WHO HAS TO...?!
WHY SHOULD I HAVE TO ALWAYS WATCH MY BACK?!
WHY AM I THE ONE WHO'S GETTING TORN UP INSIDE, DAMMIT?!
I ALMOST DIED! HOW COME THEY DON'T DIE?!

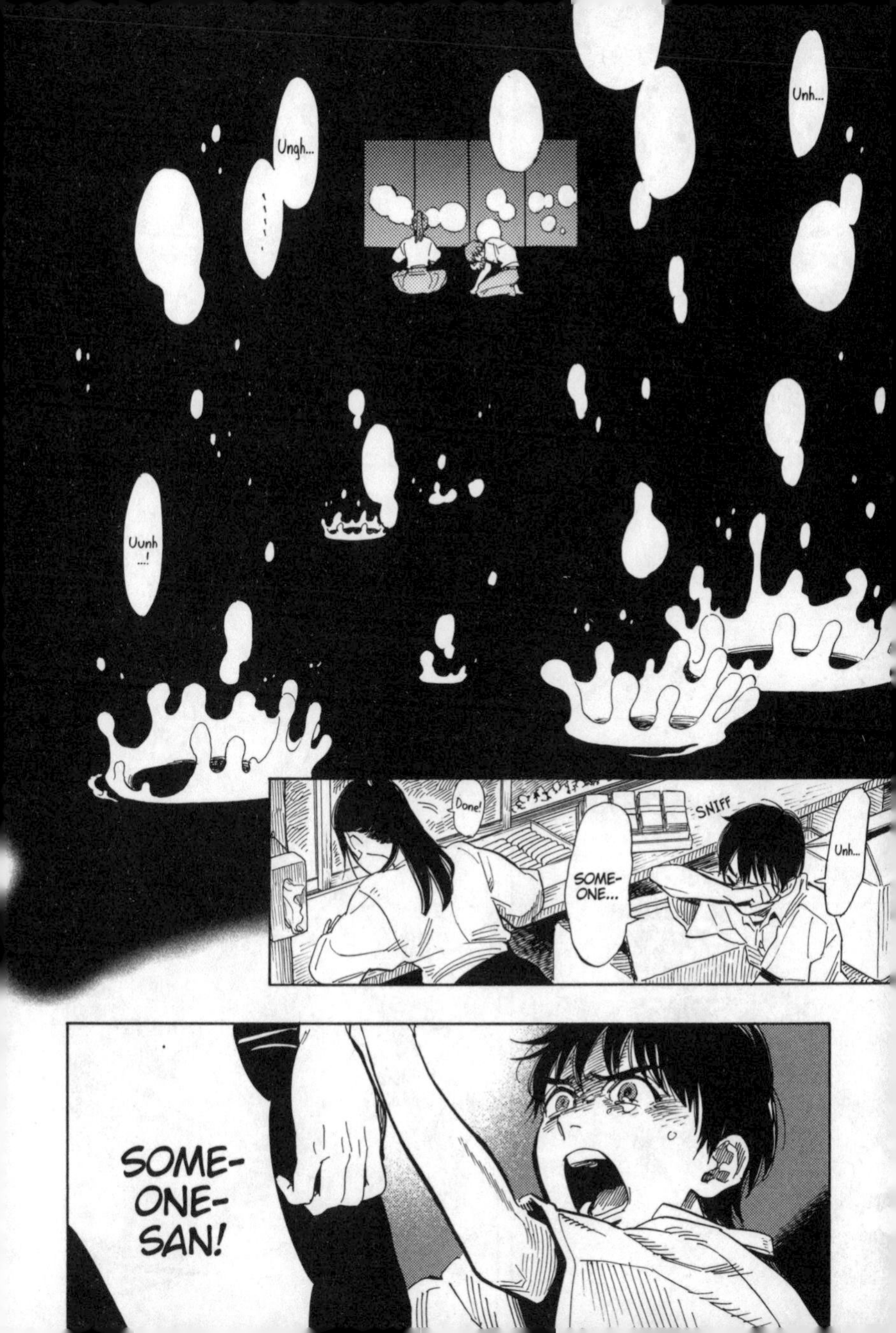
Unh...
Ungh...
Uunh!...
Unh...
SNIFF
SOME-ONE...
Done!
SOME-ONE-SAN!

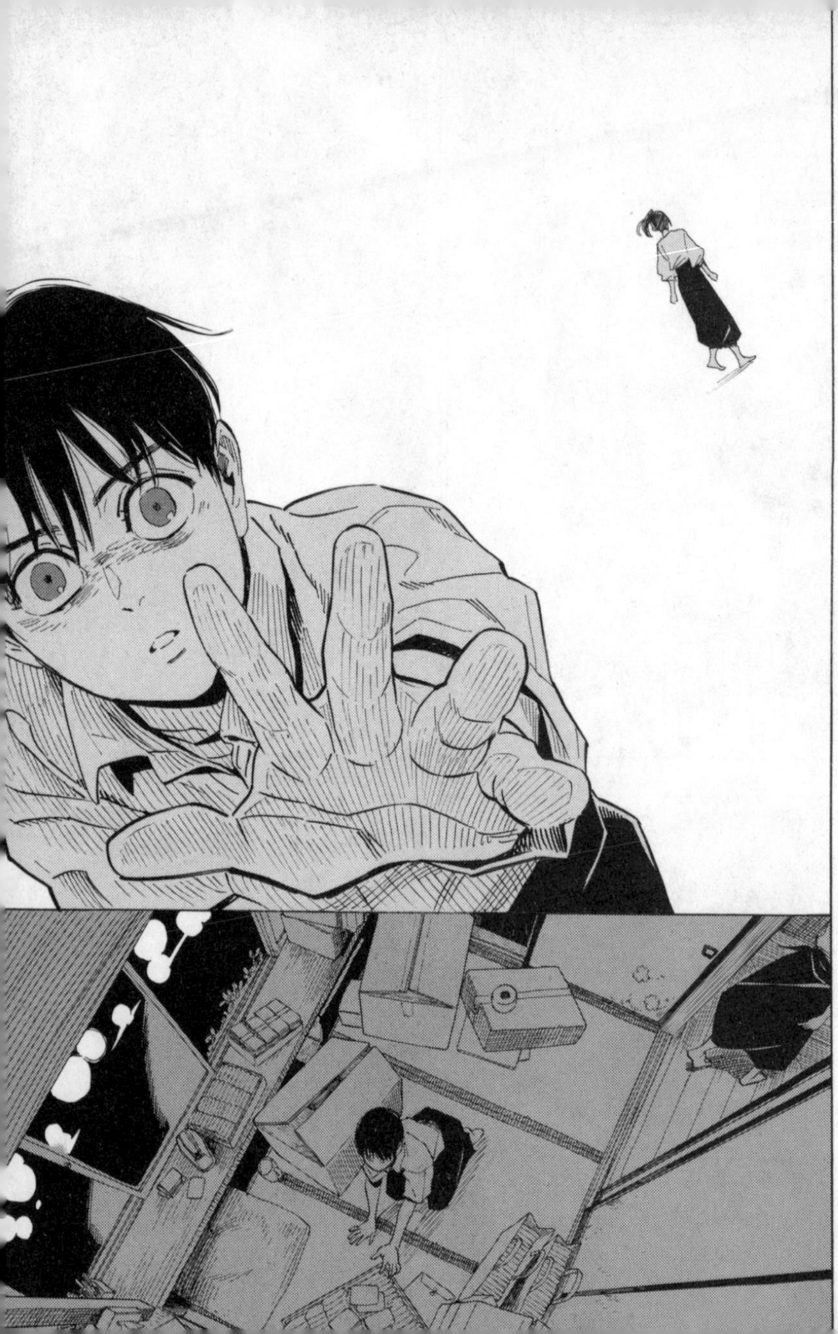

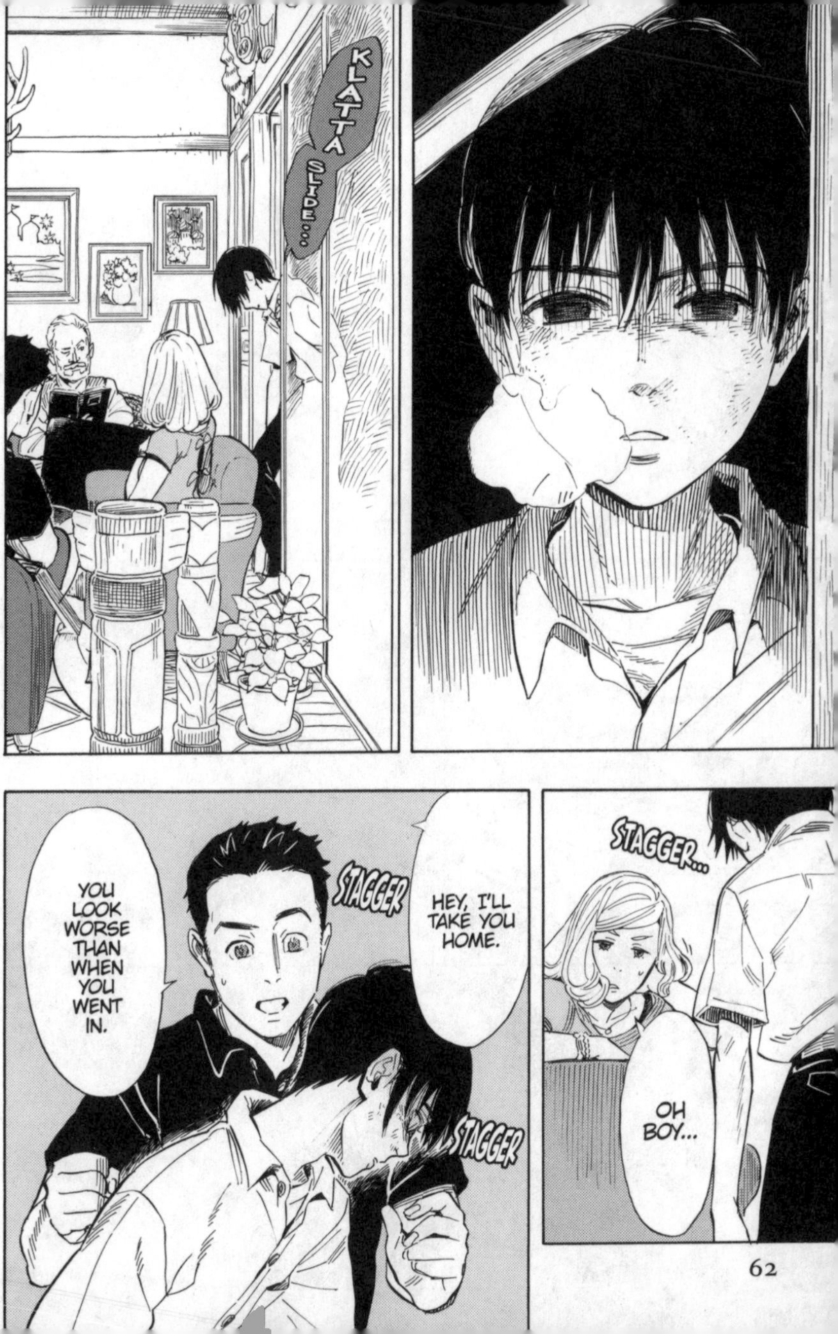
KLATTA
SLIDE...
STAGGER...
OH BOY...
HEY, I'LL TAKE YOU HOME.
STAGGER
YOU LOOK WORSE THAN WHEN YOU WENT IN.
STAGGER

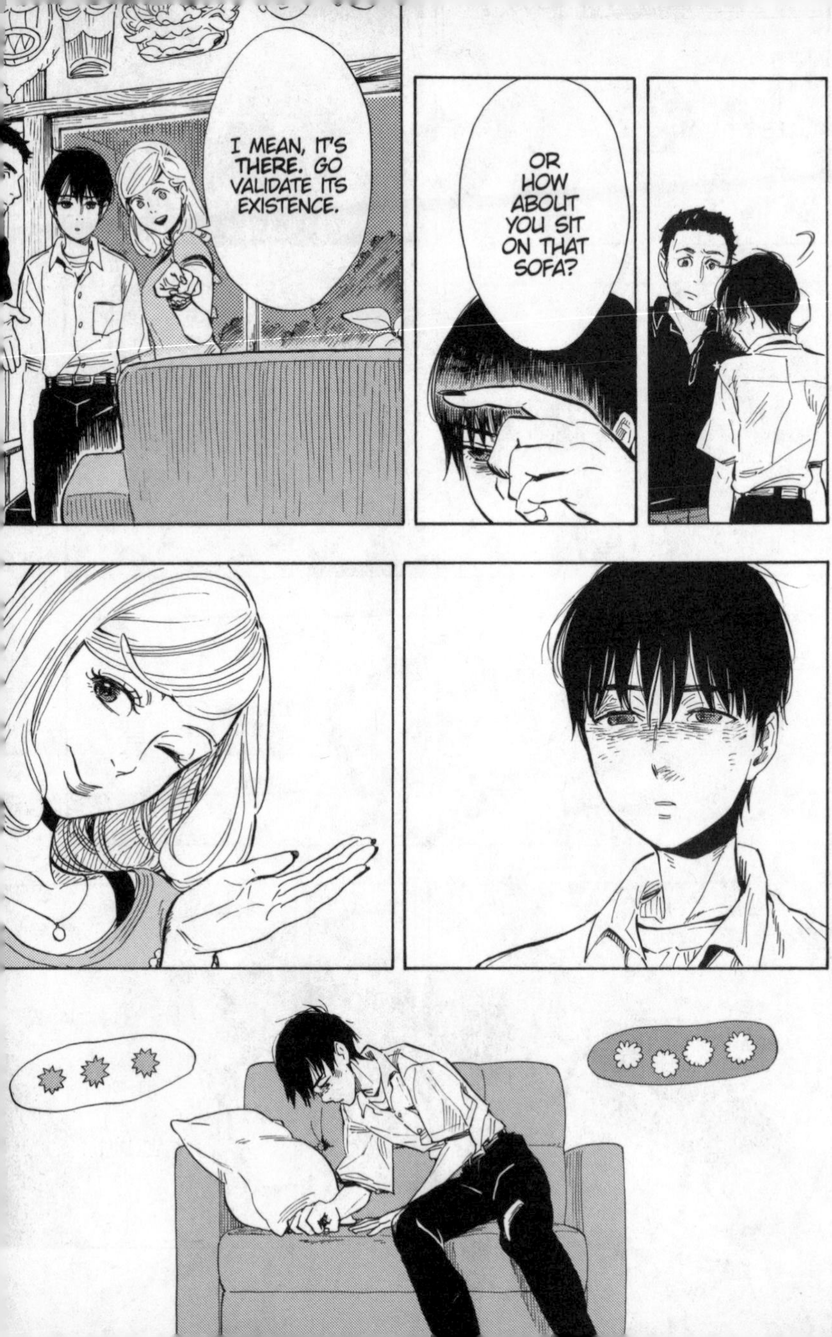
OR HOW ABOUT YOU SIT ON THAT SOFA?
I MEAN, IT'S THERE. GO VALIDATE ITS EXISTENCE.

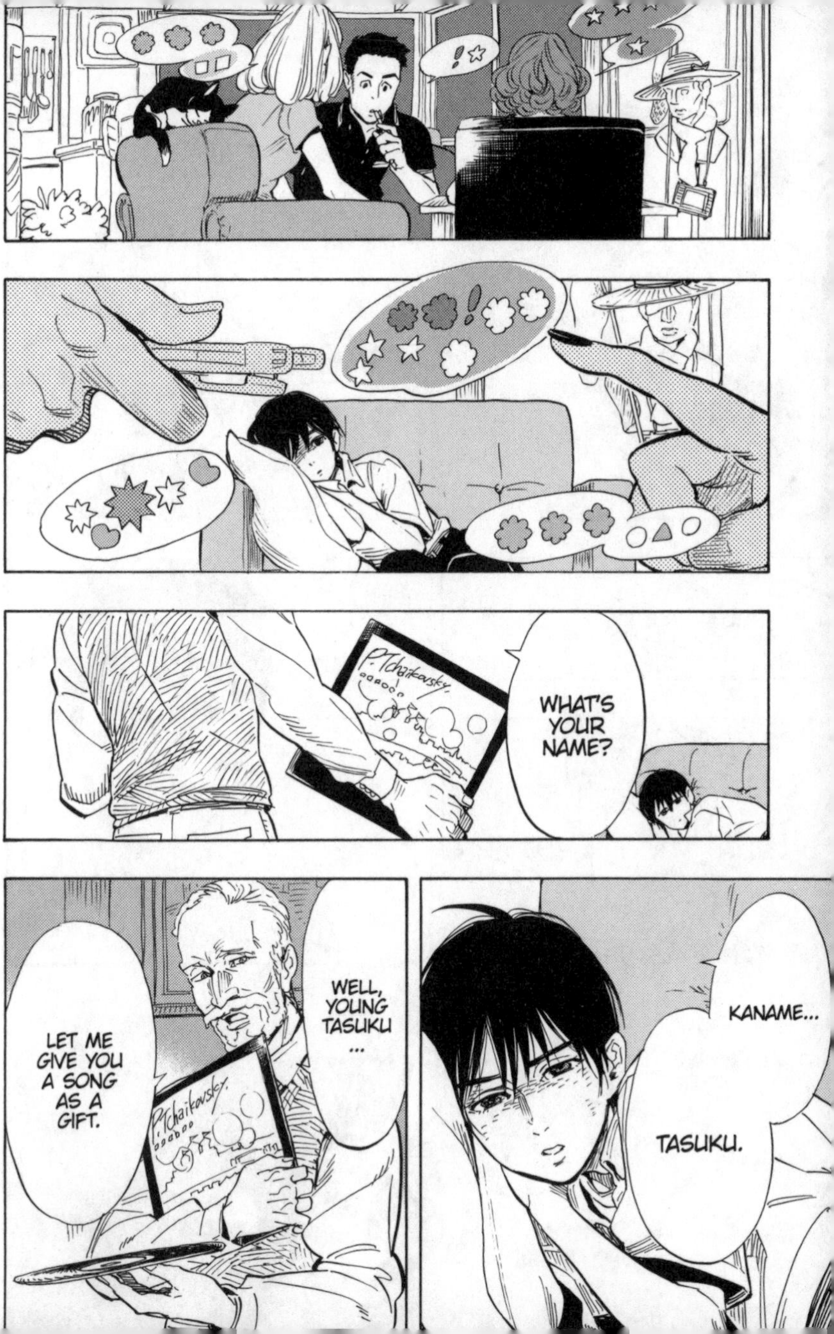
P. Tchaikovsky
WHAT'S YOUR NAME?
KANAME...
TASUKU.
WELL, YOUNG TASUKU ...
LET ME GIVE YOU A SONG AS A GIFT.
P. Tchaikovsky

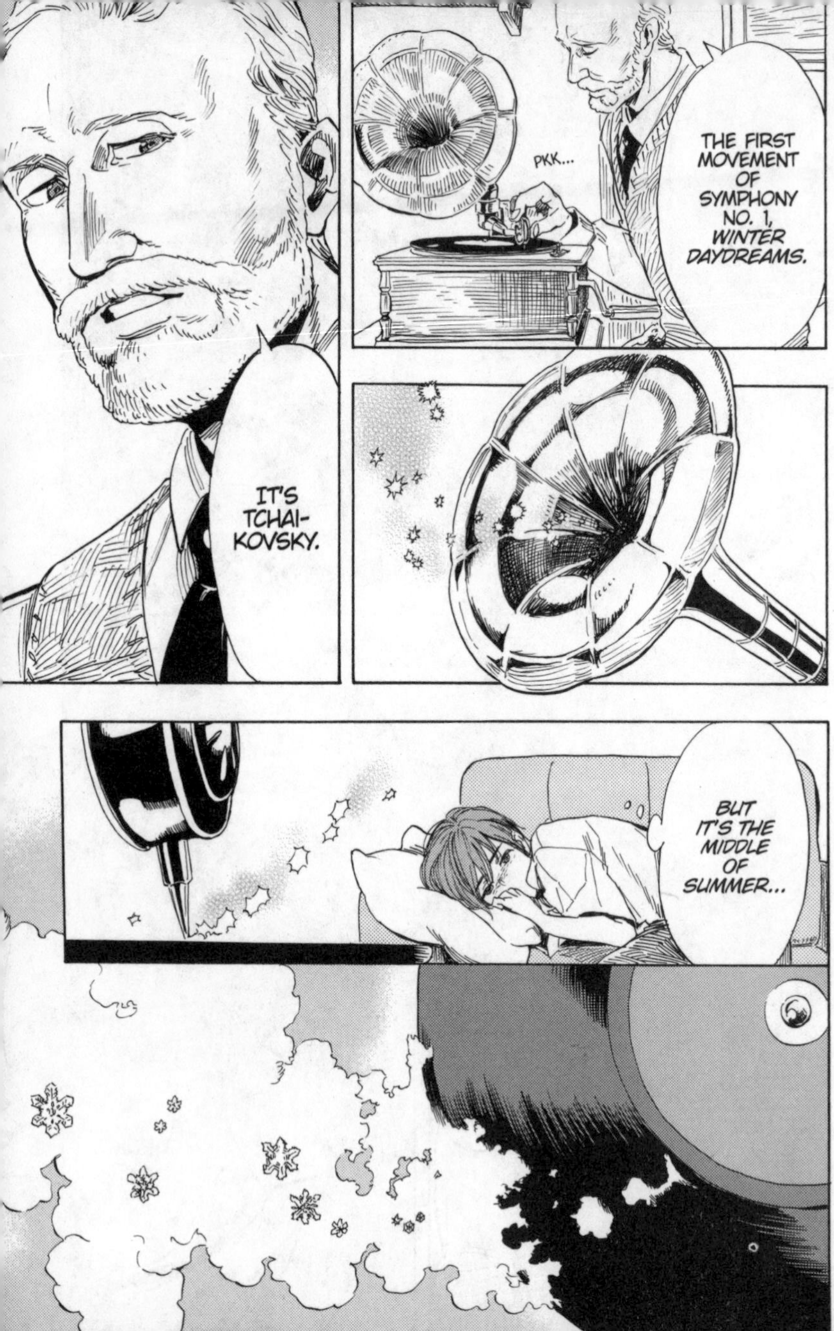
THE FIRST MOVEMENT OF SYMPHONY NO. 1, WINTER DAYDREAMS.
PKK...
IT'S TCHAI-KOVSKY.
BUT IT'S THE MIDDLE OF SUMMER...

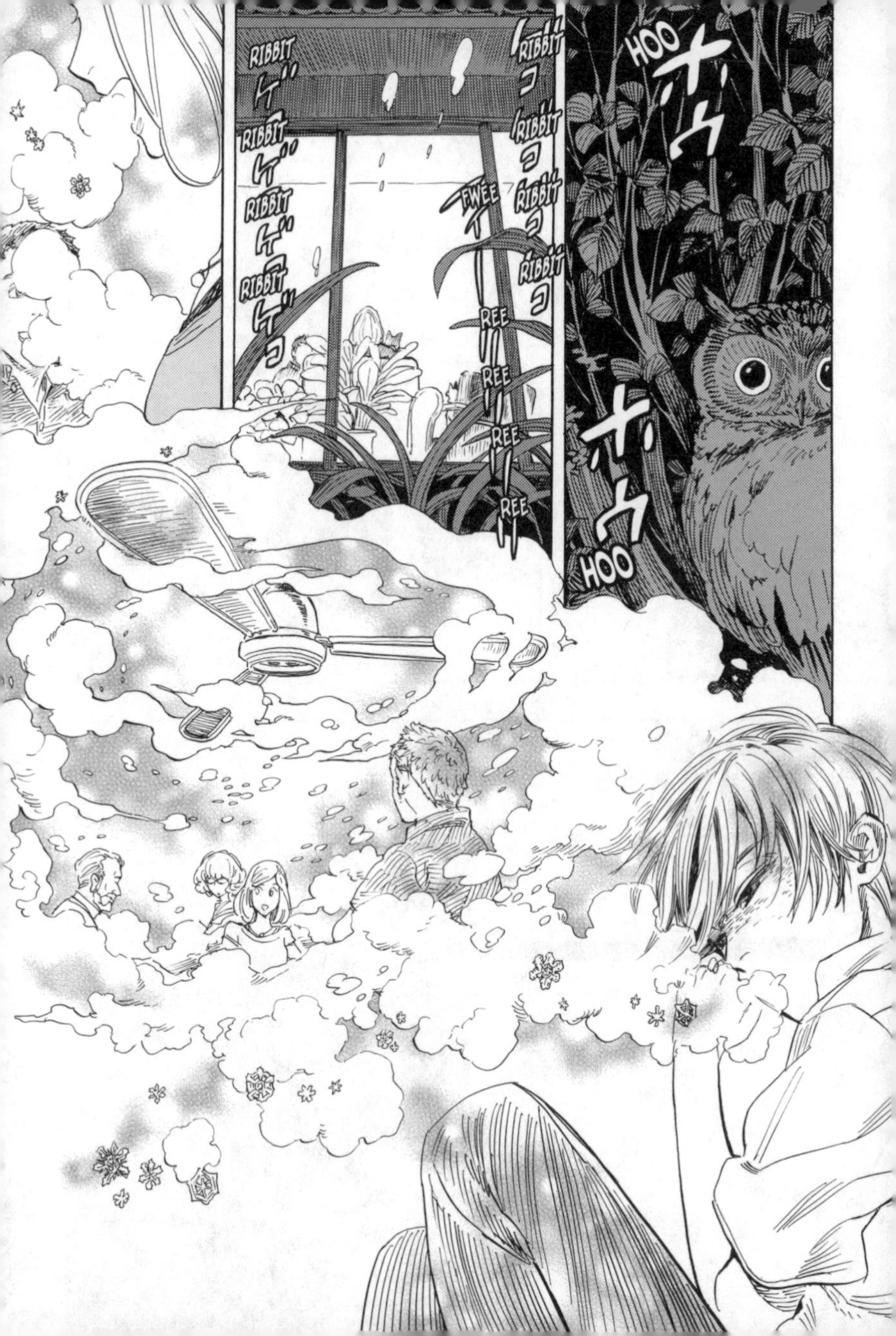
HOO
HOO
RIBBIT
RIBBIT
RIBBIT
RIBBIT
FWEE
REE
REE
REE
REE
RIBBIT
RIBBIT
RIBBIT
RIBBIT

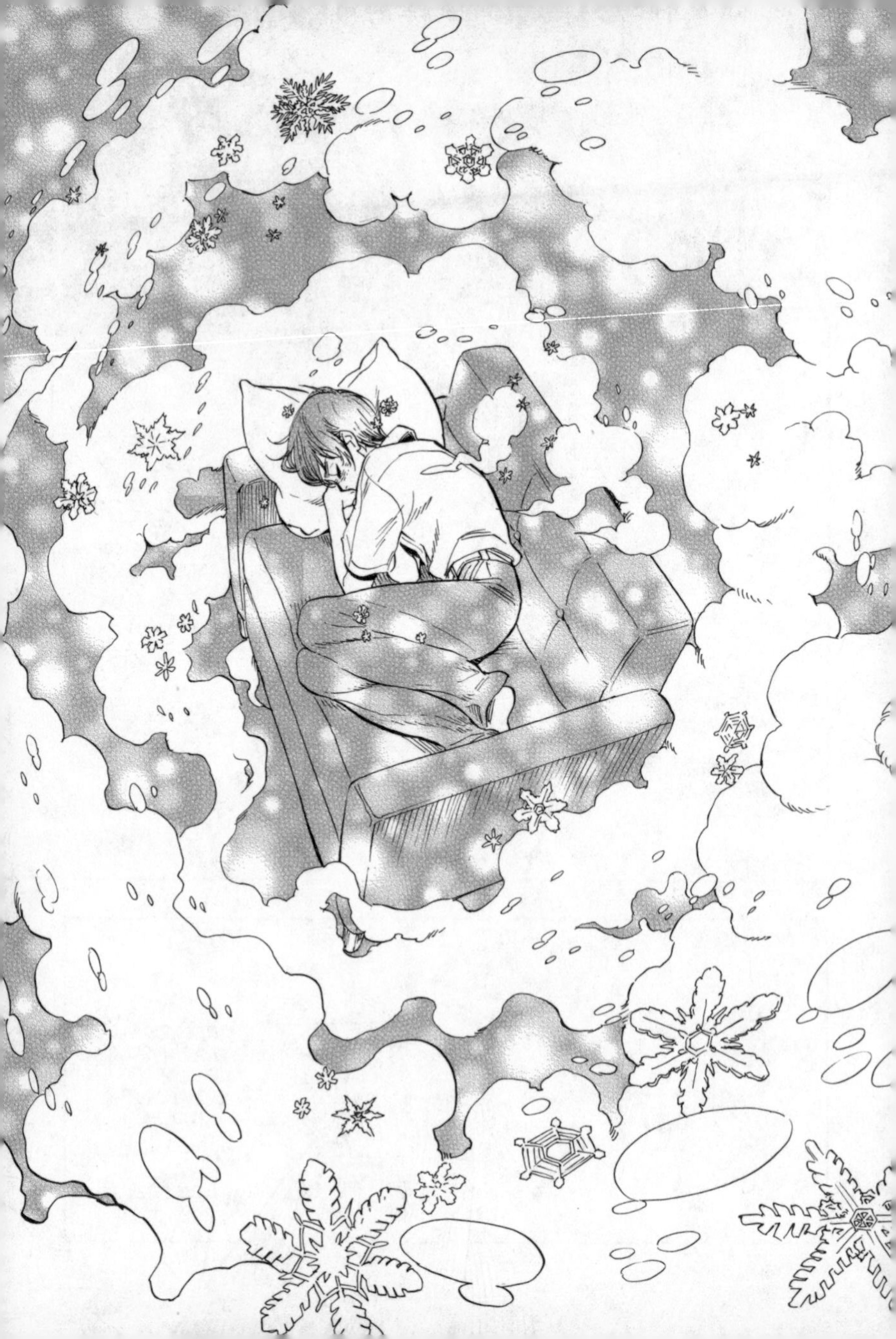

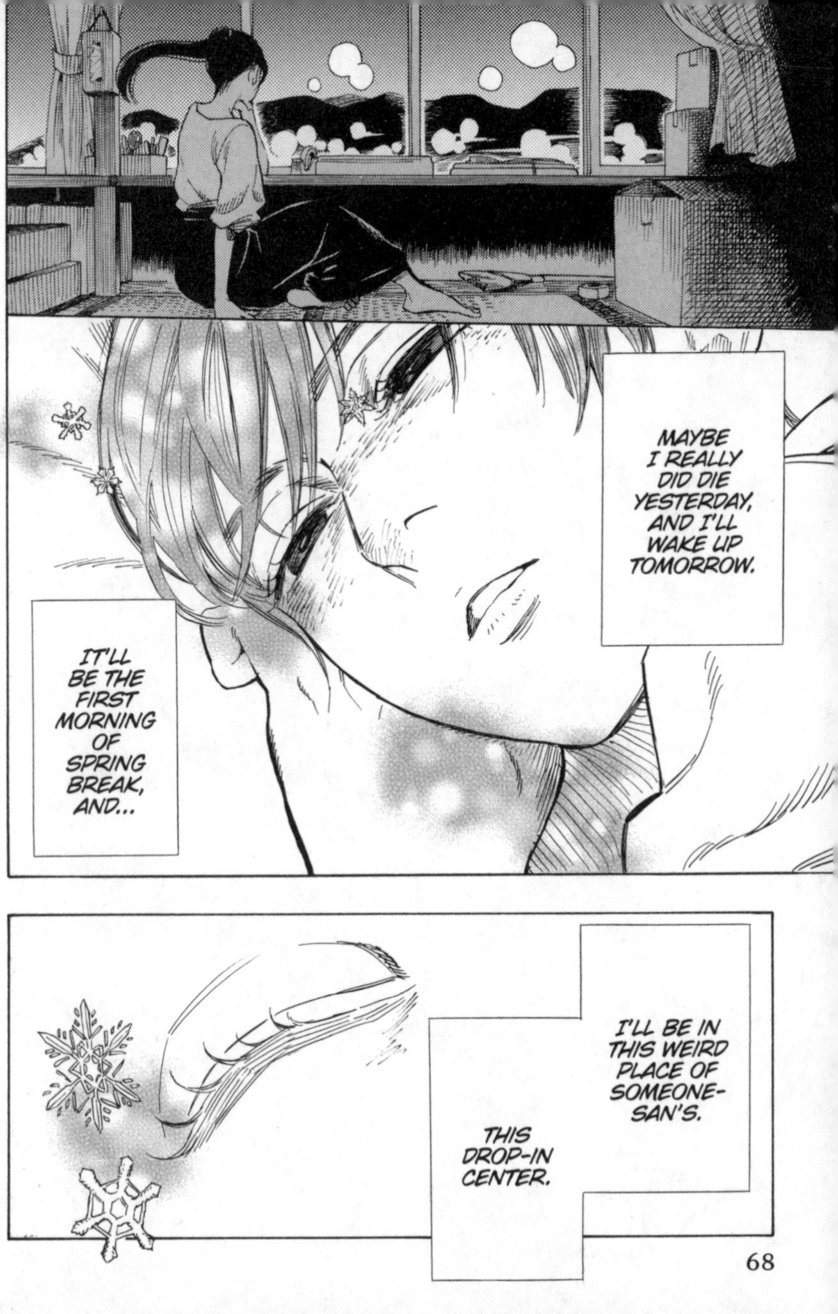
MAYBE I REALLY DID DIE YESTERDAY, AND I'LL WAKE UP TOMORROW.
IT'LL BE THE FIRST MORNING OF SPRING BREAK, AND...
I'LL BE IN THIS WEIRD PLACE OF SOMEONE-SAN'S.
THIS DROP-IN CENTER.

Our Dreams at Dusk

SHIMANAMI TASOGARE

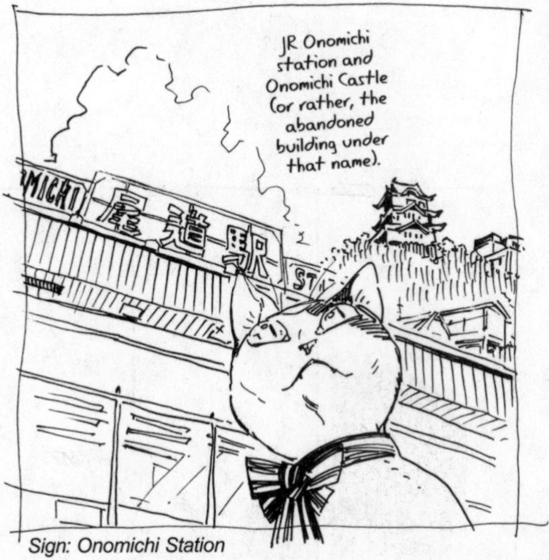
JR Onomichi station and Onomichi Castle (or rather, the abandoned building under that name).
MICHI
Sign: Onomichi Station

Chapter 3

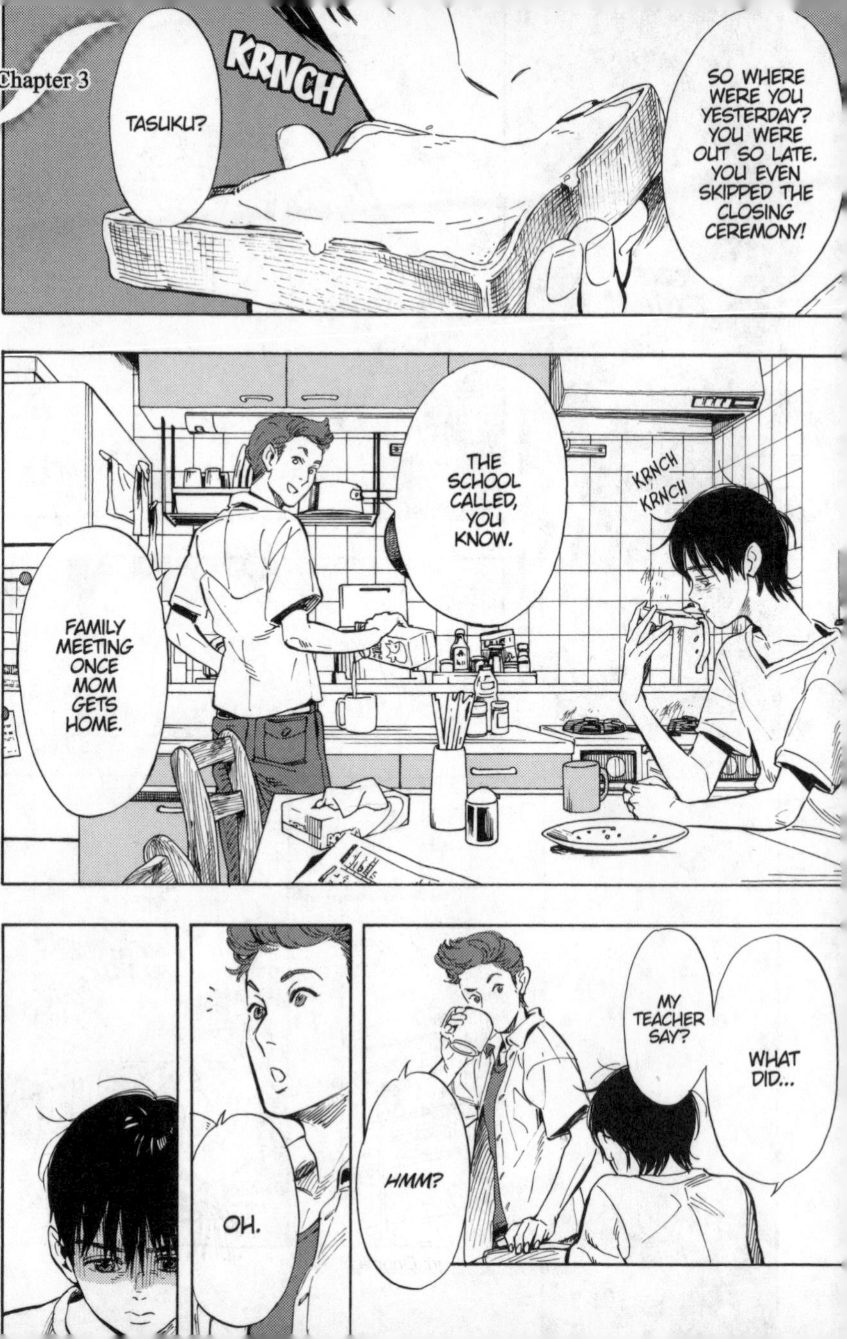
SO WHERE WERE YOU YESTERDAY? YOU WERE OUT SO LATE. YOU EVEN SKIPPED THE CLOSING CEREMONY!
KRNCH
TASUKU?
KRNCH KRNCH
THE SCHOOL CALLED, YOU KNOW.
FAMILY MEETING ONCE MOM GETS HOME.
WHAT DID...
MY TEACHER SAY?
HMM?
OH.

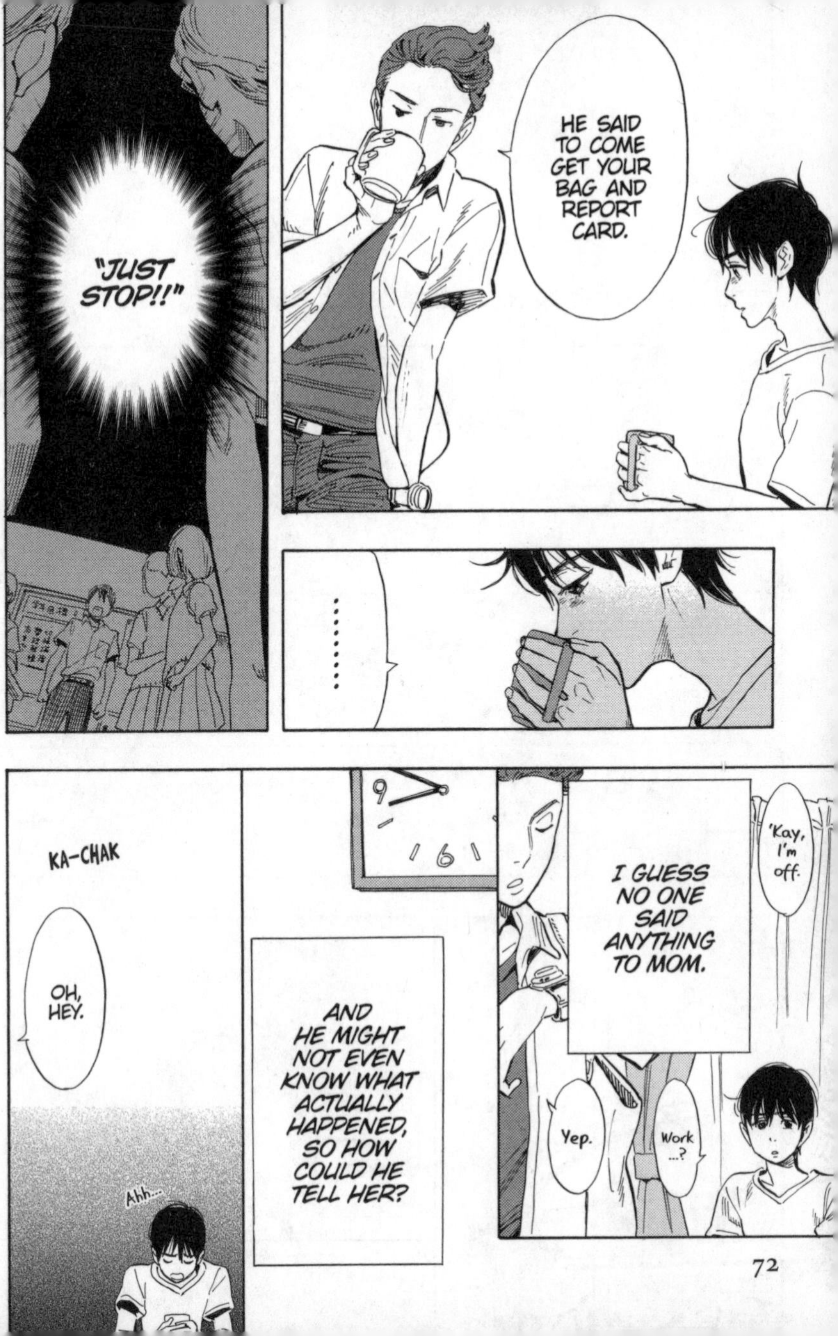
HE SAID TO COME GET YOUR BAG AND REPORT CARD.
......
"JUST STOP!!"
'Kay, I'm off.
I GUESS NO ONE SAID ANYTHING TO MOM.
Work ...?
Yep.
AND HE MIGHT NOT EVEN KNOW WHAT ACTUALLY HAPPENED, SO HOW COULD HE TELL HER?
KA-CHAK
OH, HEY.
Ahh...

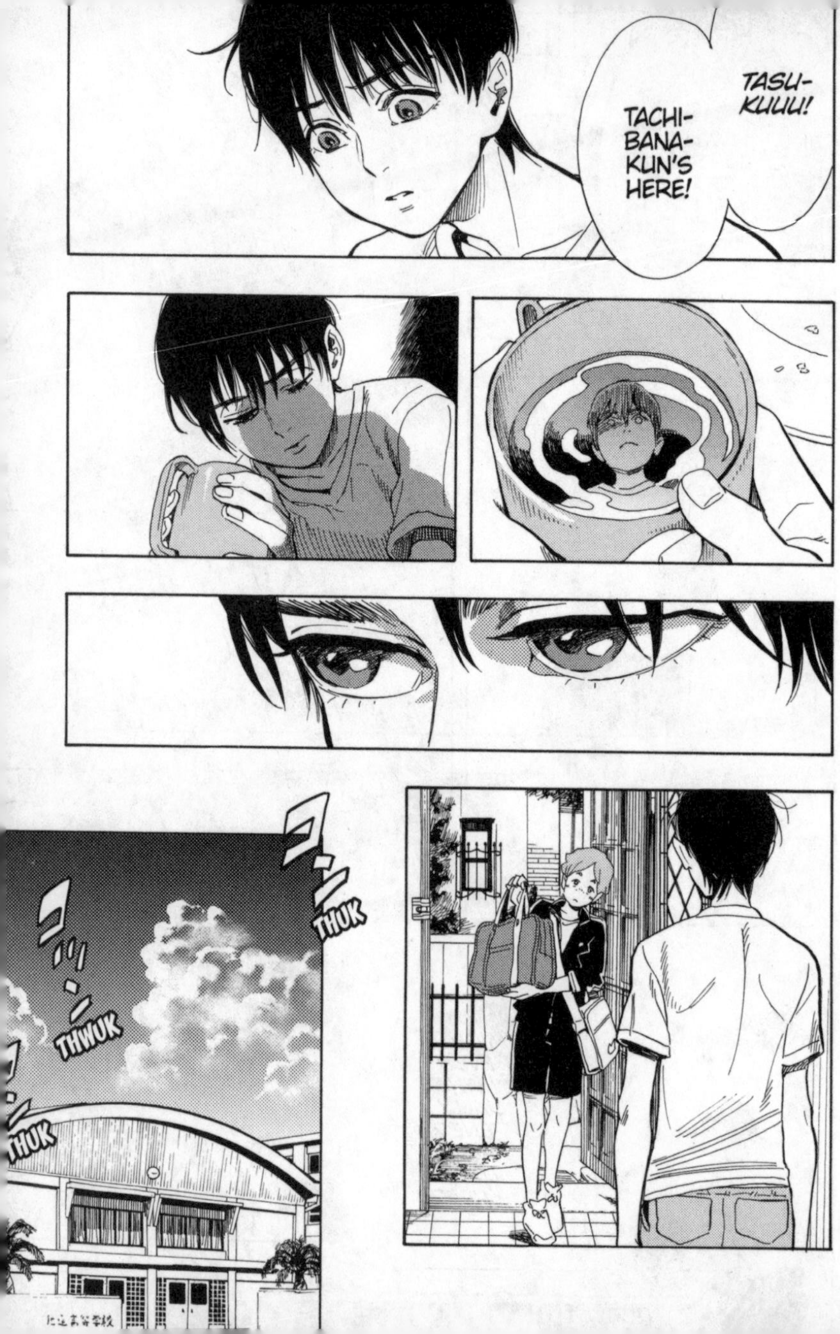
TASU-KUUU!
TACHI-BANA-KUN'S HERE!
THUK
THWUK
THUK

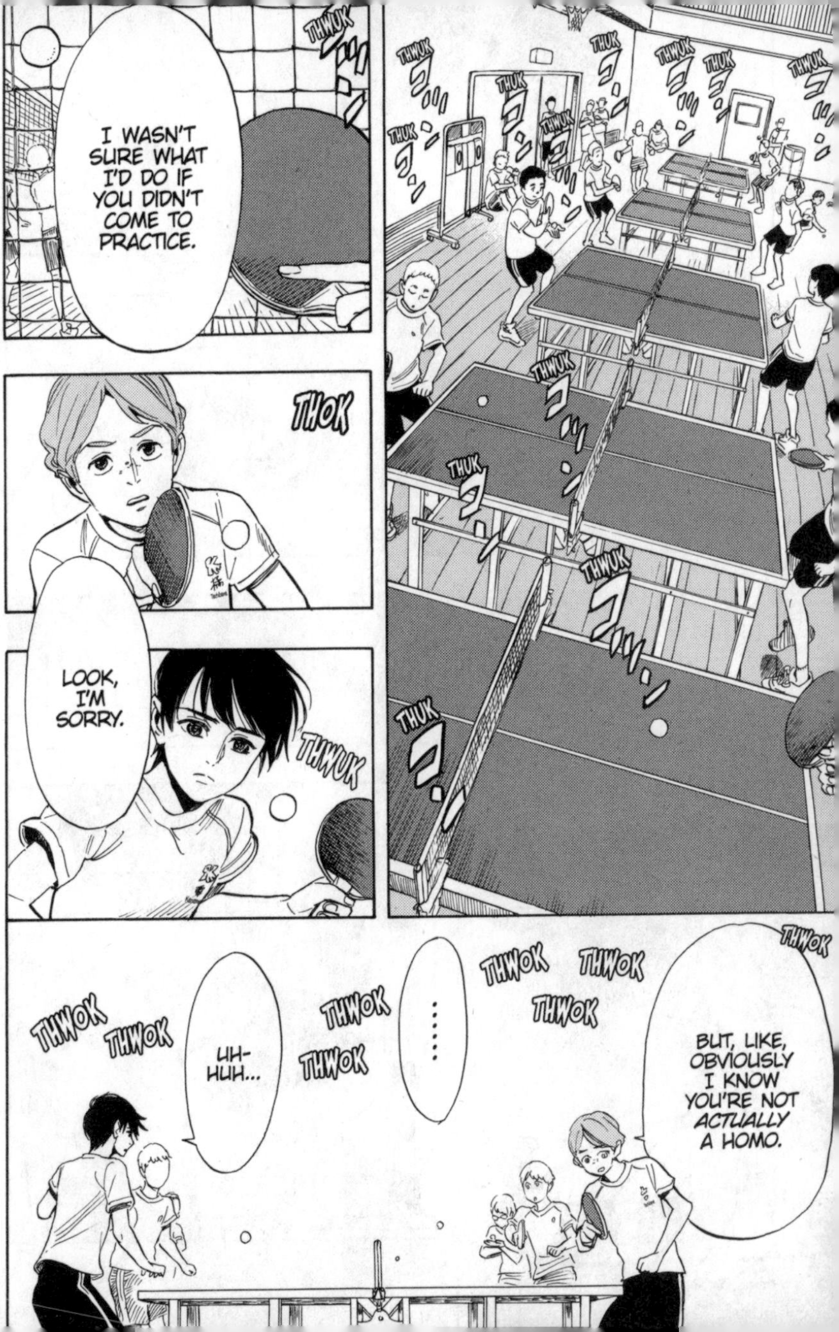
THWUK
THUK
THWUK
THUK
THWUK
THUK
THWUK
THUK
THWUK
THUK
THWUK
I WASN'T SURE WHAT I'D DO IF YOU DIDN'T COME TO PRACTICE.
THOK
LOOK, I'M SORRY.
THWUK
THWOK
BUT, LIKE, OBVIOUSLY I KNOW YOU'RE NOT *ACTUALLY* A HOMO.
THWOK
THWOK
THWOK
......
THWOK
THWOK
UH-HUH...
THWOK
THWOK

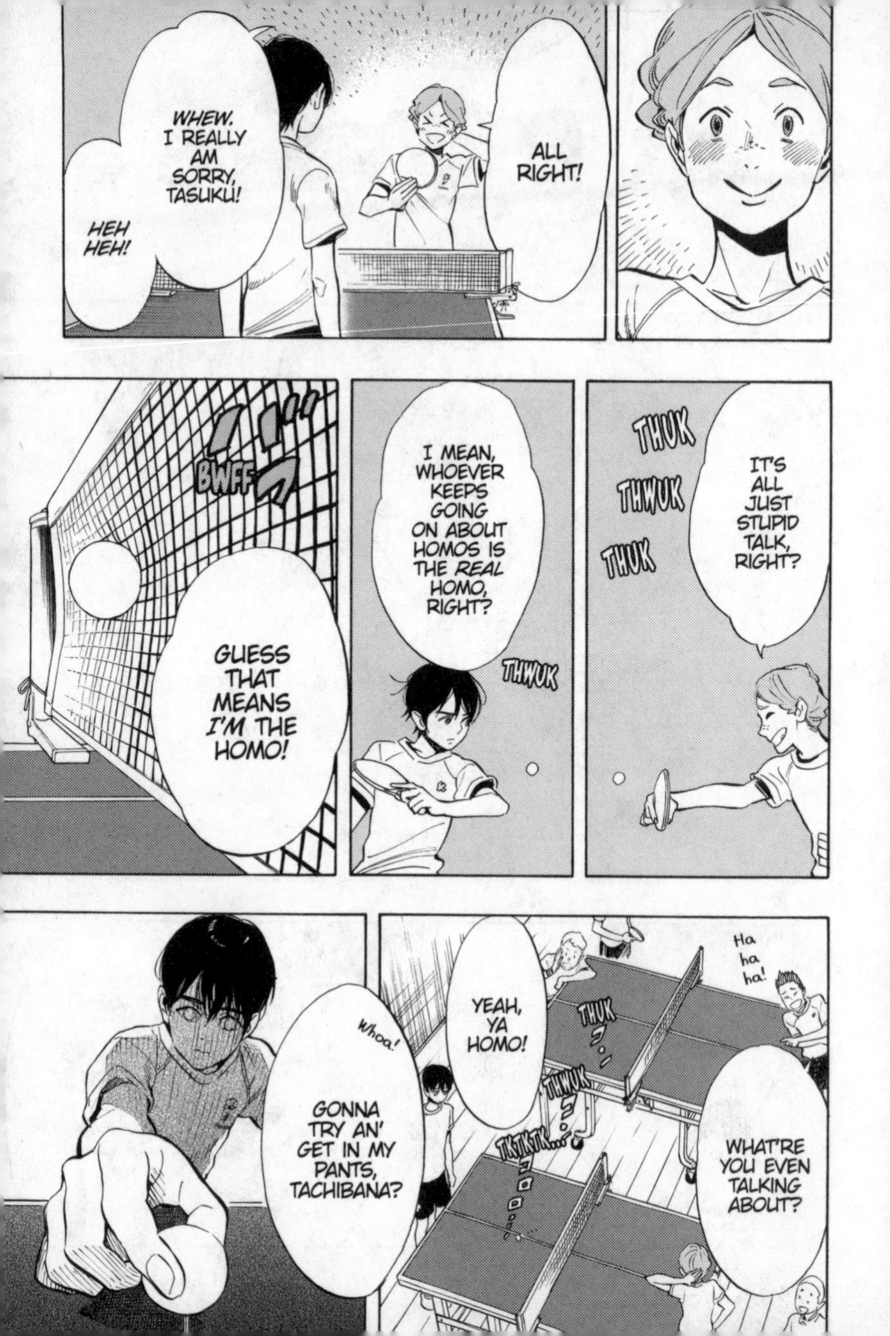
ALL RIGHT!
WHEW. I REALLY AM SORRY, TASUKU!
HEH HEH!
IT'S ALL JUST STUPID TALK, RIGHT?
THUK
THWUK
THUK
I MEAN, WHOEVER KEEPS GOING ON ABOUT HOMOS IS THE *REAL* HOMO, RIGHT?
THWUK
BWFF
GUESS THAT MEANS *I'M* THE HOMO!
Ha ha ha!
YEAH, YA HOMO!
THUK
THWUK
TKTKTK...
WHAT'RE YOU EVEN TALKING ABOUT?
Whoa!
GONNA TRY AN' GET IN MY PANTS, TACHIBANA?

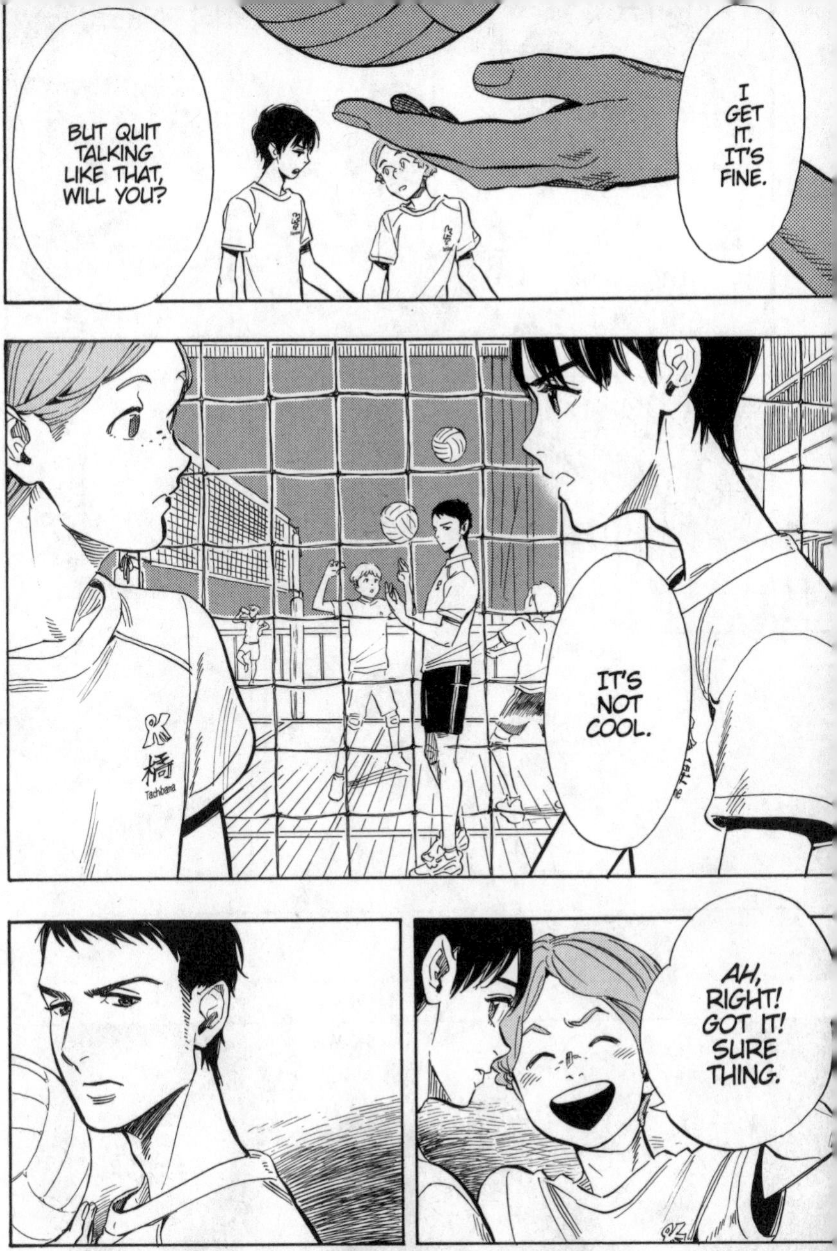
I GET IT. IT'S FINE.
BUT QUIT TALKING LIKE THAT, WILL YOU?
IT'S NOT COOL.
Tachibana
AH, RIGHT! GOT IT! SURE THING.

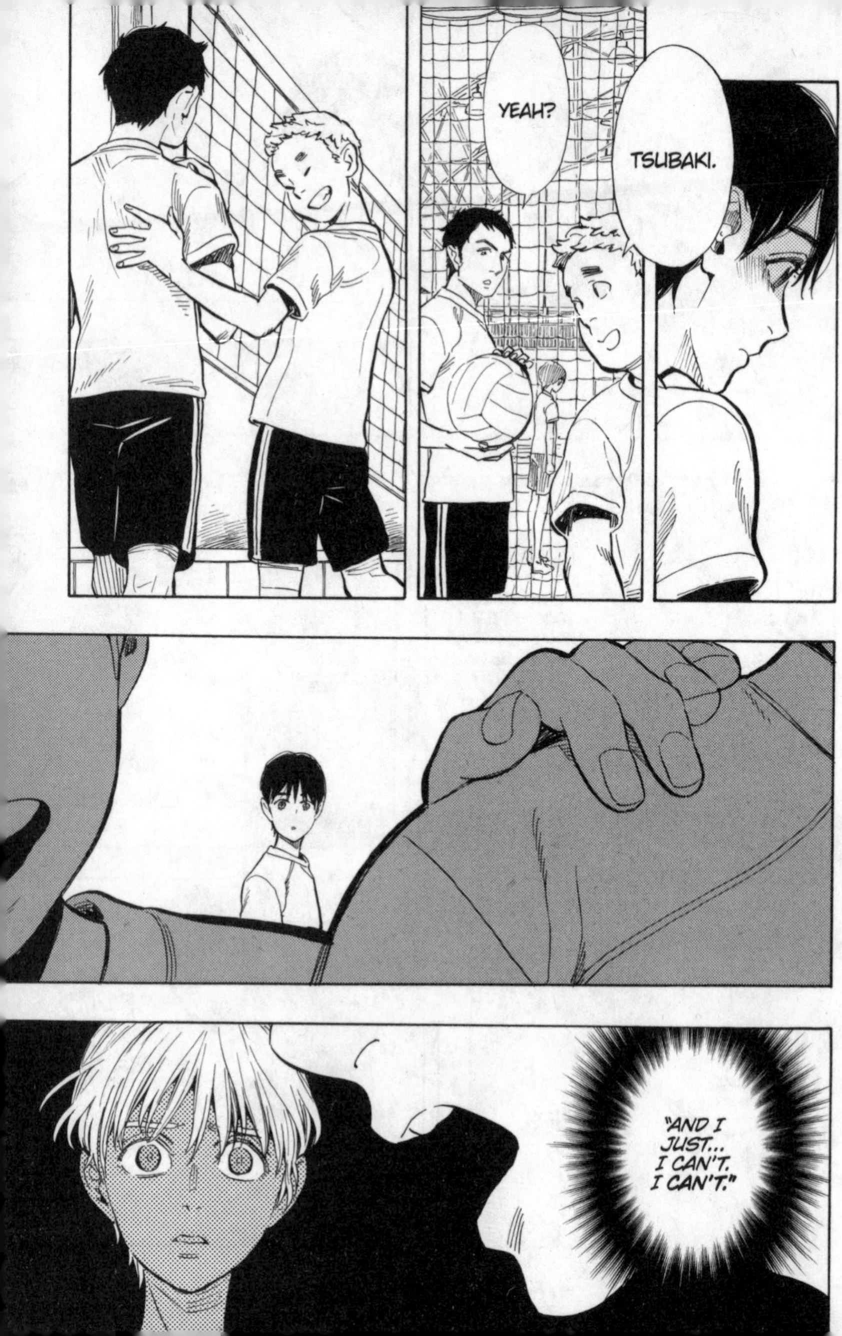
TSUBAKI.
YEAH?
"AND I JUST... I CAN'T. I CAN'T."

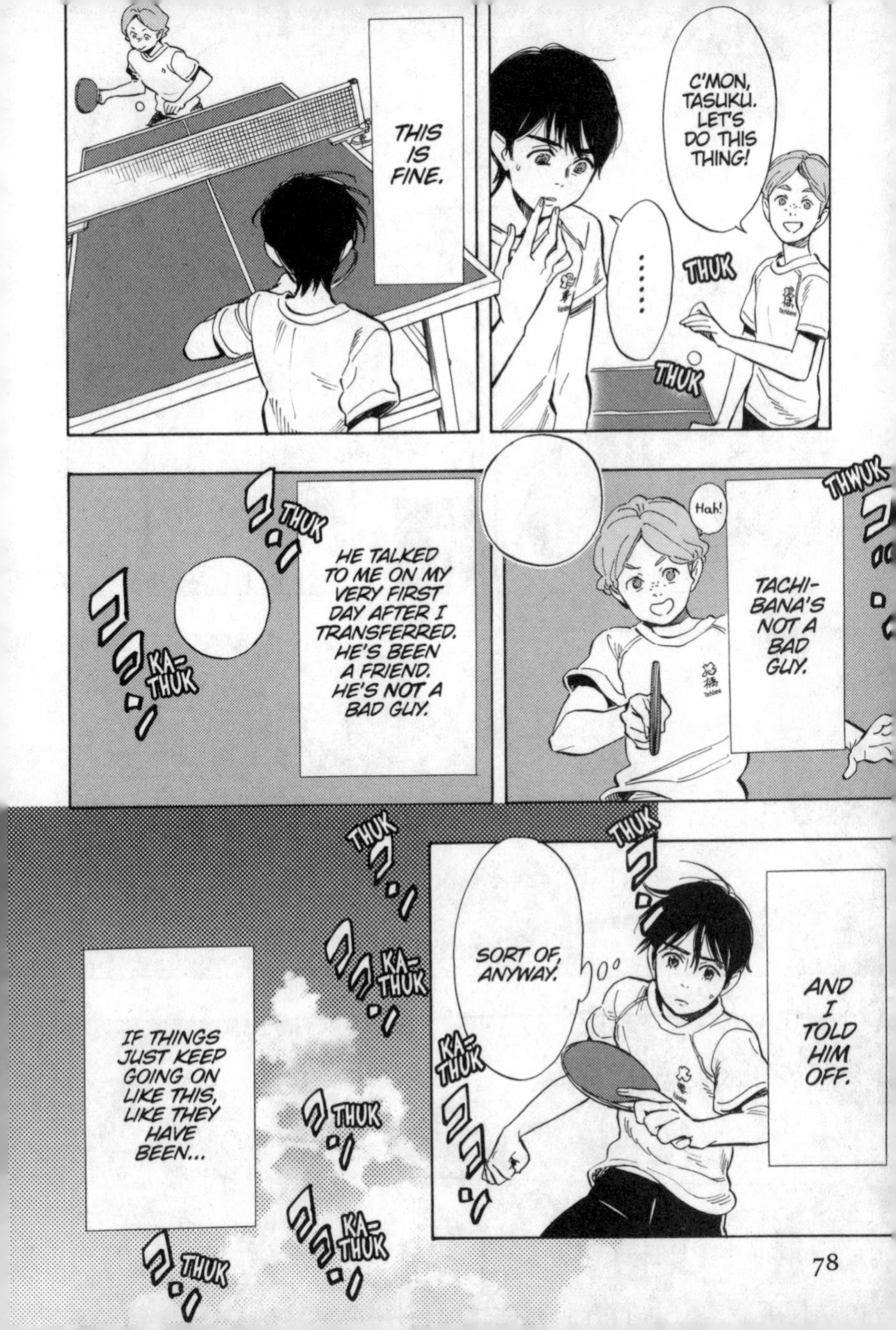
C'MON, TASUKU. LET'S DO THIS THING!
......
THUK
THUK
THIS IS FINE.
THWUK
Hah!
TACHI-BANA'S NOT A BAD GUY.
THUK
KA-THUK
HE TALKED TO ME ON MY VERY FIRST DAY AFTER I TRANSFERRED. HE'S BEEN A FRIEND. HE'S NOT A BAD GUY.
THUK
AND I TOLD HIM OFF.
SORT OF, ANYWAY.
KA-THUK
THUK
KA-THUK
IF THINGS JUST KEEP GOING ON LIKE THIS, LIKE THEY HAVE BEEN...
THUK
KA-THUK
THUK

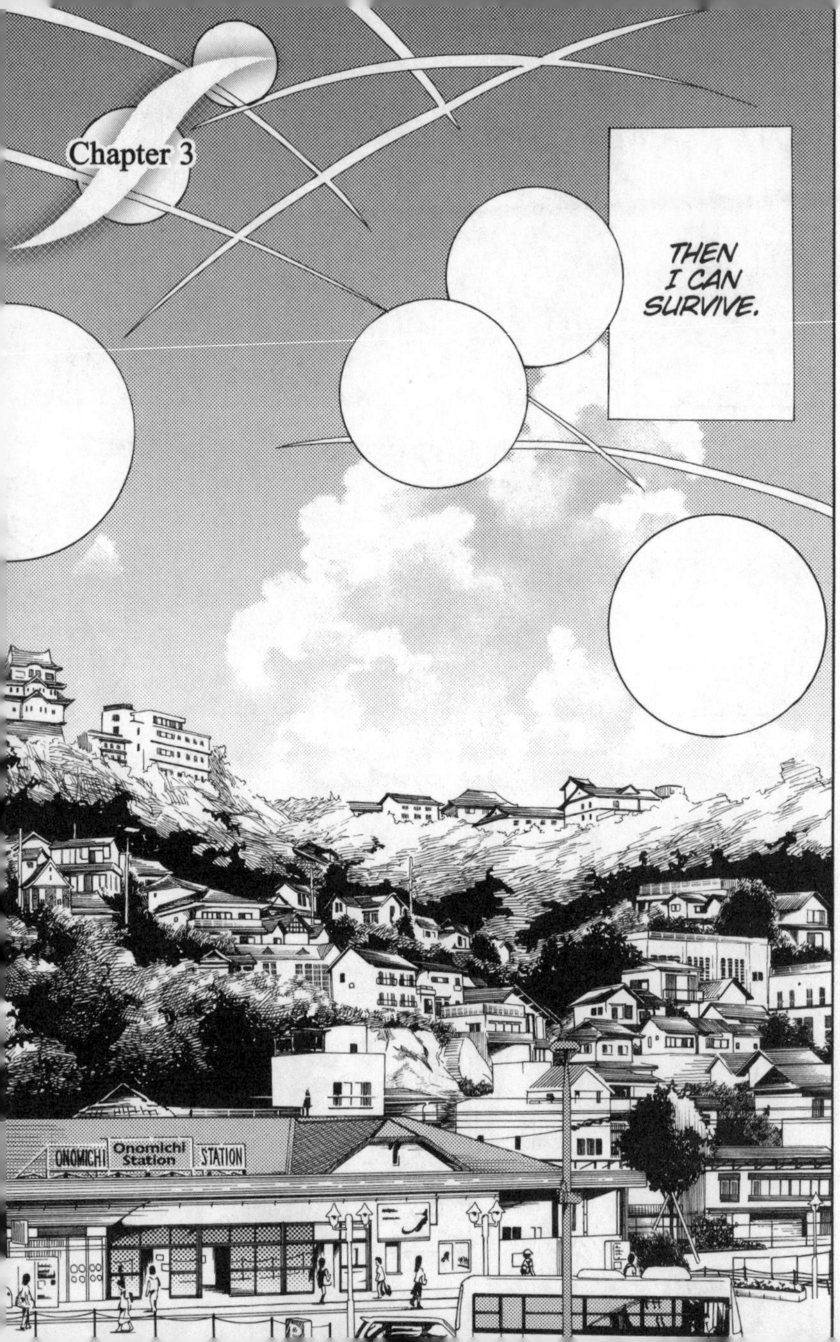
Chapter 3
THEN I CAN SURVIVE.
ONOMICHI
Onomichi Station
STATION

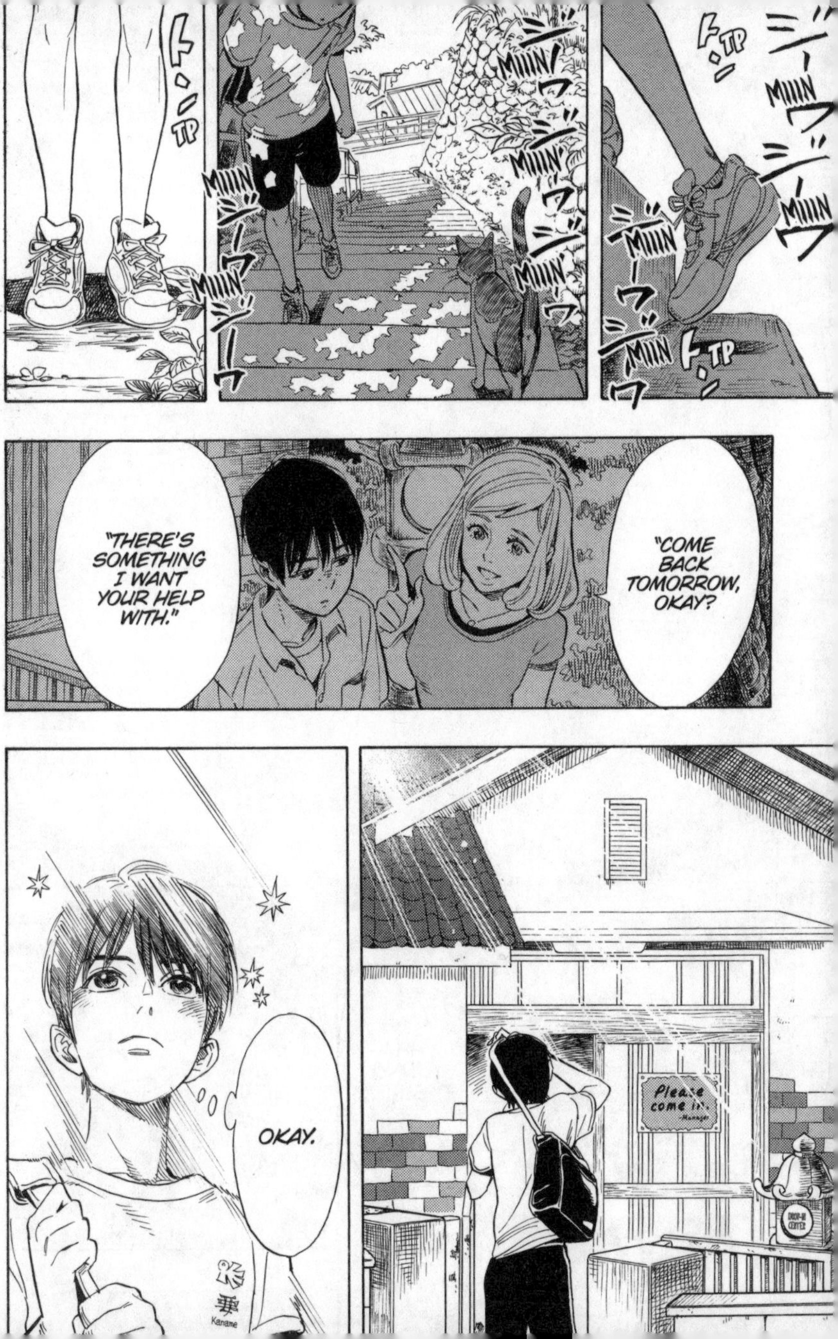

TP
MIIN
MIIN
MIIN
MIIN
TP
MIIN
MIIN
MIIN
MIIN
MIIN
MIIN
TP
"COME BACK TOMORROW, OKAY?"
"THERE'S SOMETHING I WANT YOUR HELP WITH."
Please come in.
-Manager
DROP-IN CENTER
OKAY.
要
Kaname

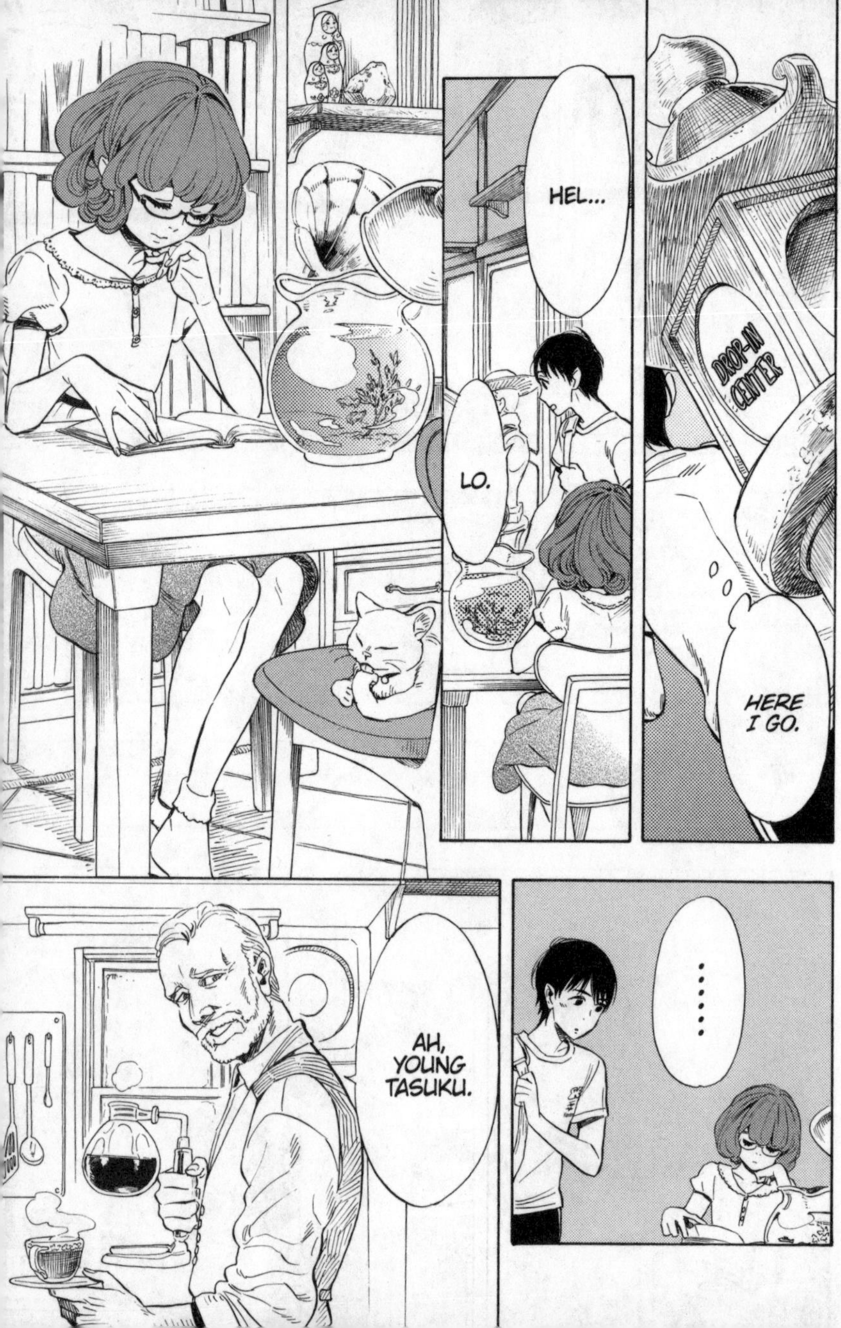
DROP-IN CENTER
HERE I GO.
HEL...
LO.
......
AH, YOUNG TASUKU.

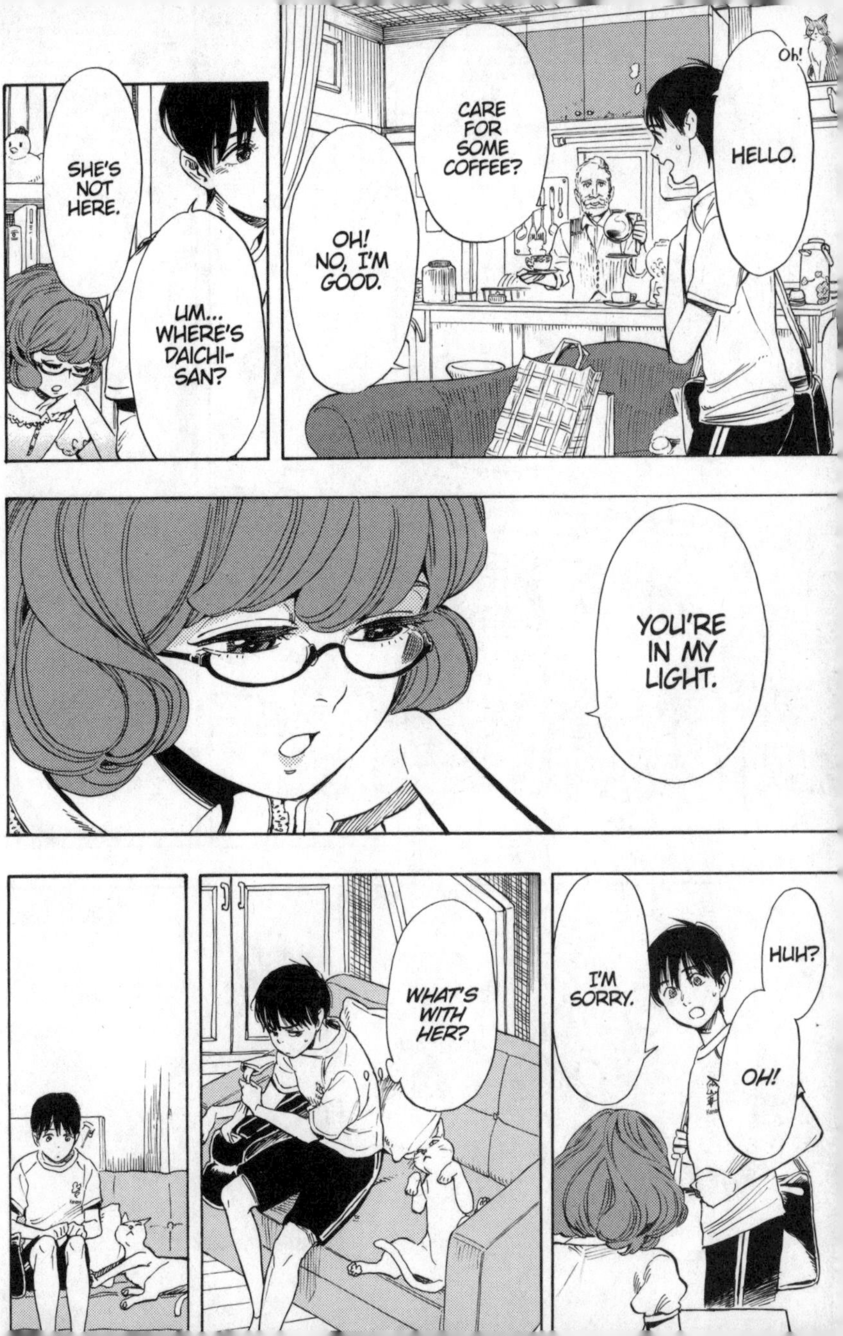
Oh!
HELLO.
CARE FOR SOME COFFEE?
OH! NO, I'M GOOD.
UM... WHERE'S DAICHI-SAN?
SHE'S NOT HERE.
YOU'RE IN MY LIGHT.
HUH?
OH!
I'M SORRY.
WHAT'S WITH HER?

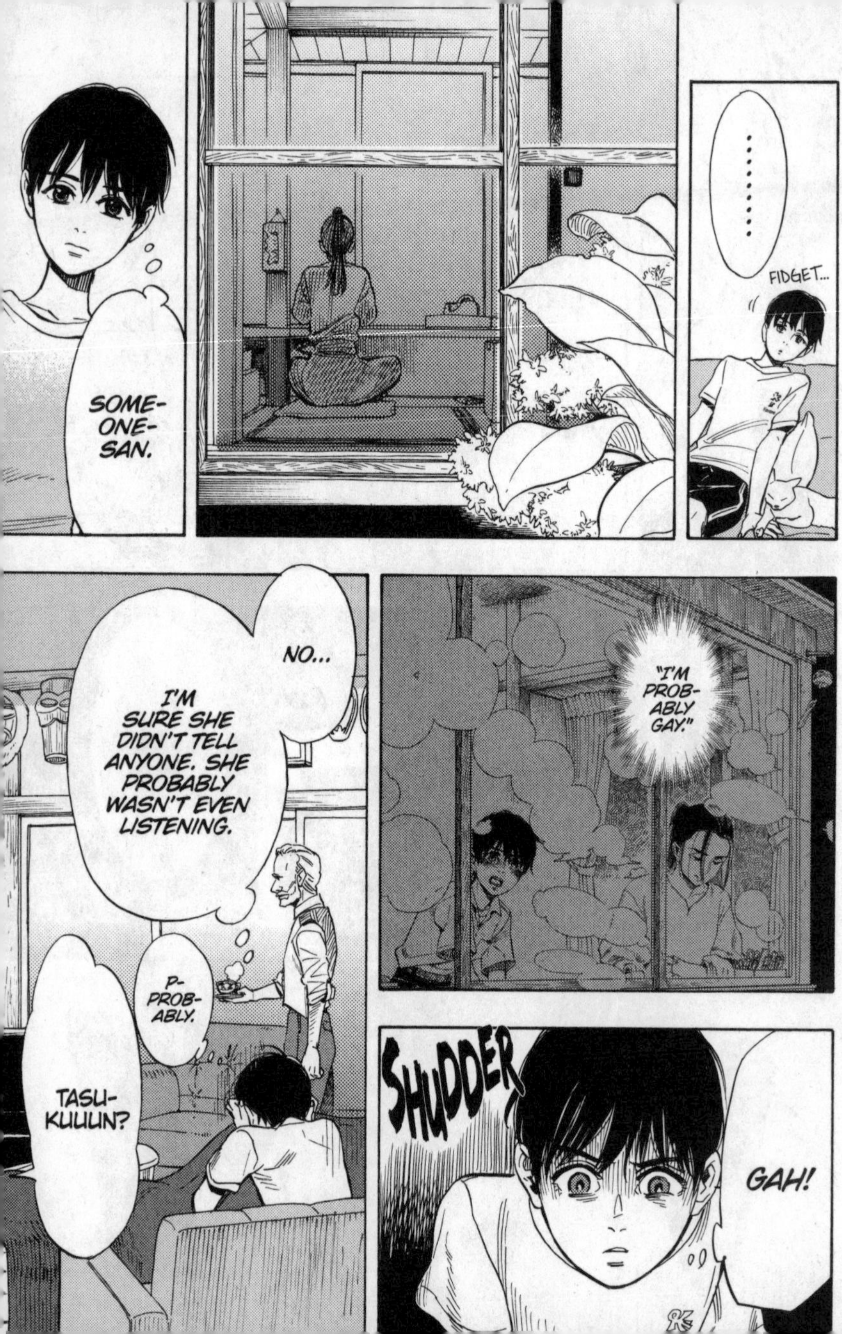
......
FIDGET...
SOME-ONE-SAN.
"I'M PROBABLY GAY."
SHUDDER
GAH!
NO...
I'M SURE SHE DIDN'T TELL ANYONE. SHE PROBABLY WASN'T EVEN LISTENING.
P-PROBABLY.
TASU-KUUUN?

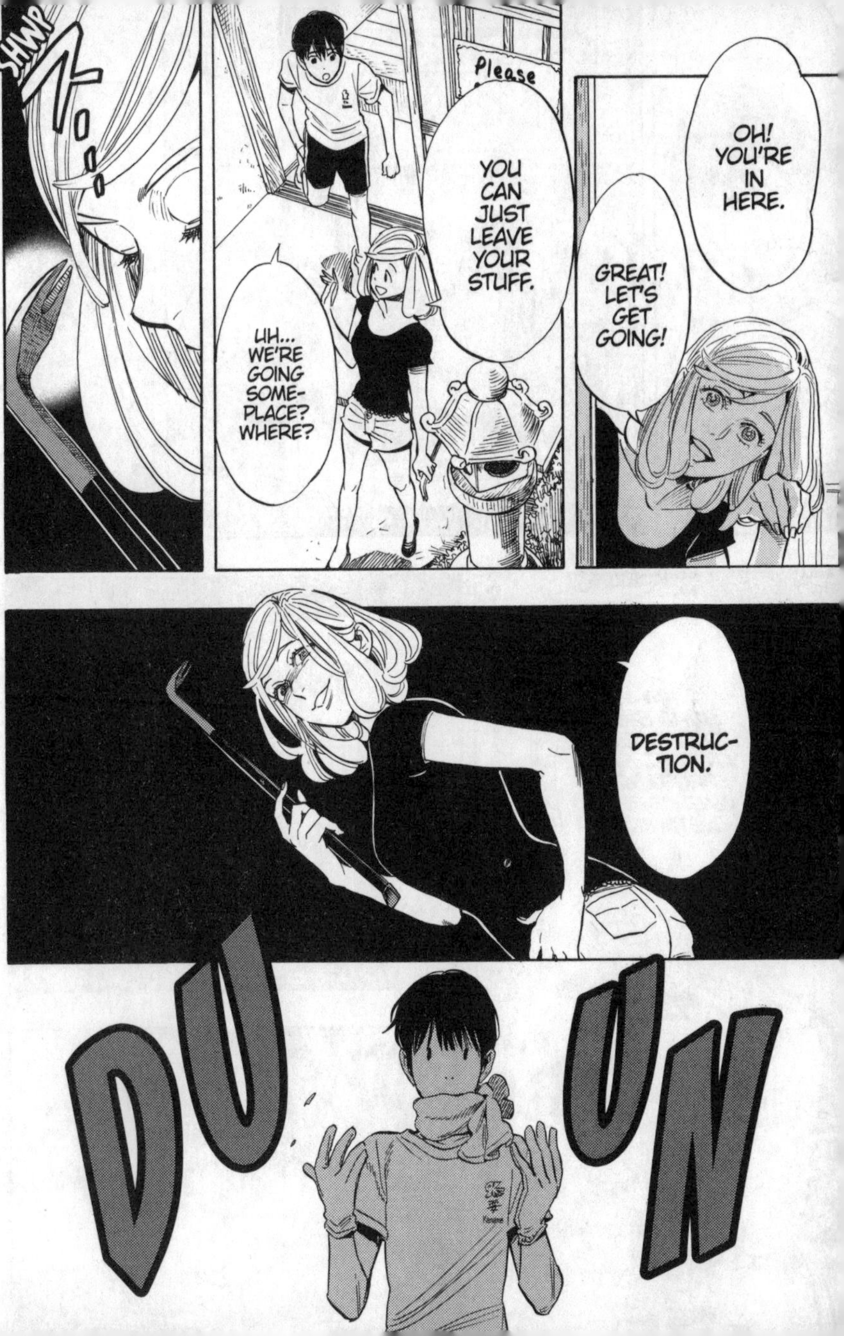
OH! YOU'RE IN HERE.
GREAT! LET'S GET GOING!
Please
YOU CAN JUST LEAVE YOUR STUFF.
UH... WE'RE GOING SOME-PLACE? WHERE?
SHWP
DESTRUC-TION.
DUUN

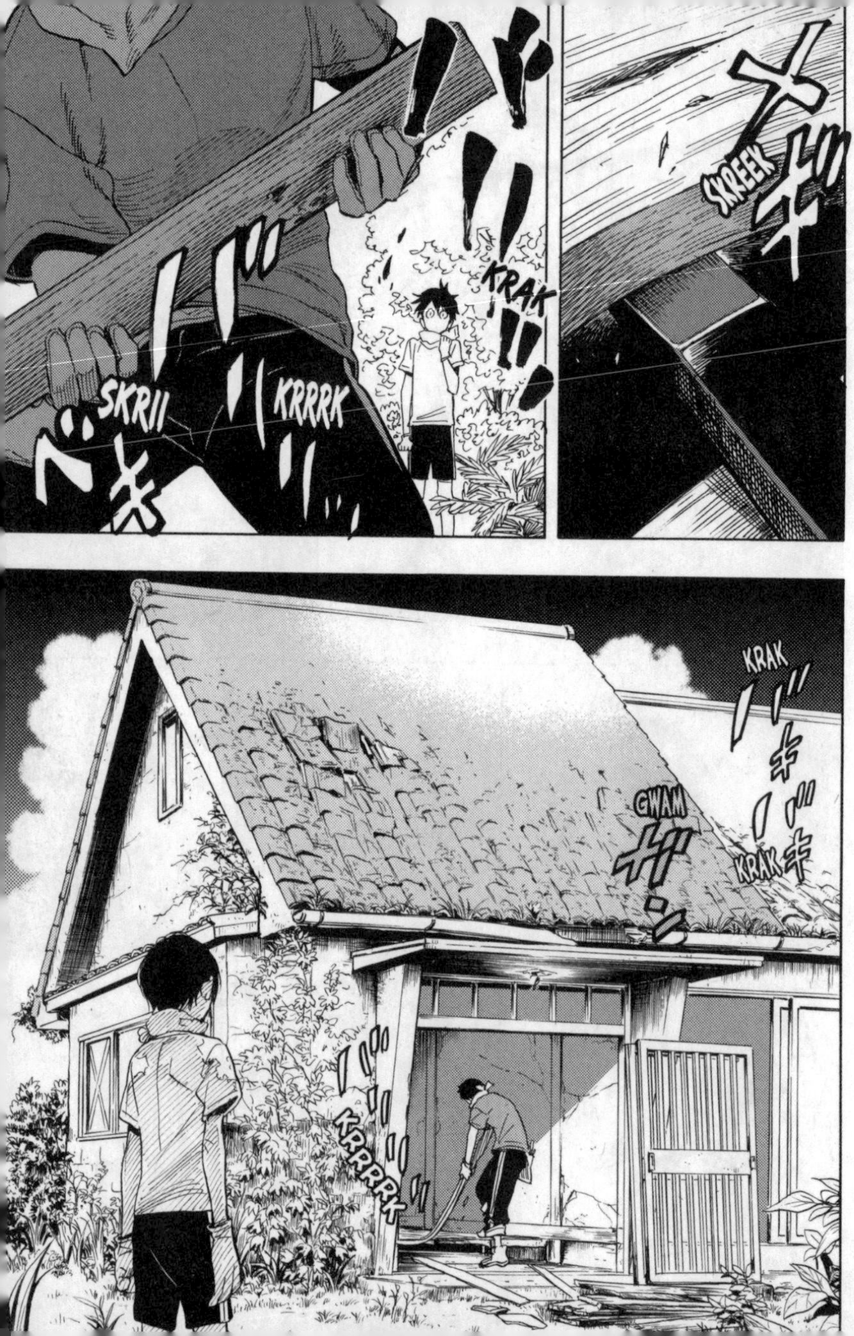
SKREEK
KRAK
SKRII
KRRRK
KRAK
GWAM
KRAK
KRRRRK

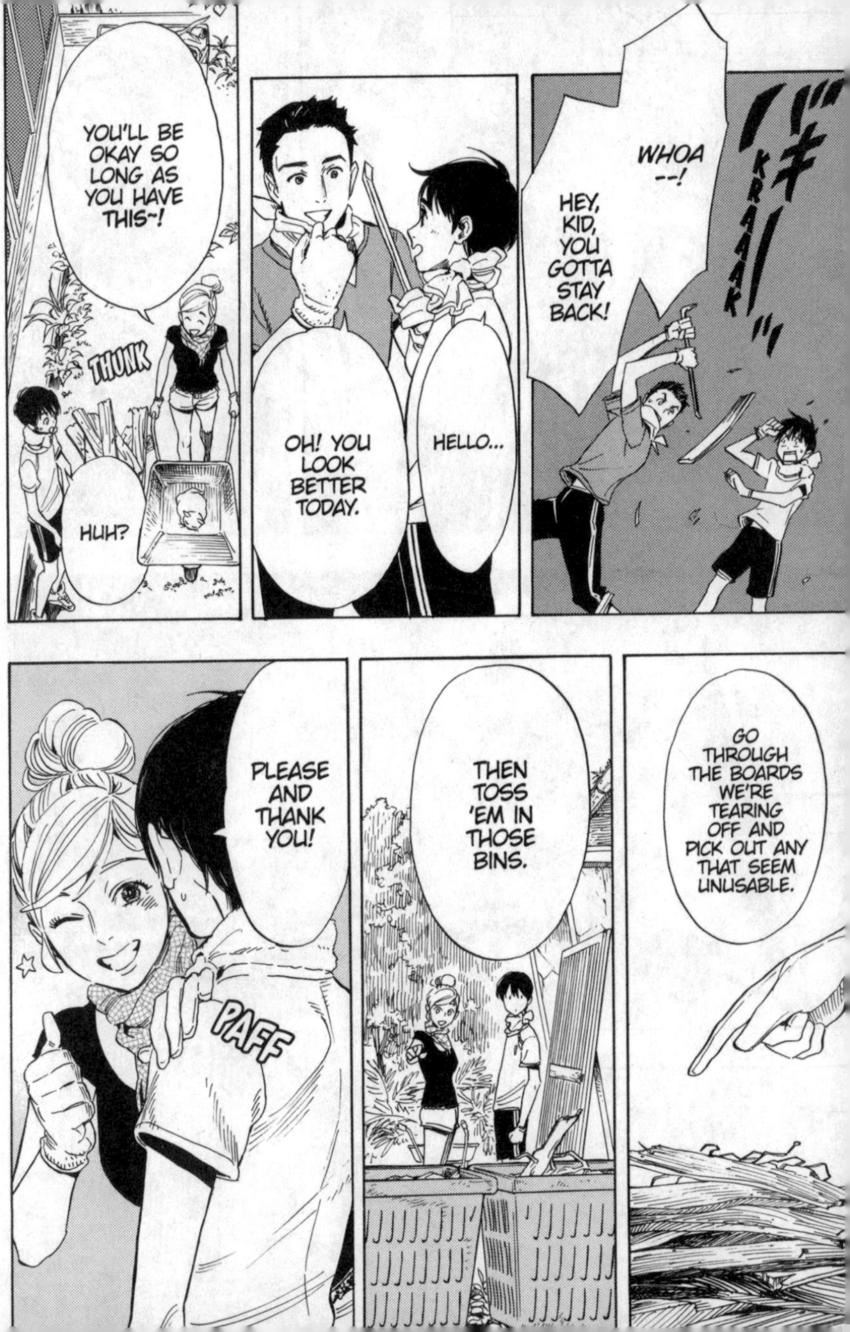
KRAAAK
WHOA --!
HEY, KID, YOU GOTTA STAY BACK!
HELLO...
OH! YOU LOOK BETTER TODAY.
YOU'LL BE OKAY SO LONG AS YOU HAVE THIS~!
THUNK
HUH?
GO THROUGH THE BOARDS WE'RE TEARING OFF AND PICK OUT ANY THAT SEEM UNUSABLE.
THEN TOSS 'EM IN THOSE BINS.
PLEASE AND THANK YOU!
PAFF

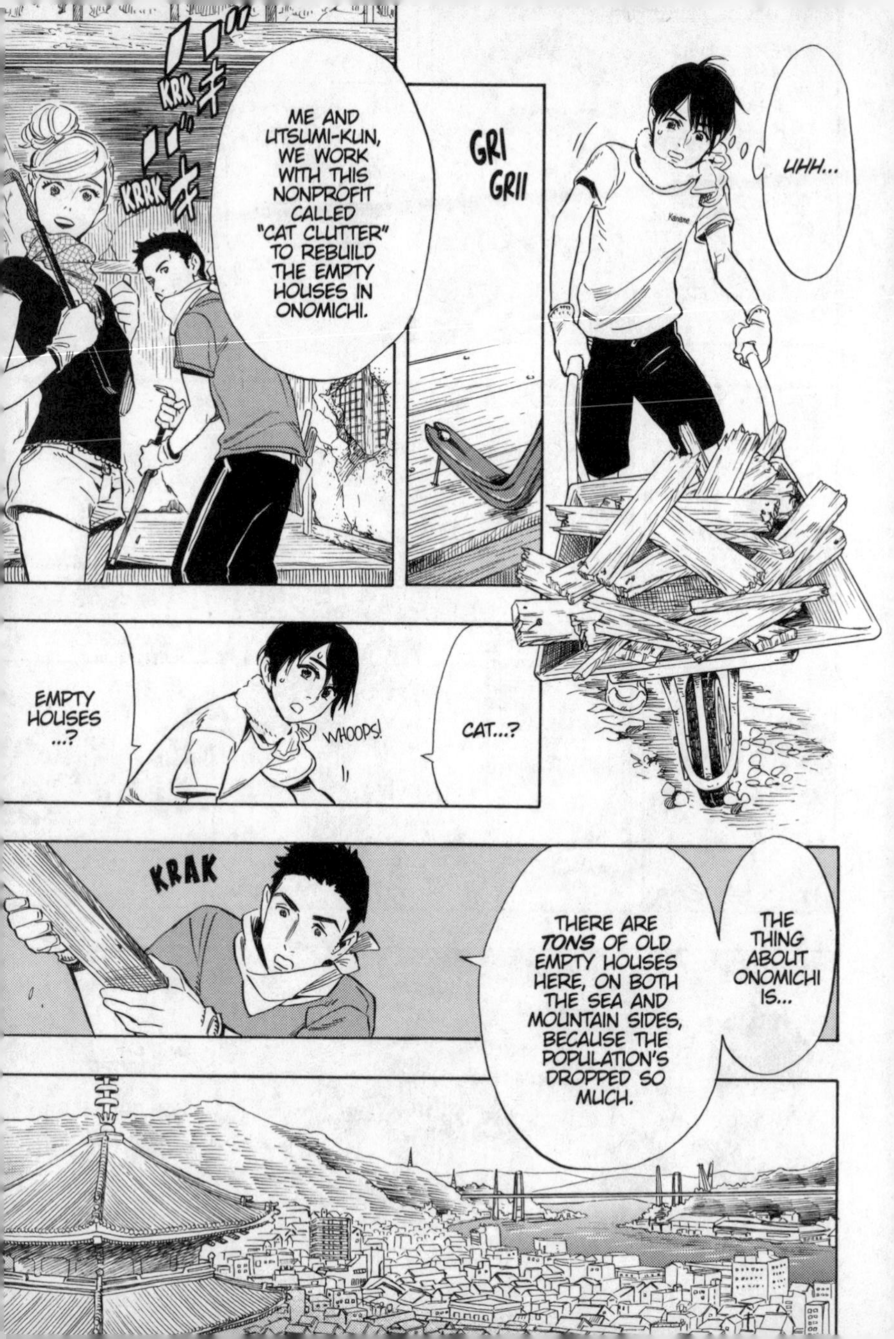
UHH...
Kaname
GRI GRII
ME AND UTSUMI-KUN, WE WORK WITH THIS NONPROFIT CALLED "CAT CLUTTER" TO REBUILD THE EMPTY HOUSES IN ONOMICHI.
KRK
KRRK
CAT...?
WHOOPS!
EMPTY HOUSES ...?
THE THING ABOUT ONOMICHI IS...
THERE ARE *TONS* OF OLD EMPTY HOUSES HERE, ON BOTH THE SEA AND MOUNTAIN SIDES, BECAUSE THE POPULATION'S DROPPED SO MUCH.
KRAK

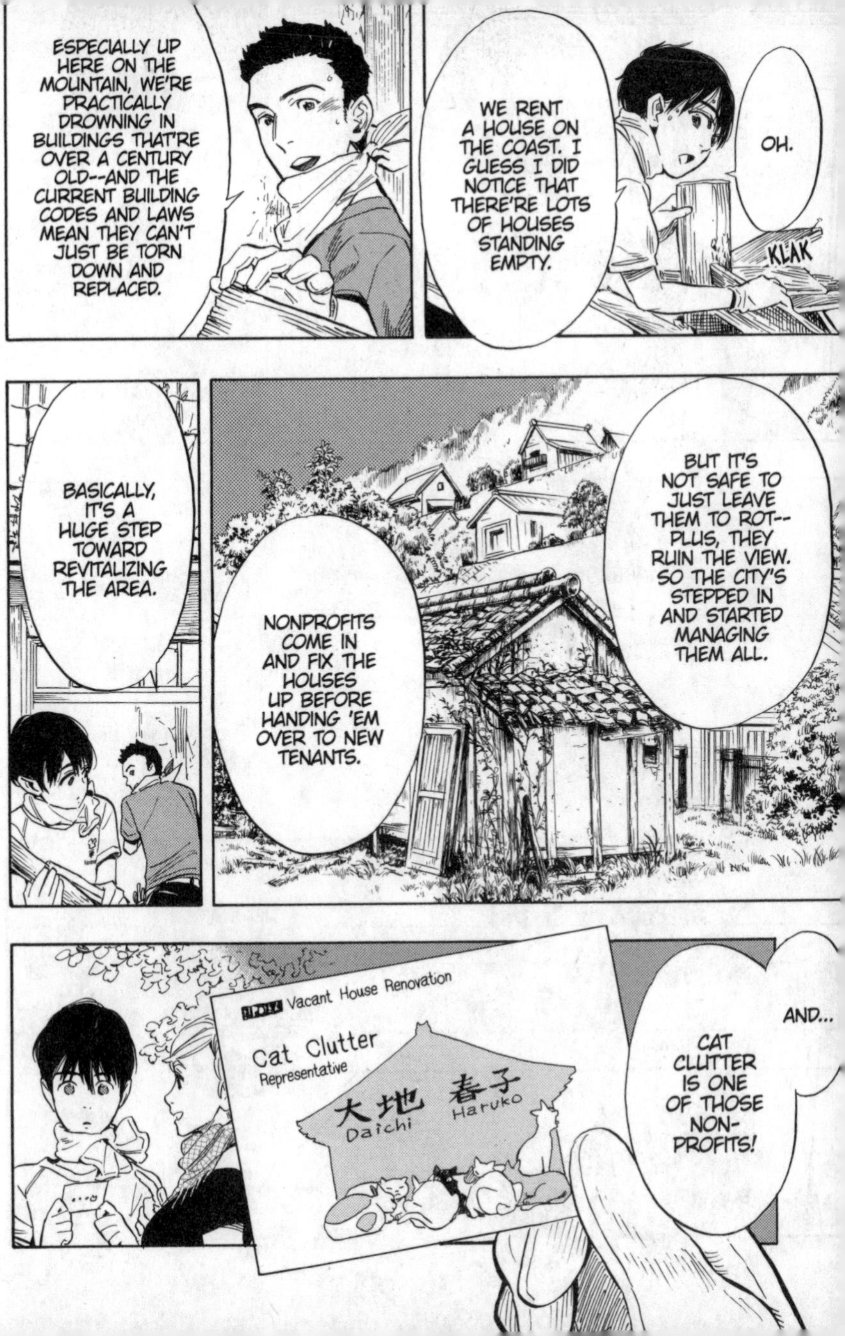
OH.
KLAK
WE RENT A HOUSE ON THE COAST. I GUESS I DID NOTICE THAT THERE'RE LOTS OF HOUSES STANDING EMPTY.
ESPECIALLY UP HERE ON THE MOUNTAIN, WE'RE PRACTICALLY DROWNING IN BUILDINGS THAT'RE OVER A CENTURY OLD--AND THE CURRENT BUILDING CODES AND LAWS MEAN THEY CAN'T JUST BE TORN DOWN AND REPLACED.
BUT IT'S NOT SAFE TO JUST LEAVE THEM TO ROT--PLUS, THEY RUIN THE VIEW. SO THE CITY'S STEPPED IN AND STARTED MANAGING THEM ALL.
NONPROFITS COME IN AND FIX THE HOUSES UP BEFORE HANDING 'EM OVER TO NEW TENANTS.
BASICALLY, IT'S A HUGE STEP TOWARD REVITALIZING THE AREA.
AND...
CAT CLUTTER IS ONE OF THOSE NON-PROFITS!
Vacant House Renovation
Cat Clutter
Representative
大地 春子
Daichi Haruko

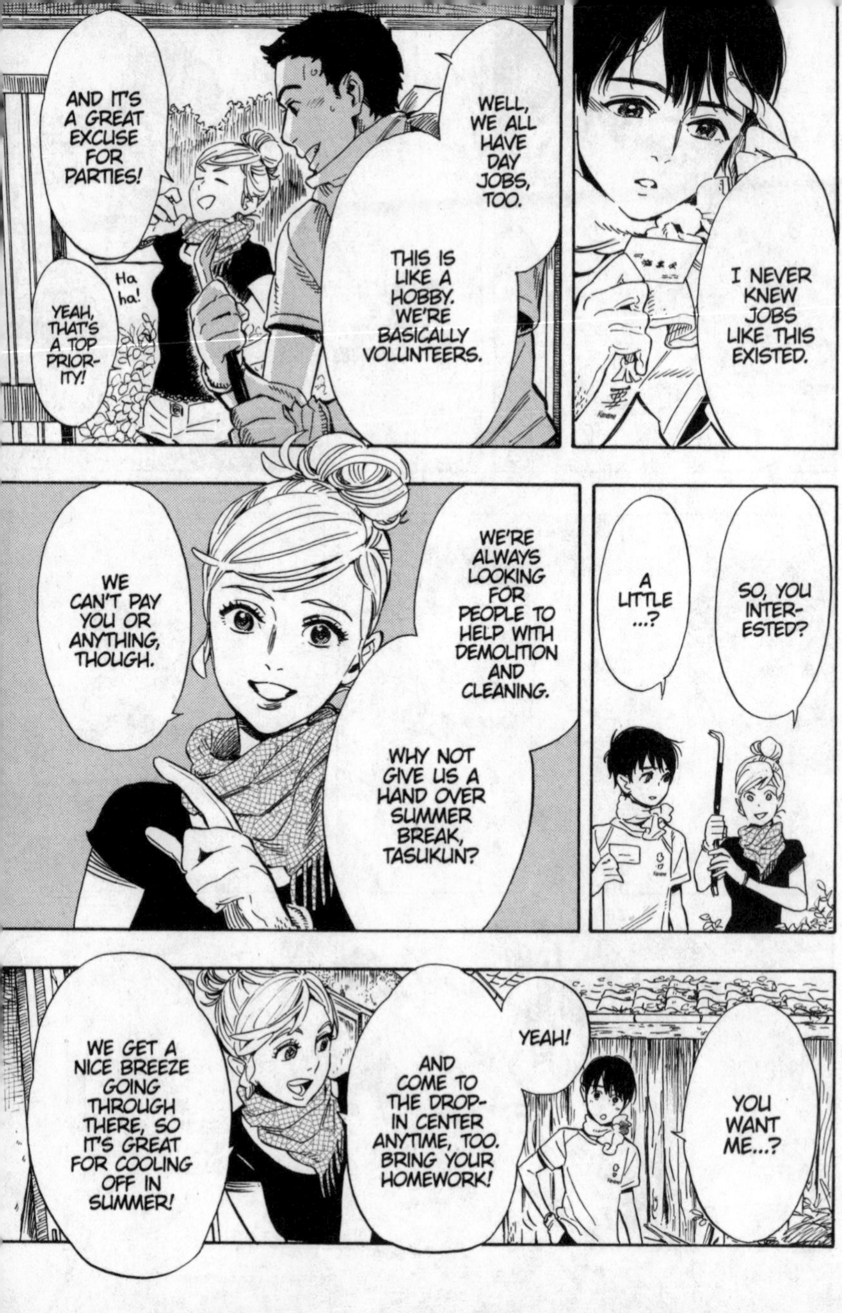
I NEVER KNEW JOBS LIKE THIS EXISTED.
WELL, WE ALL HAVE DAY JOBS, TOO.
THIS IS LIKE A HOBBY. WE'RE BASICALLY VOLUNTEERS.
AND IT'S A GREAT EXCUSE FOR PARTIES!
Ha ha!
YEAH, THAT'S A TOP PRIOR-ITY!
SO, YOU INTER-ESTED?
A LITTLE ...?
WE'RE ALWAYS LOOKING FOR PEOPLE TO HELP WITH DEMOLITION AND CLEANING.
WHY NOT GIVE US A HAND OVER SUMMER BREAK, TASUKUN?
WE CAN'T PAY YOU OR ANYTHING, THOUGH.
YOU WANT ME...?
YEAH!
AND COME TO THE DROP-IN CENTER ANYTIME, TOO. BRING YOUR HOMEWORK!
WE GET A NICE BREEZE GOING THROUGH THERE, SO IT'S GREAT FOR COOLING OFF IN SUMMER!

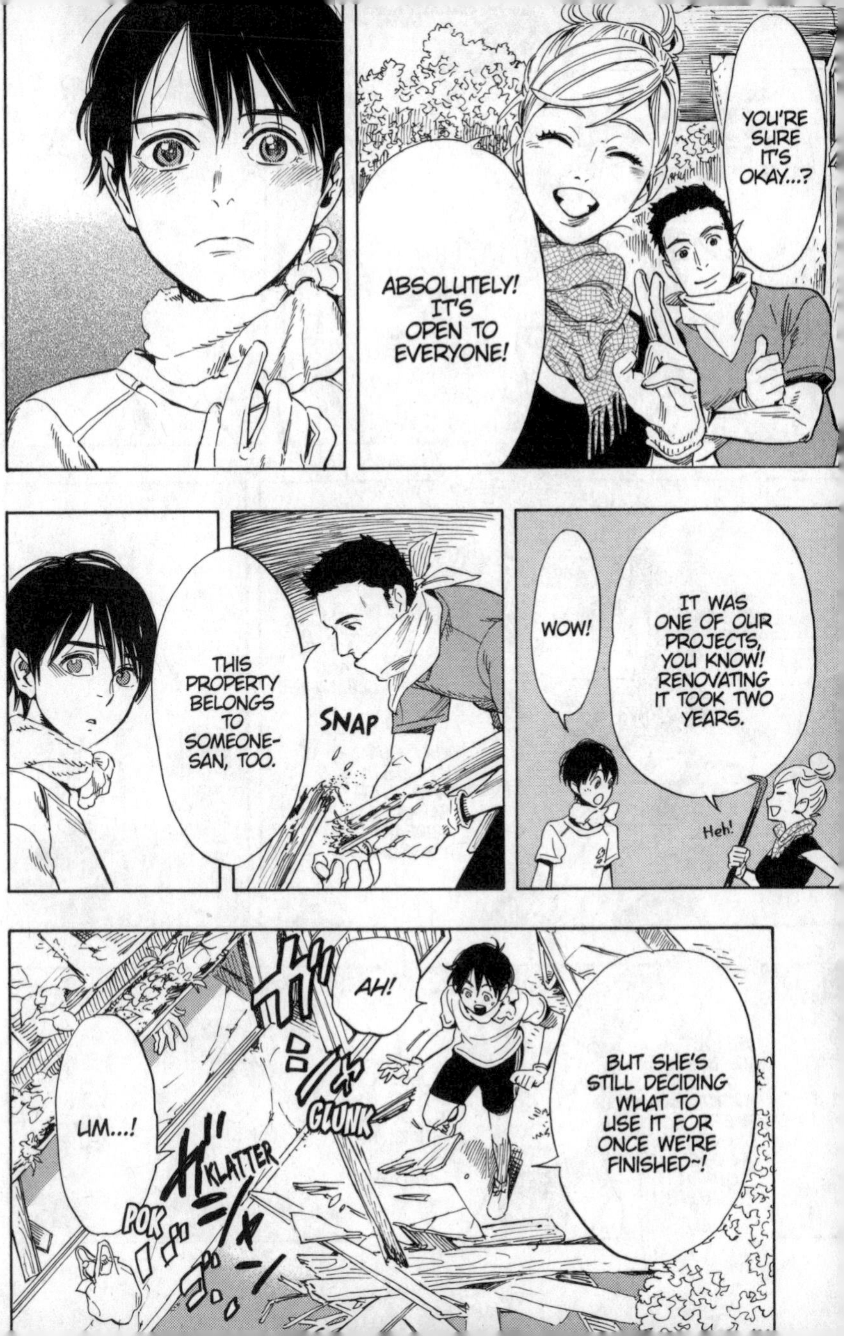
YOU'RE SURE IT'S OKAY...?
ABSOLUTELY! IT'S OPEN TO EVERYONE!
IT WAS ONE OF OUR PROJECTS, YOU KNOW! RENOVATING IT TOOK TWO YEARS.
WOW!
Heh!
THIS PROPERTY BELONGS TO SOMEONE-SAN, TOO.
SNAP
BUT SHE'S STILL DECIDING WHAT TO USE IT FOR ONCE WE'RE FINISHED~!
AH!
GLUNK
UM...!
KLATTER
POK

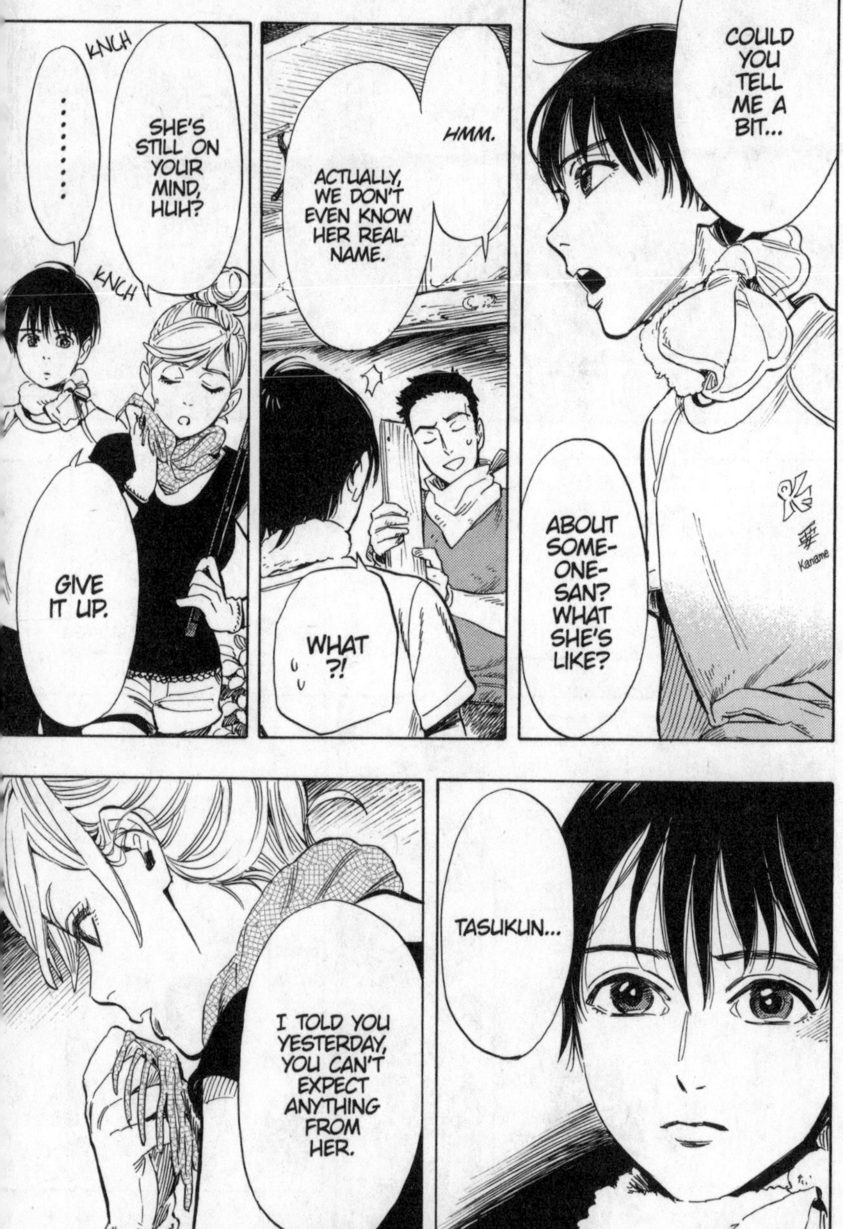
COULD YOU TELL ME A BIT...
ABOUT SOME-ONE-SAN? WHAT SHE'S LIKE?
要
Kaname
HMM.
ACTUALLY, WE DON'T EVEN KNOW HER REAL NAME.
WHAT ?!
SHE'S STILL ON YOUR MIND, HUH?
KNCH
....
KNCH
GIVE IT UP.
TASUKUN...
I TOLD YOU YESTERDAY, YOU CAN'T EXPECT ANYTHING FROM HER.

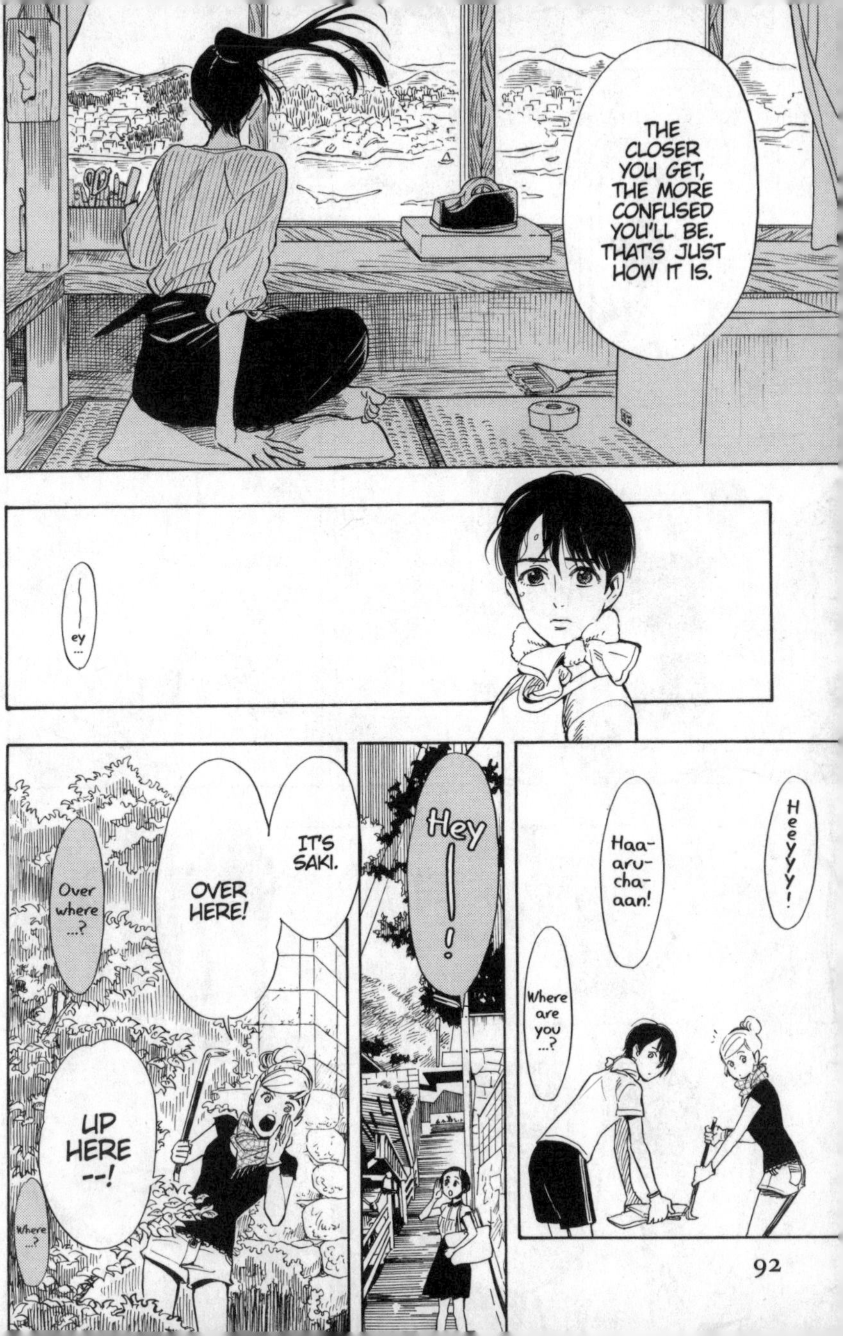
THE CLOSER YOU GET, THE MORE CONFUSED YOU'LL BE. THAT'S JUST HOW IT IS.
—ey...
Heeyyy!
Haa-aru-cha-aan!
Where are you...?
Hey—!
IT'S SAKI.
OVER HERE!
Over where...?
UP HERE--!
Where...?

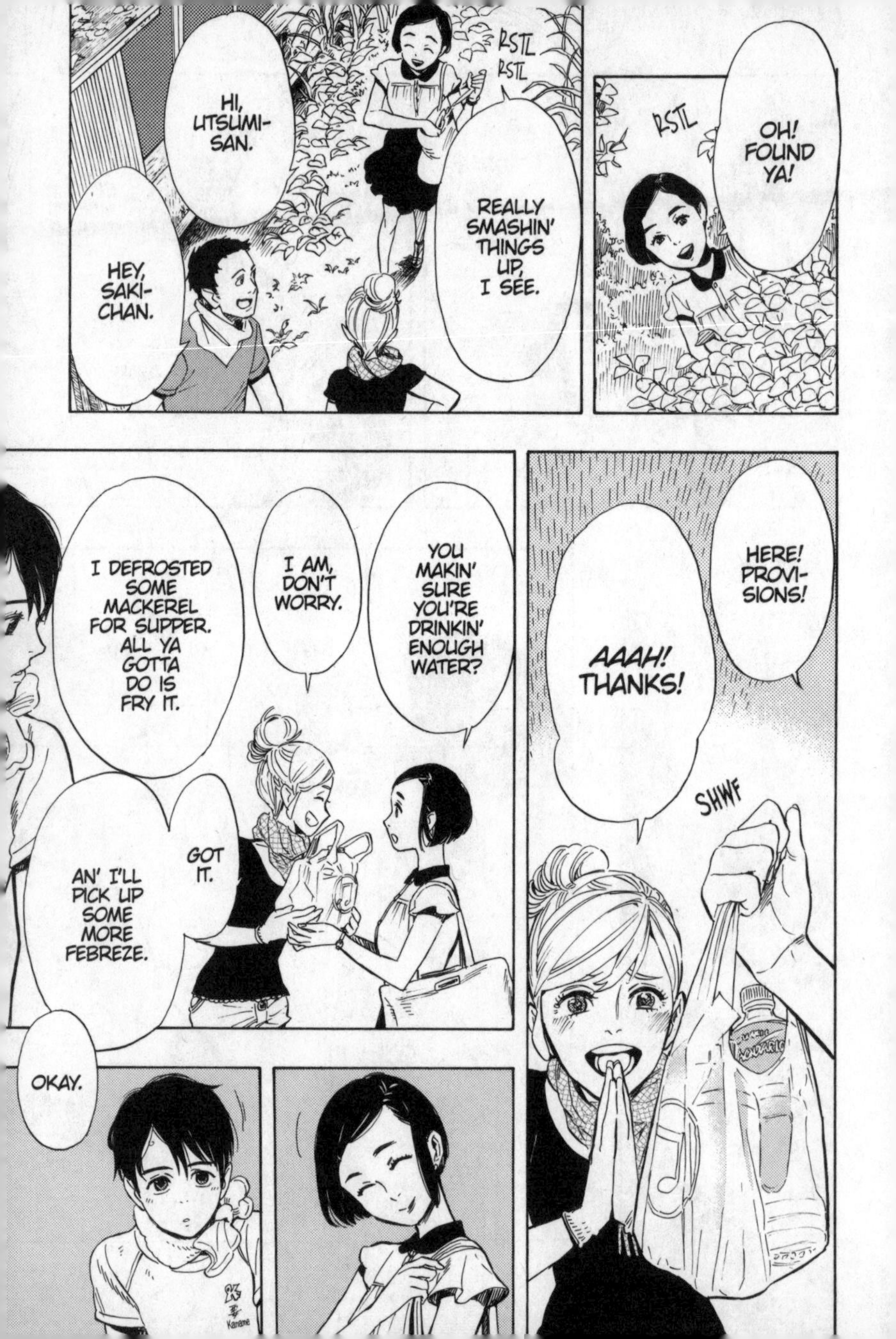
RSTL
OH! FOUND YA!
RSTL RSTL
REALLY SMASHIN' THINGS UP, I SEE.
HI, UTSUMI-SAN.
HEY, SAKI-CHAN.
HERE! PROVISIONS!
AAAH! THANKS!
SHWF
YOU MAKIN' SURE YOU'RE DRINKIN' ENOUGH WATER?
I AM, DON'T WORRY.
I DEFROSTED SOME MACKEREL FOR SUPPER. ALL YA GOTTA DO IS FRY IT.
GOT IT.
AN' I'LL PICK UP SOME MORE FEBREZE.
OKAY.

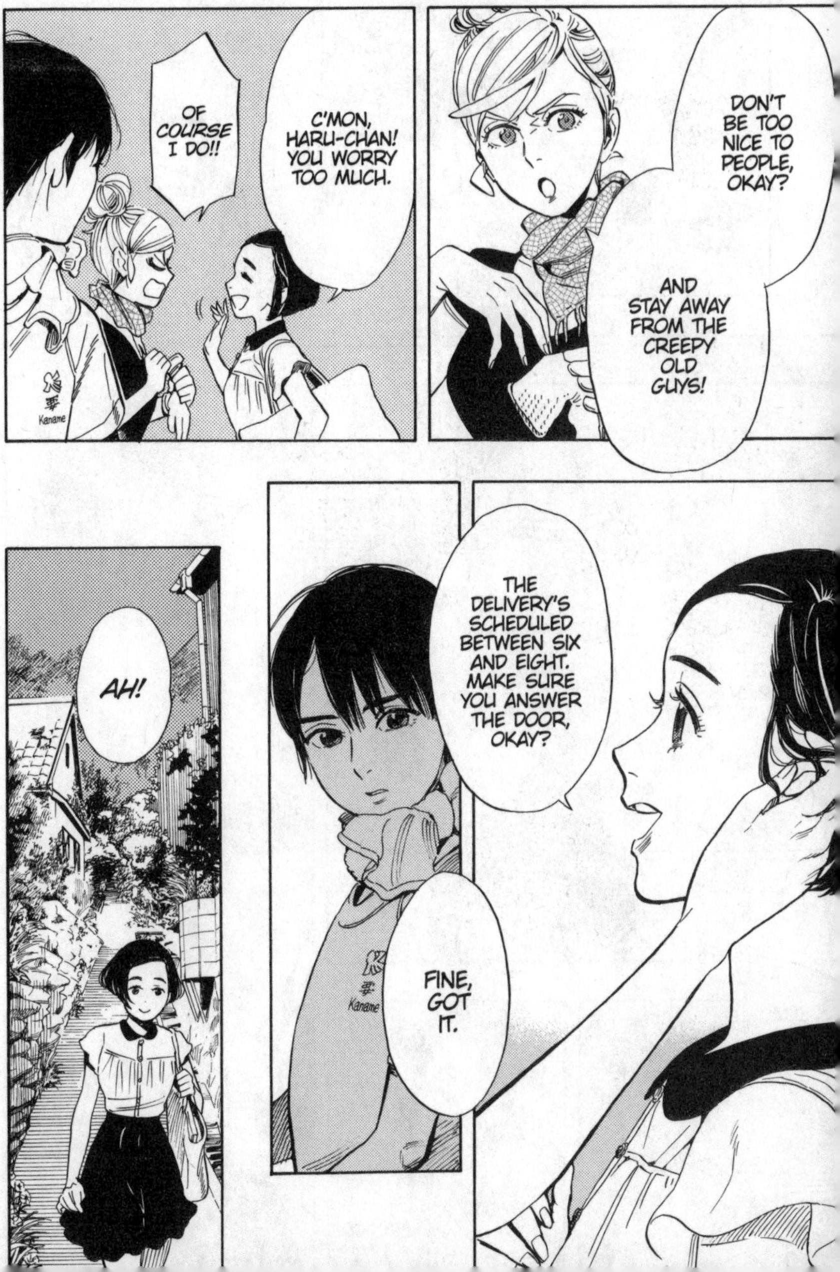
DON'T BE TOO NICE TO PEOPLE, OKAY?
AND STAY AWAY FROM THE CREEPY OLD GUYS!
C'MON, HARU-CHAN! YOU WORRY TOO MUCH.
OF COURSE I DO!!
Kaname
THE DELIVERY'S SCHEDULED BETWEEN SIX AND EIGHT. MAKE SURE YOU ANSWER THE DOOR, OKAY?
FINE, GOT IT.
Kaname
AH!

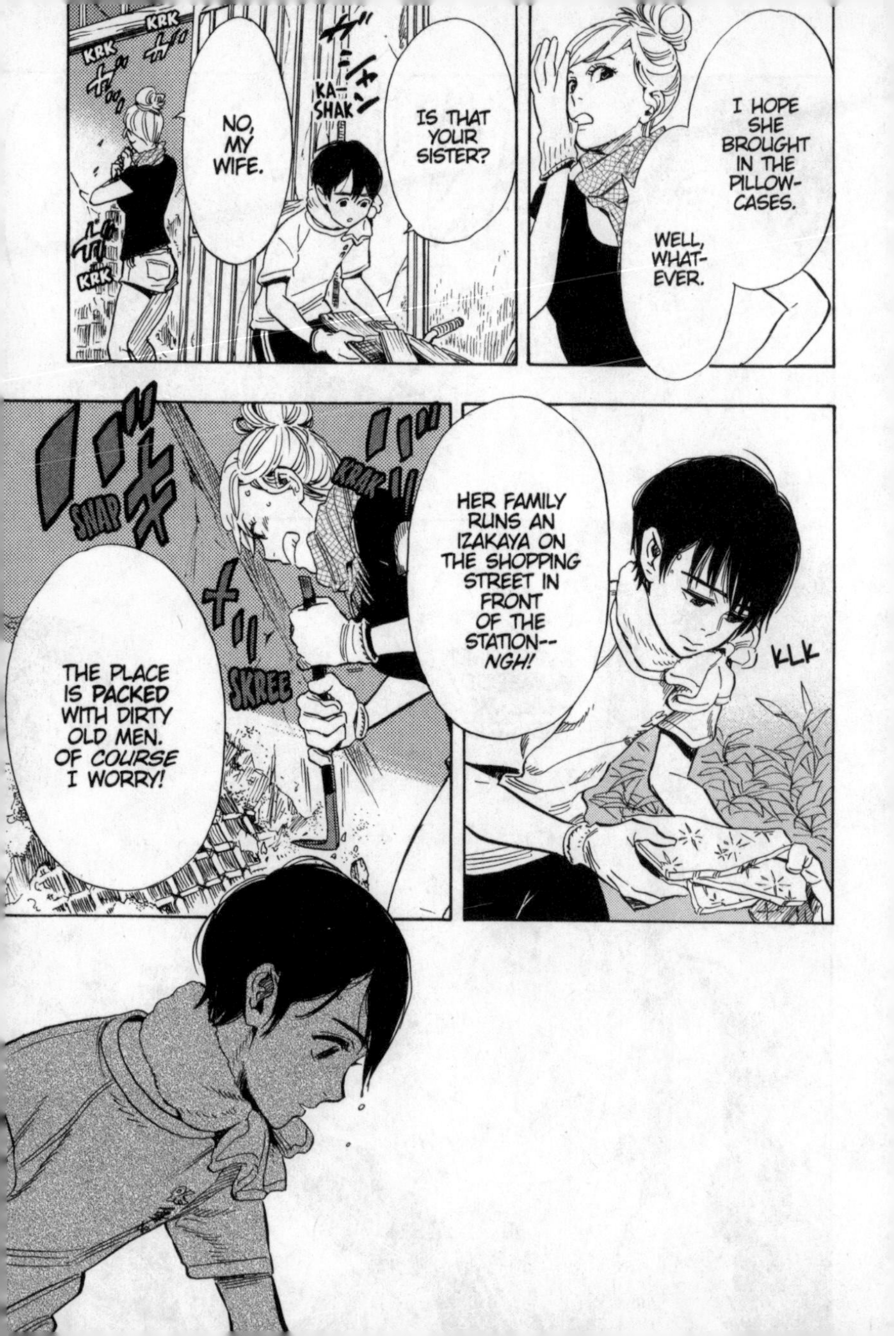
I HOPE SHE BROUGHT IN THE PILLOW-CASES.
WELL, WHAT-EVER.
IS THAT YOUR SISTER?
KA-SHAK
NO, MY WIFE.
KRK
KRK
KRK
KRK
HER FAMILY RUNS AN IZAKAYA ON THE SHOPPING STREET IN FRONT OF THE STATION--NGH!
KLK
KRAK
SNAP
SKREE
THE PLACE IS PACKED WITH DIRTY OLD MEN. OF COURSE I WORRY!

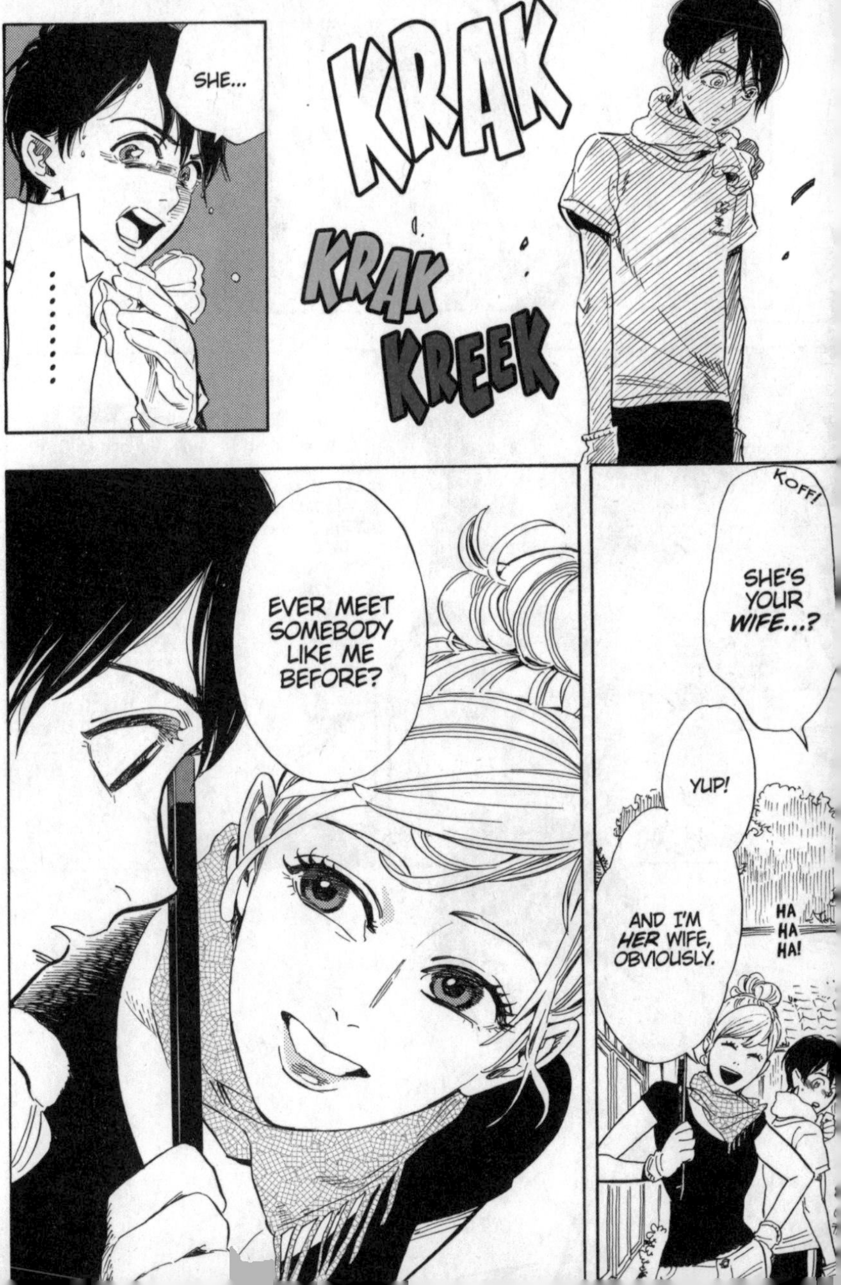
KRAK
KRAK
KREEK
SHE...
......
KOFF!
SHE'S YOUR WIFE...?
YUP!
AND I'M HER WIFE, OBVIOUSLY.
HA HA HA!
EVER MEET SOMEBODY LIKE ME BEFORE?

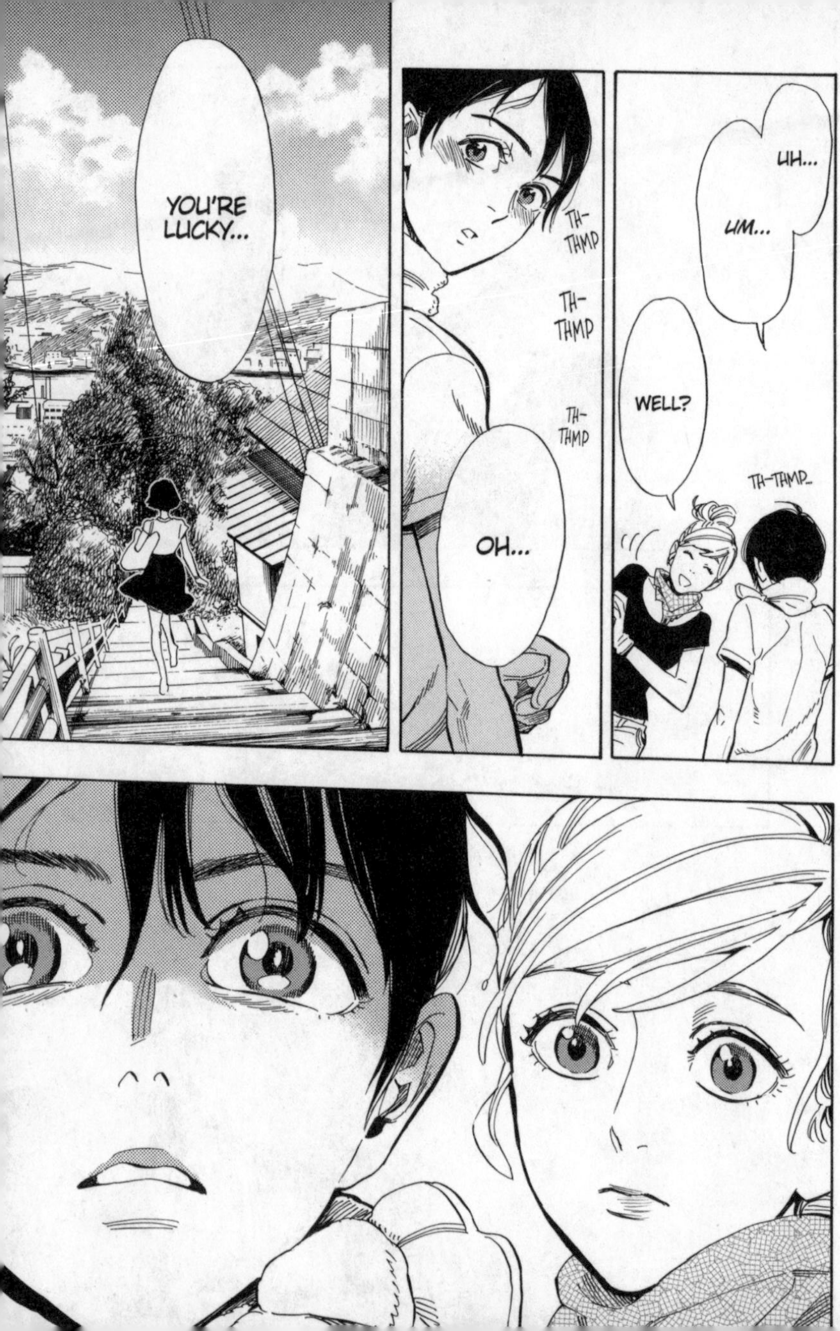
UH...
UM...
WELL?
TH-THMP...
TH-THMP
TH-THMP
TH-THMP
OH...
YOU'RE LUCKY...

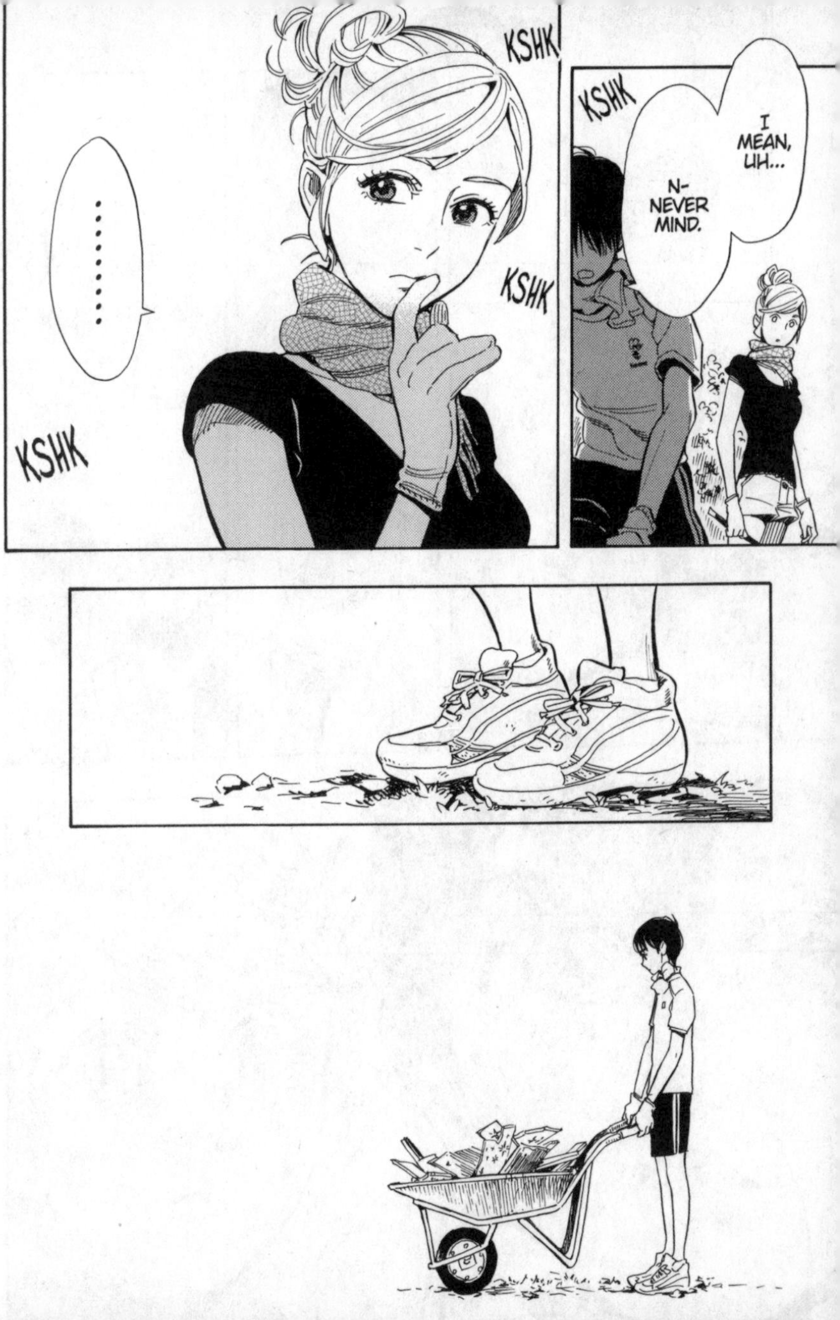
KSHK
I MEAN, UH...
N-NEVER MIND.
KSHK
KSHK
......
KSHK

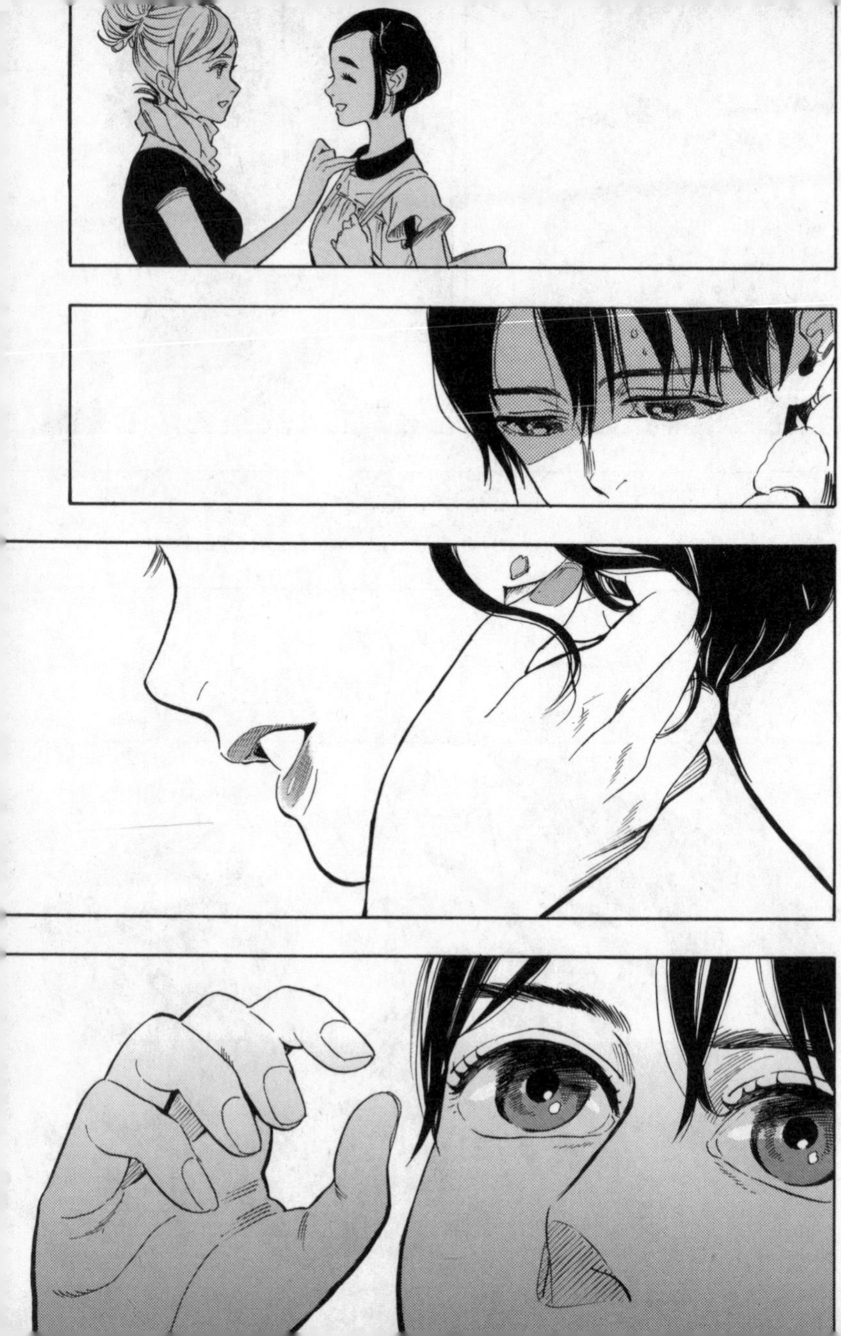

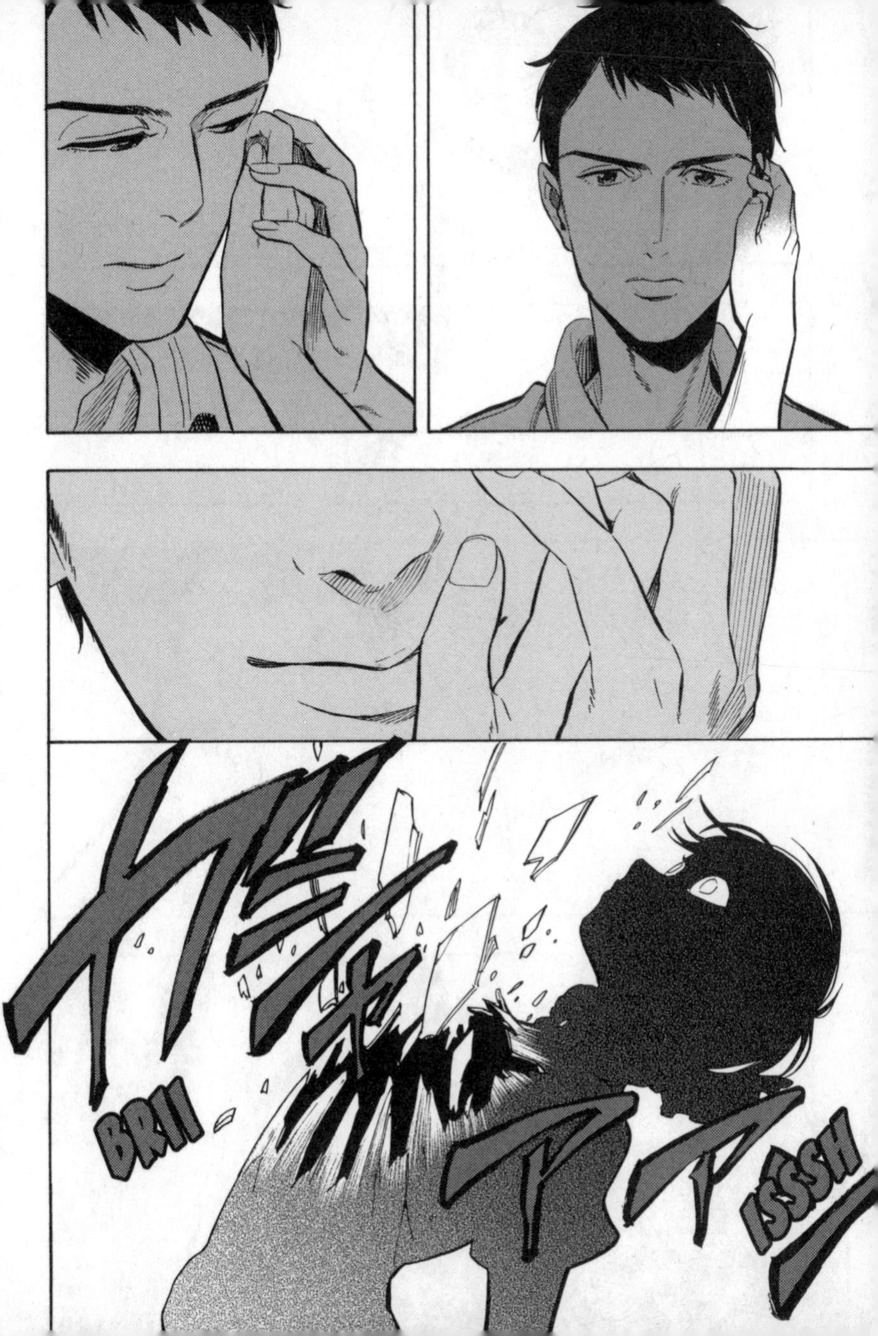
BRII
ISSSH

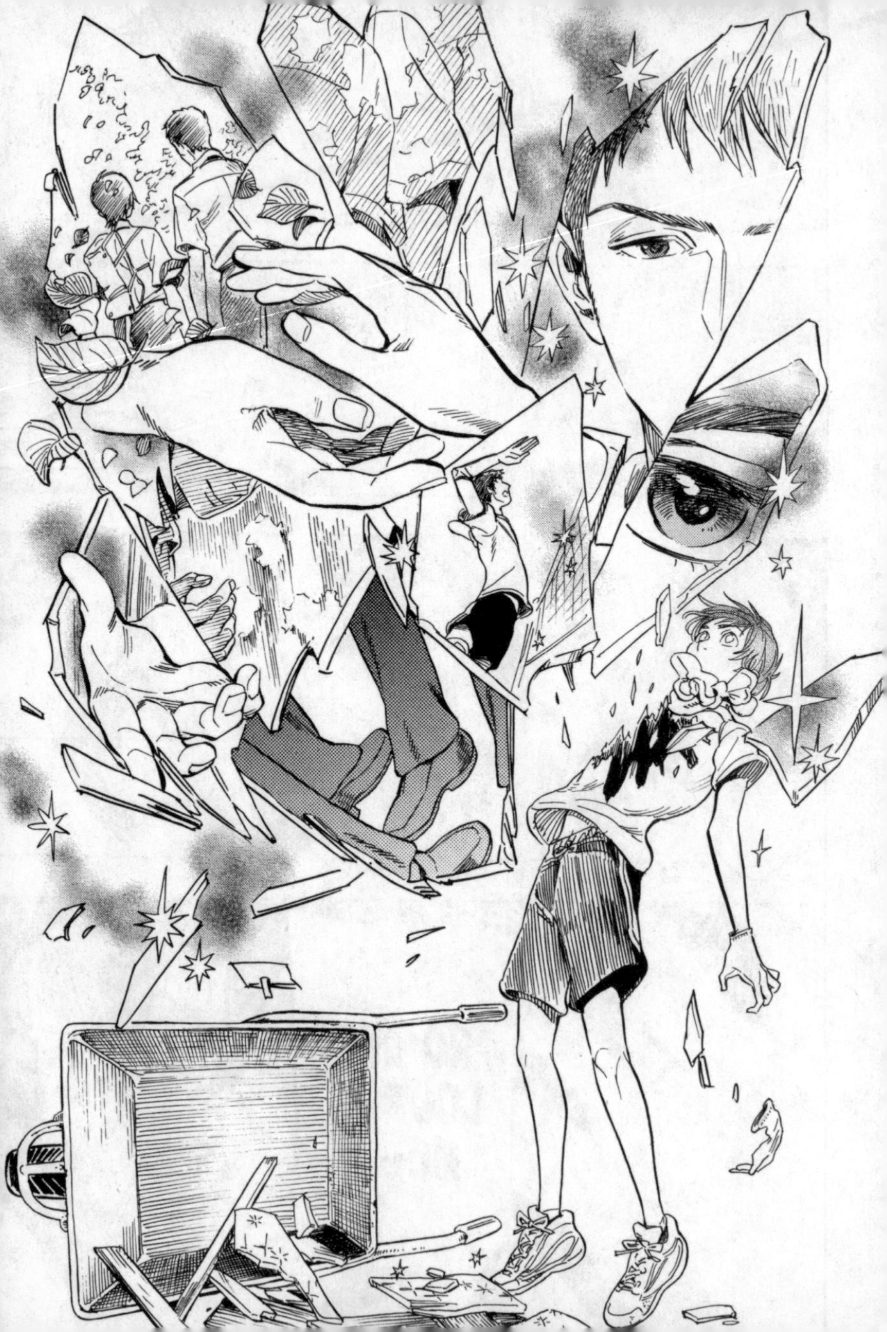

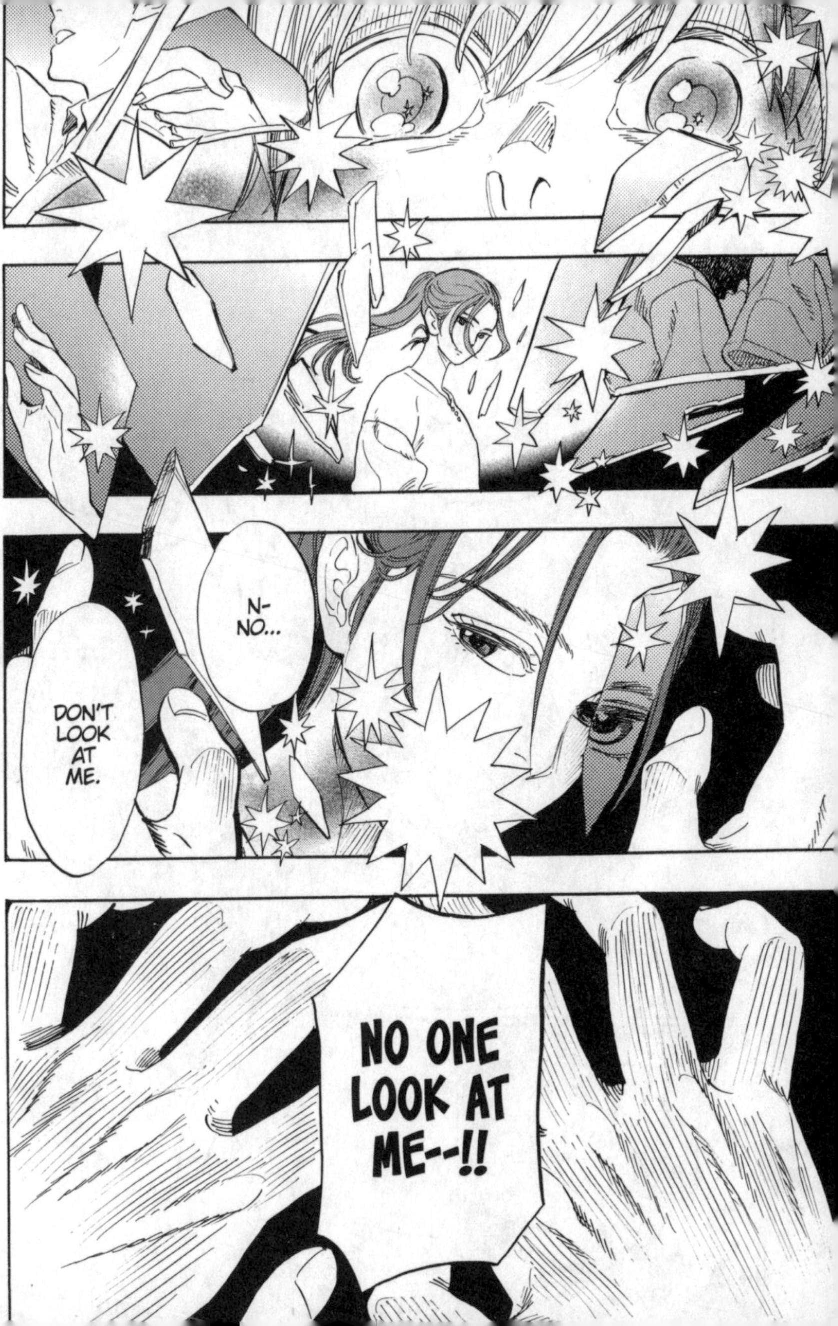
N-NO...
DON'T LOOK AT ME.
NO ONE LOOK AT ME--!!

Our Dreams at Dusk
SHIMANAMI TASOGARE

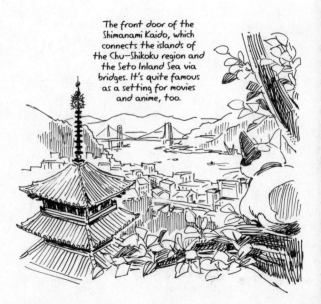

The front door of the Shimanami Kaido, which connects the islands of the Chu-Shikoku region and the Seto Inland Sea via bridges. It's quite famous as a setting for movies and anime, too.

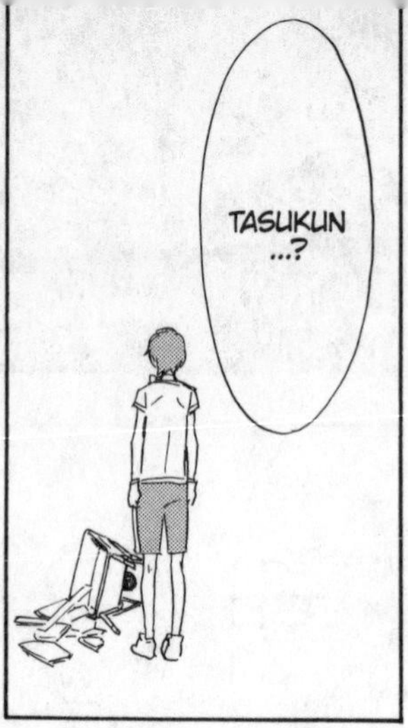
TASUKUN ...?

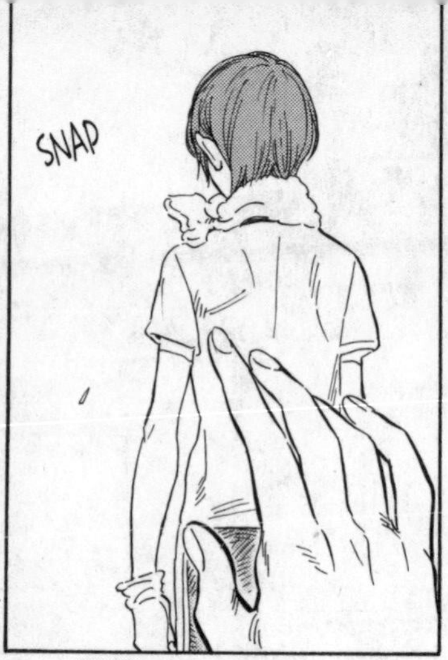
SNAP

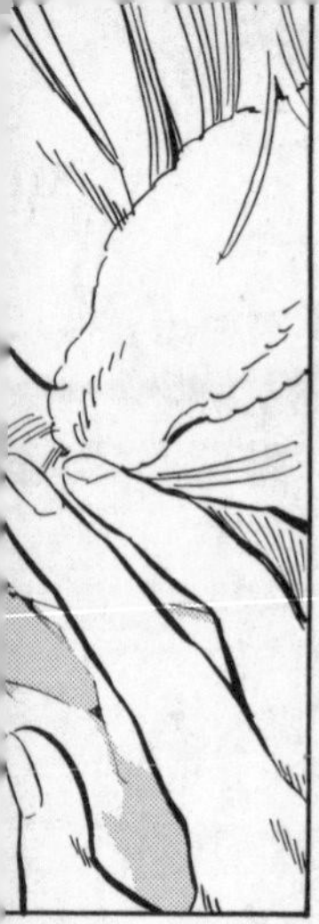

Chapter 4

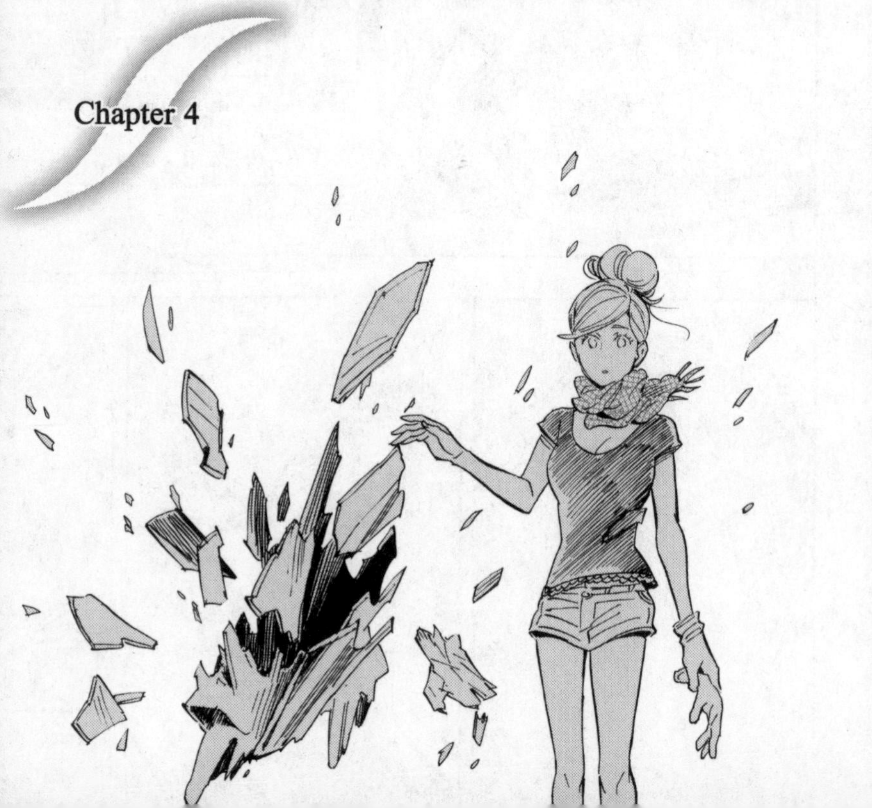

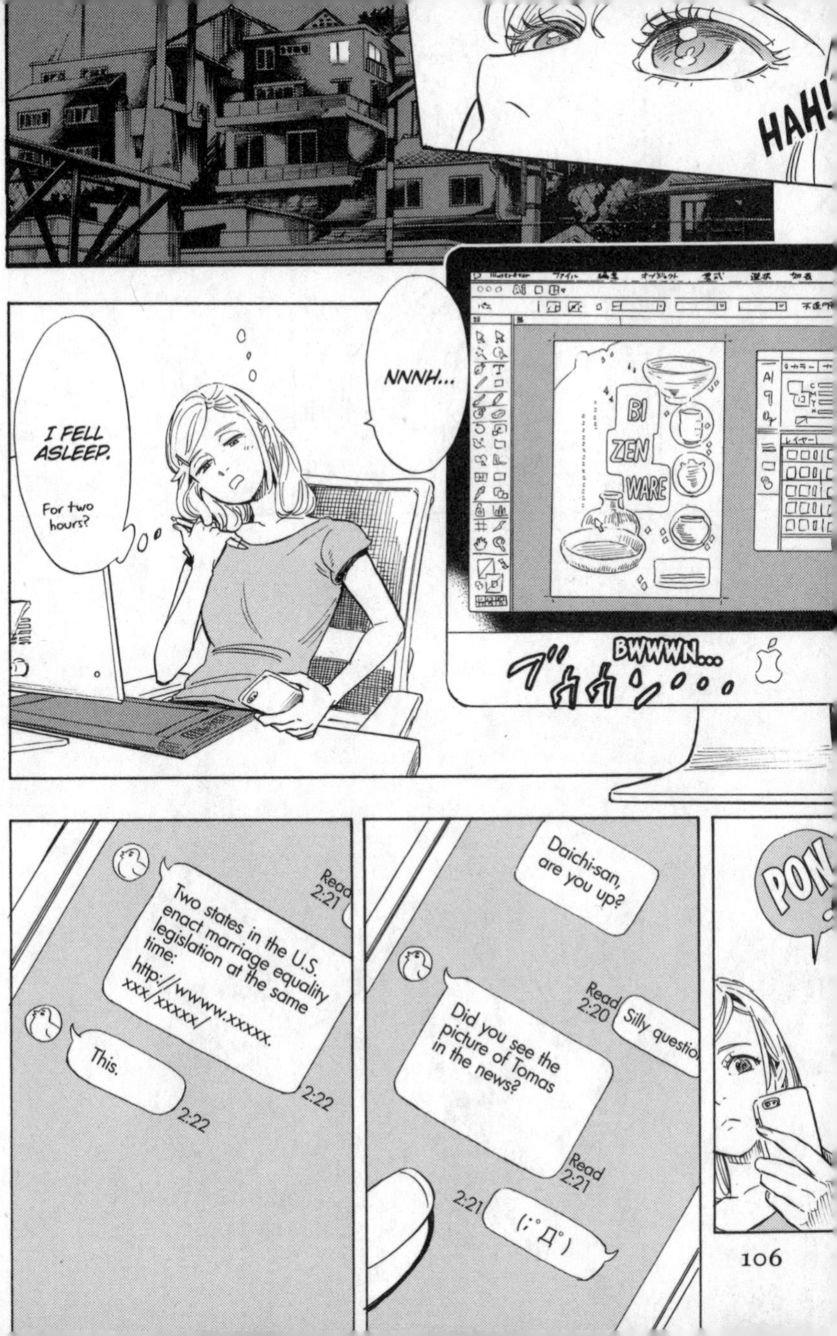
HAH!
NNNH...
I FELL ASLEEP.
For two hours?
BI ZEN WARE
BWWWN...
PON
Daichi-san, are you up?
Read 2:20
Silly questio
Did you see the picture of Tomas in the news?
Read 2:21
2:21
(;ﾟДﾟ)
Read 2:21
Two states in the U.S. enact marriage equality legislation at the same time: http://wwww.xxxxx.xxx/xxxxx/
2:22
This.
2:22

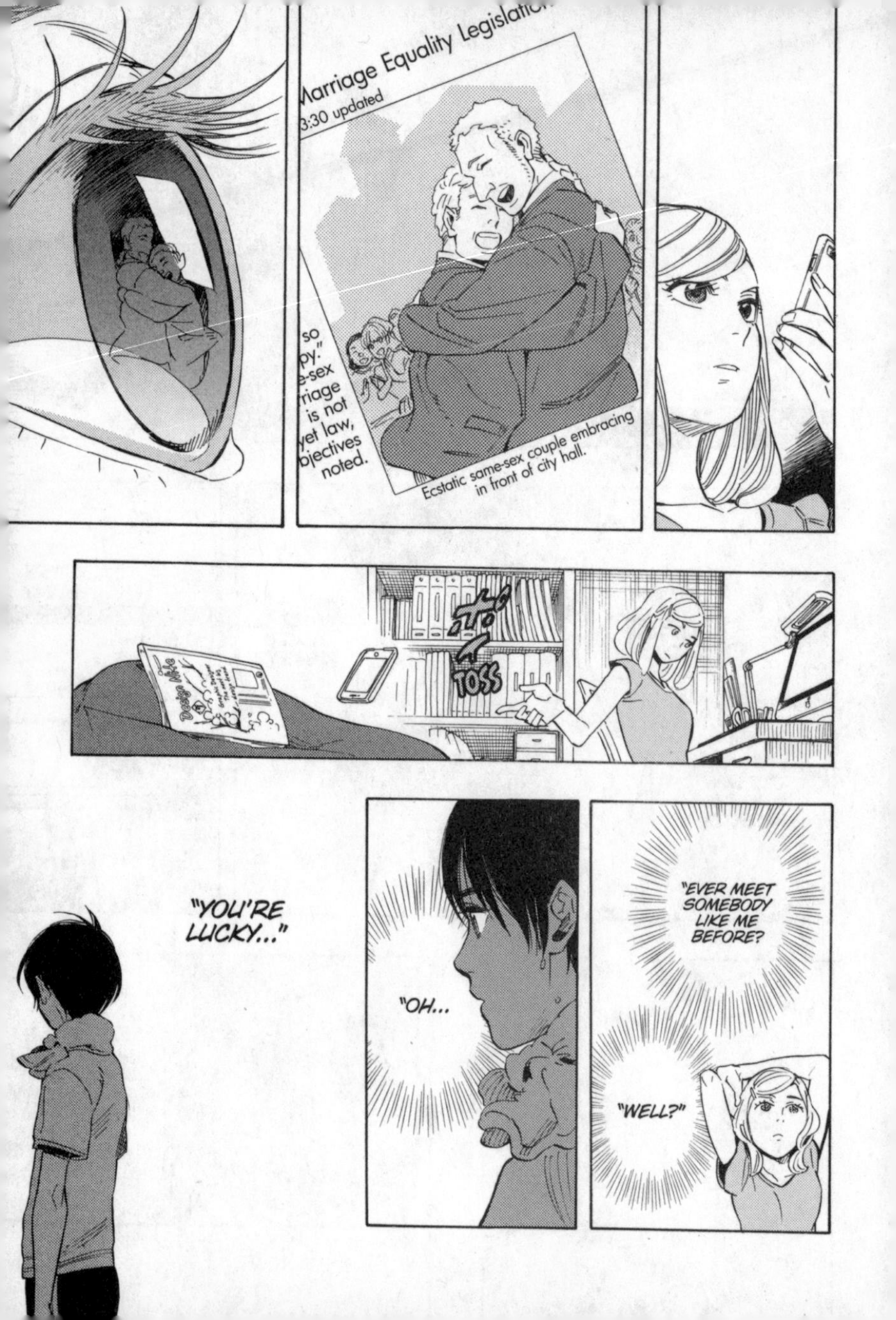

Marriage Equality Legislatio
3:30 updated
"so
py."
e-sex
rriage
is not
yet law,
bjectives
noted.
Ecstatic same-sex couple embracing in front of city hall.
TOSS
"EVER MEET SOMEBODY LIKE ME BEFORE?
"WELL?"
"OH...
"YOU'RE LUCKY..."

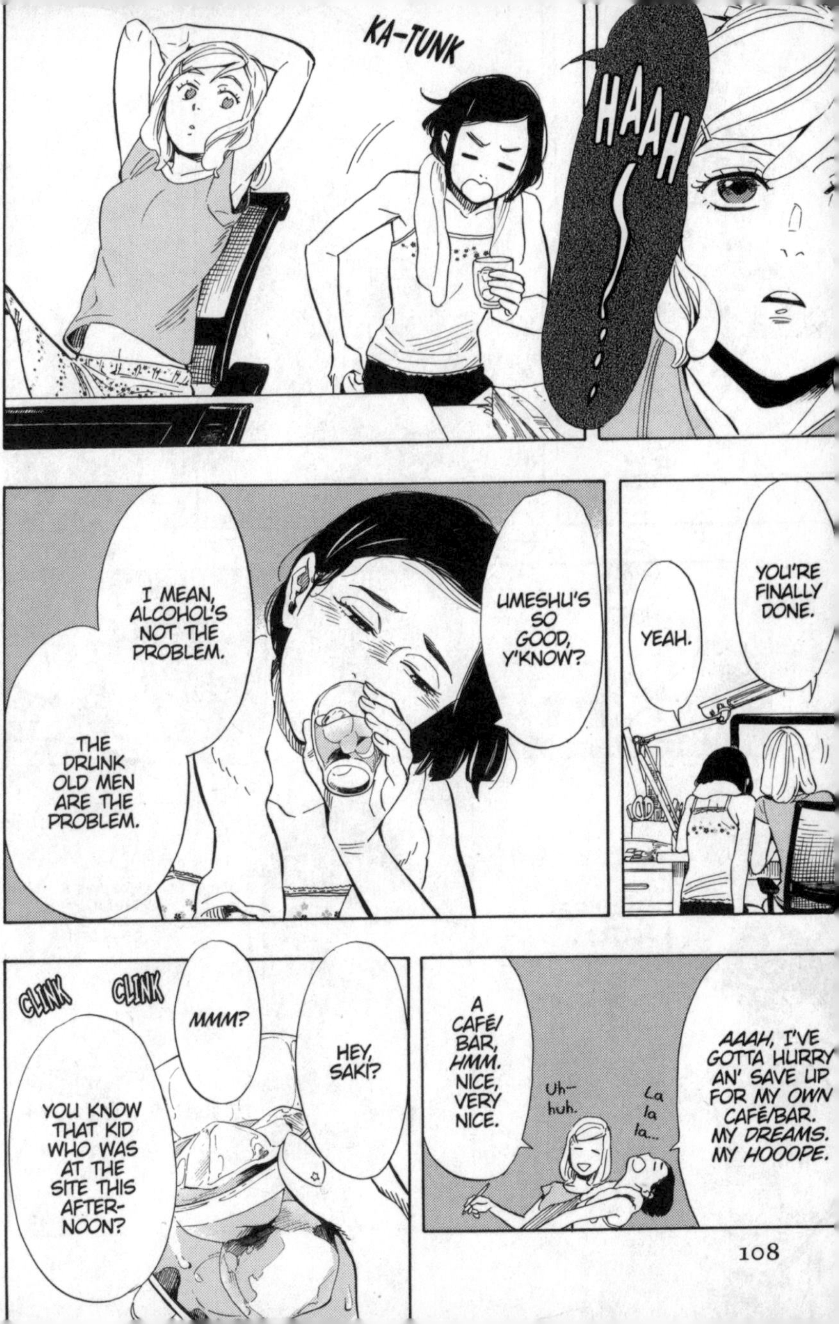
HAAH
KA-TUNK
YOU'RE FINALLY DONE.
YEAH.
UMESHU'S SO GOOD, Y'KNOW?
I MEAN, ALCOHOL'S NOT THE PROBLEM.
THE DRUNK OLD MEN ARE THE PROBLEM.
AAAH, I'VE GOTTA HURRY AN' SAVE UP FOR MY OWN CAFÉ/BAR. MY DREAMS. MY HOOOPE.
La la la...
Uh-huh.
A CAFÉ/BAR, HMM. NICE, VERY NICE.
HEY, SAKI?
MMM?
YOU KNOW THAT KID WHO WAS AT THE SITE THIS AFTER-NOON?
CLINK
CLINK

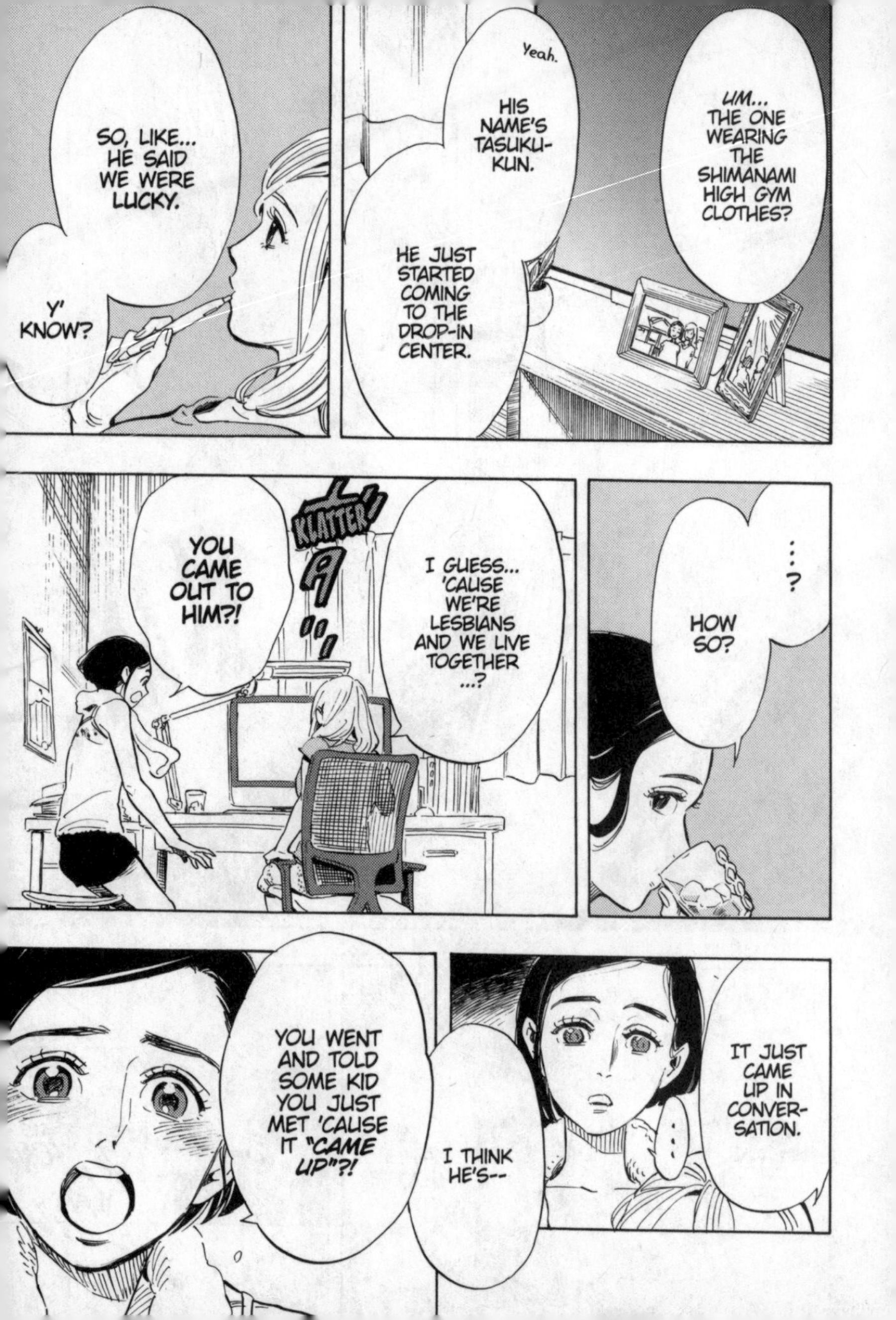
UM... THE ONE WEARING THE SHIMANAMI HIGH GYM CLOTHES?
Yeah.
HIS NAME'S TASUKU-KUN.
HE JUST STARTED COMING TO THE DROP-IN CENTER.
SO, LIKE... HE SAID WE WERE LUCKY.
Y' KNOW?
...?
HOW SO?
I GUESS... 'CAUSE WE'RE LESBIANS AND WE LIVE TOGETHER ...?
KLATTER
YOU CAME OUT TO HIM?!
IT JUST CAME UP IN CONVER-SATION.
...
I THINK HE'S--
YOU WENT AND TOLD SOME KID YOU JUST MET 'CAUSE IT "CAME UP"?!

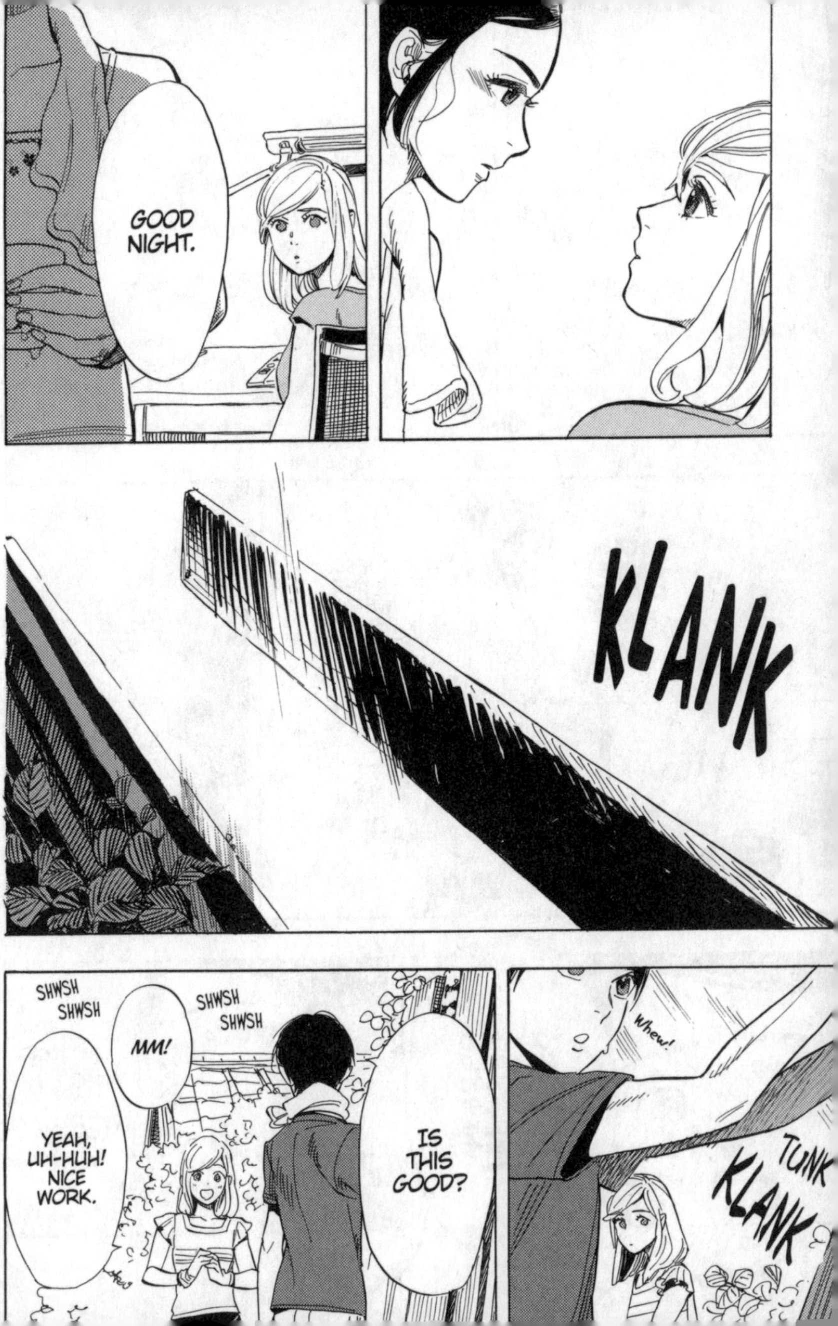
GOOD NIGHT.
KLANK
Whew!
TUNK
KLANK
IS THIS GOOD?
SHWSH SHWSH
MM!
SHWSH SHWSH
YEAH, UH-HUH! NICE WORK.

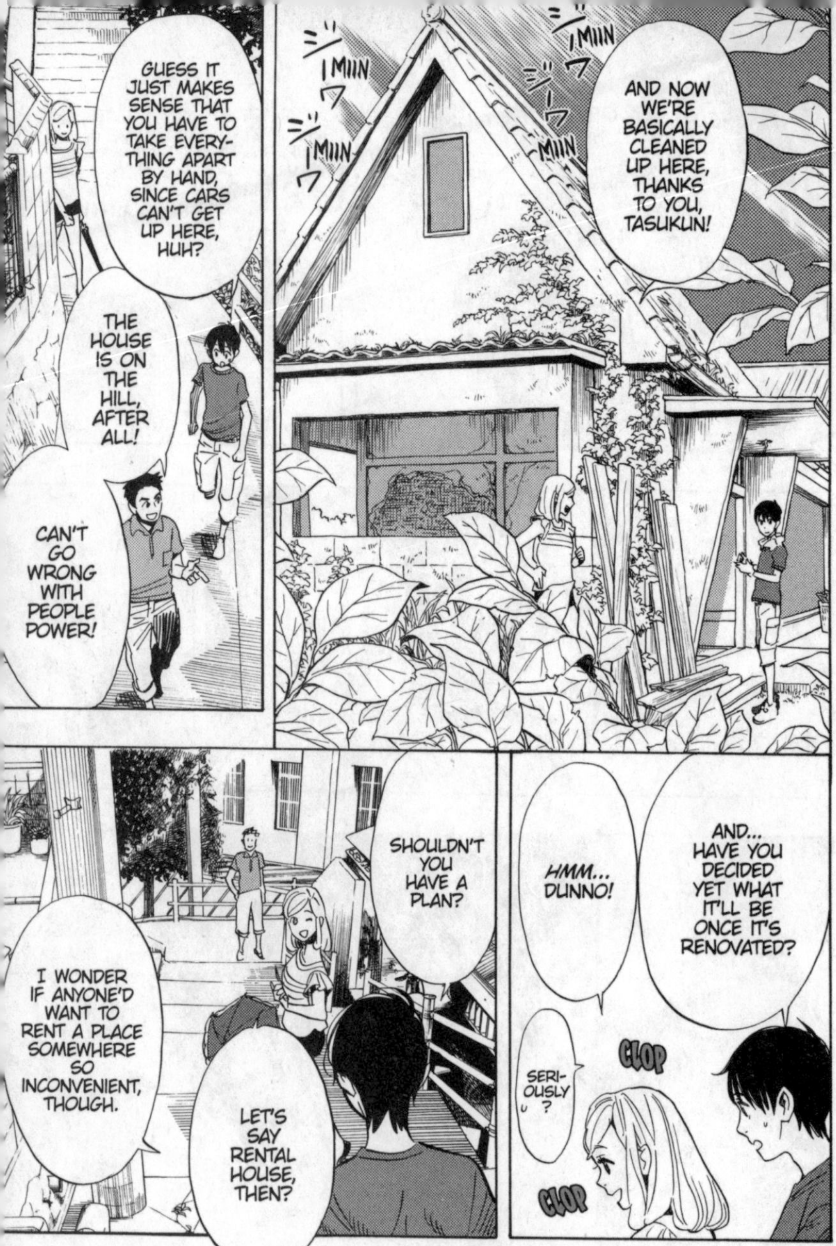
MIIN
MIIN
MIIN
MIIN
AND NOW WE'RE BASICALLY CLEANED UP HERE, THANKS TO YOU, TASUKUN!
GUESS IT JUST MAKES SENSE THAT YOU HAVE TO TAKE EVERY-THING APART BY HAND, SINCE CARS CAN'T GET UP HERE, HUH?
THE HOUSE IS ON THE HILL, AFTER ALL!
CAN'T GO WRONG WITH PEOPLE POWER!
AND... HAVE YOU DECIDED YET WHAT IT'LL BE ONCE IT'S RENOVATED?
HMM... DUNNO!
SERI-OUSLY?
CLOP
CLOP
SHOULDN'T YOU HAVE A PLAN?
I WONDER IF ANYONE'D WANT TO RENT A PLACE SOMEWHERE SO INCONVENIENT, THOUGH.
LET'S SAY RENTAL HOUSE, THEN?

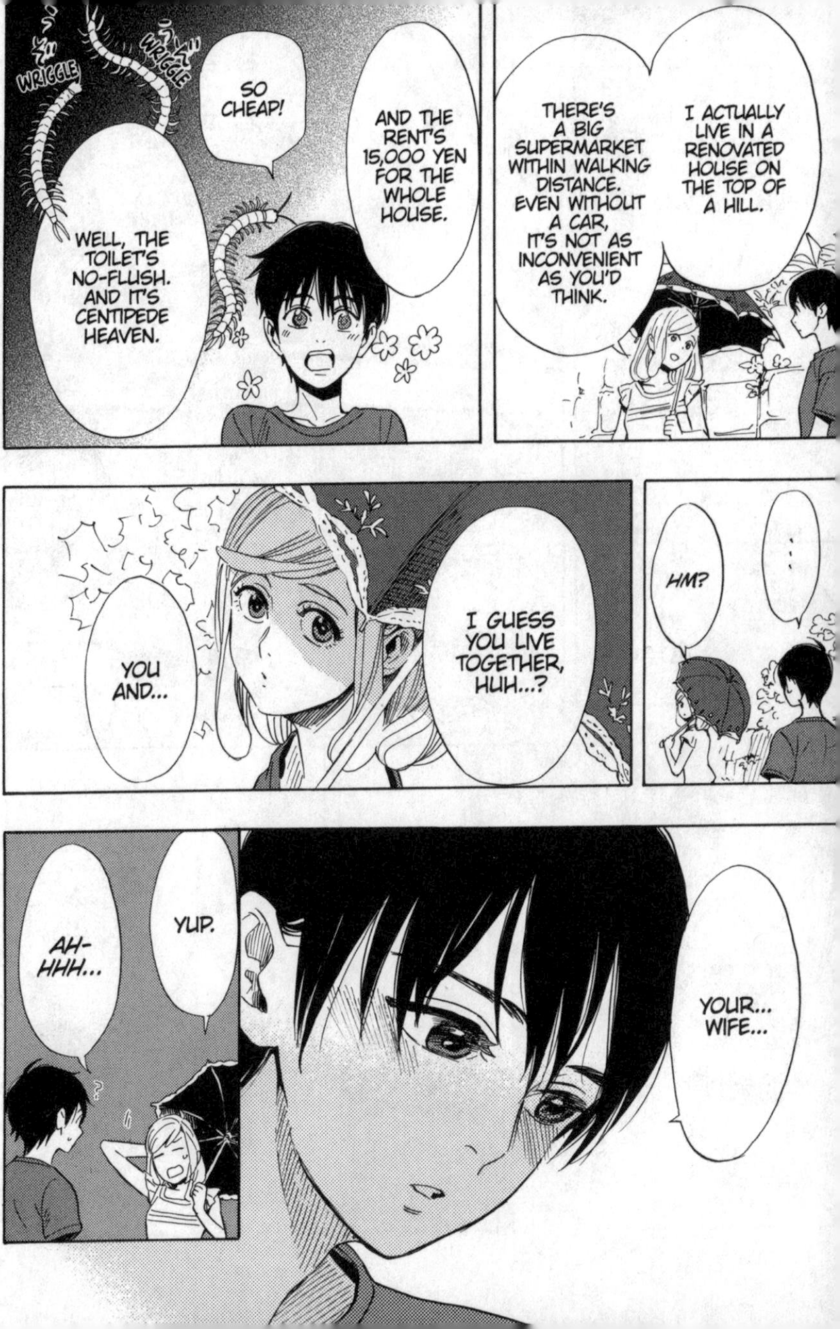
I ACTUALLY LIVE IN A RENOVATED HOUSE ON THE TOP OF A HILL.
THERE'S A BIG SUPERMARKET WITHIN WALKING DISTANCE. EVEN WITHOUT A CAR, IT'S NOT AS INCONVENIENT AS YOU'D THINK.
AND THE RENT'S 15,000 YEN FOR THE WHOLE HOUSE.
SO CHEAP!
WELL, THE TOILET'S NO-FLUSH. AND IT'S CENTIPEDE HEAVEN.
WRIGGLE
WRIGGLE
...
HM?
I GUESS YOU LIVE TOGETHER, HUH...?
YOU AND...
YOUR... WIFE...
YUP.
AH-HHH...

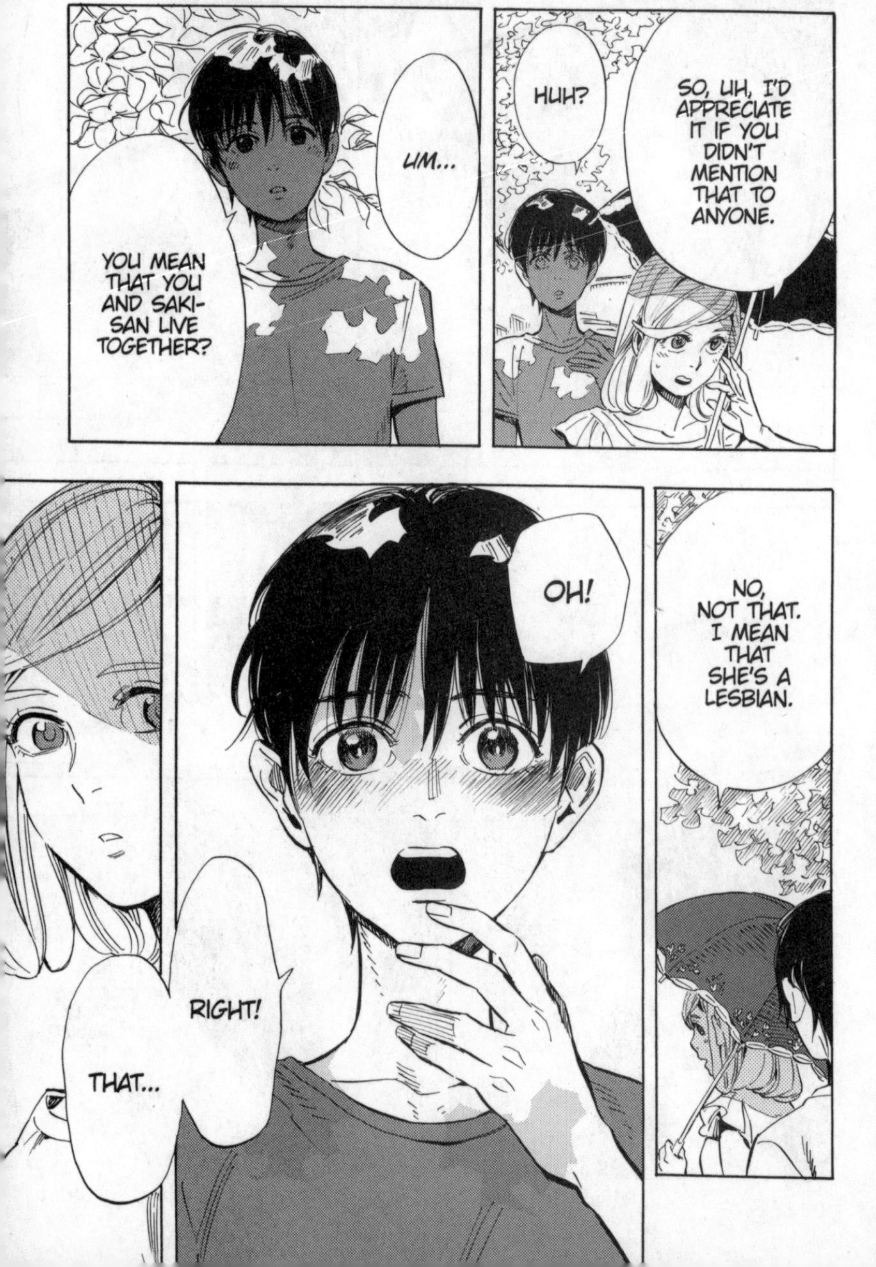
SO, UH, I'D APPRECIATE IT IF YOU DIDN'T MENTION THAT TO ANYONE.
HUH?
UM...
YOU MEAN THAT YOU AND SAKI-SAN LIVE TOGETHER?
NO, NOT THAT. I MEAN THAT SHE'S A LESBIAN.
OH!
RIGHT!
THAT...

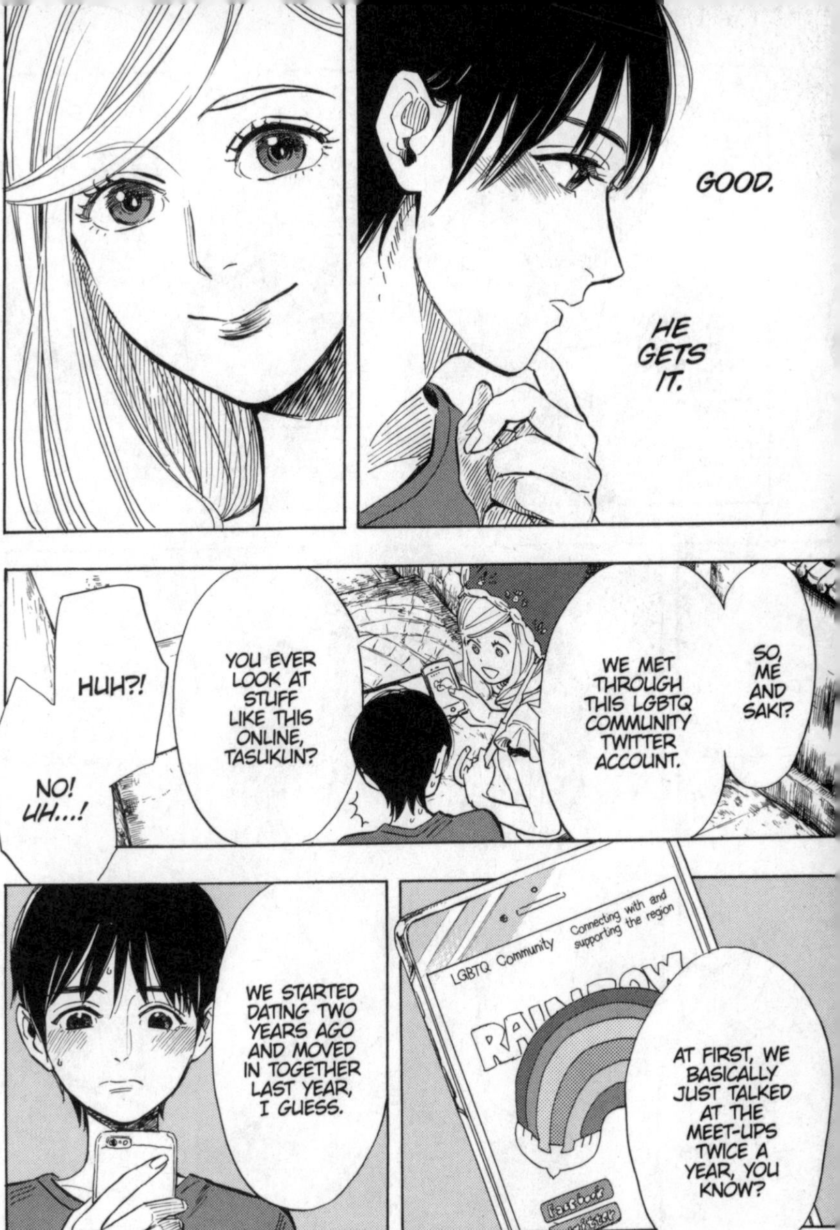
GOOD.
HE GETS IT.
SO, ME AND SAKI?
WE MET THROUGH THIS LGBTQ COMMUNITY TWITTER ACCOUNT.
YOU EVER LOOK AT STUFF LIKE THIS ONLINE, TASUKUN?
HUH?!
NO! UH...!
LGBTQ Community
Connecting with and supporting the region
AT FIRST, WE BASICALLY JUST TALKED AT THE MEET-UPS TWICE A YEAR, YOU KNOW?
WE STARTED DATING TWO YEARS AGO AND MOVED IN TOGETHER LAST YEAR, I GUESS.

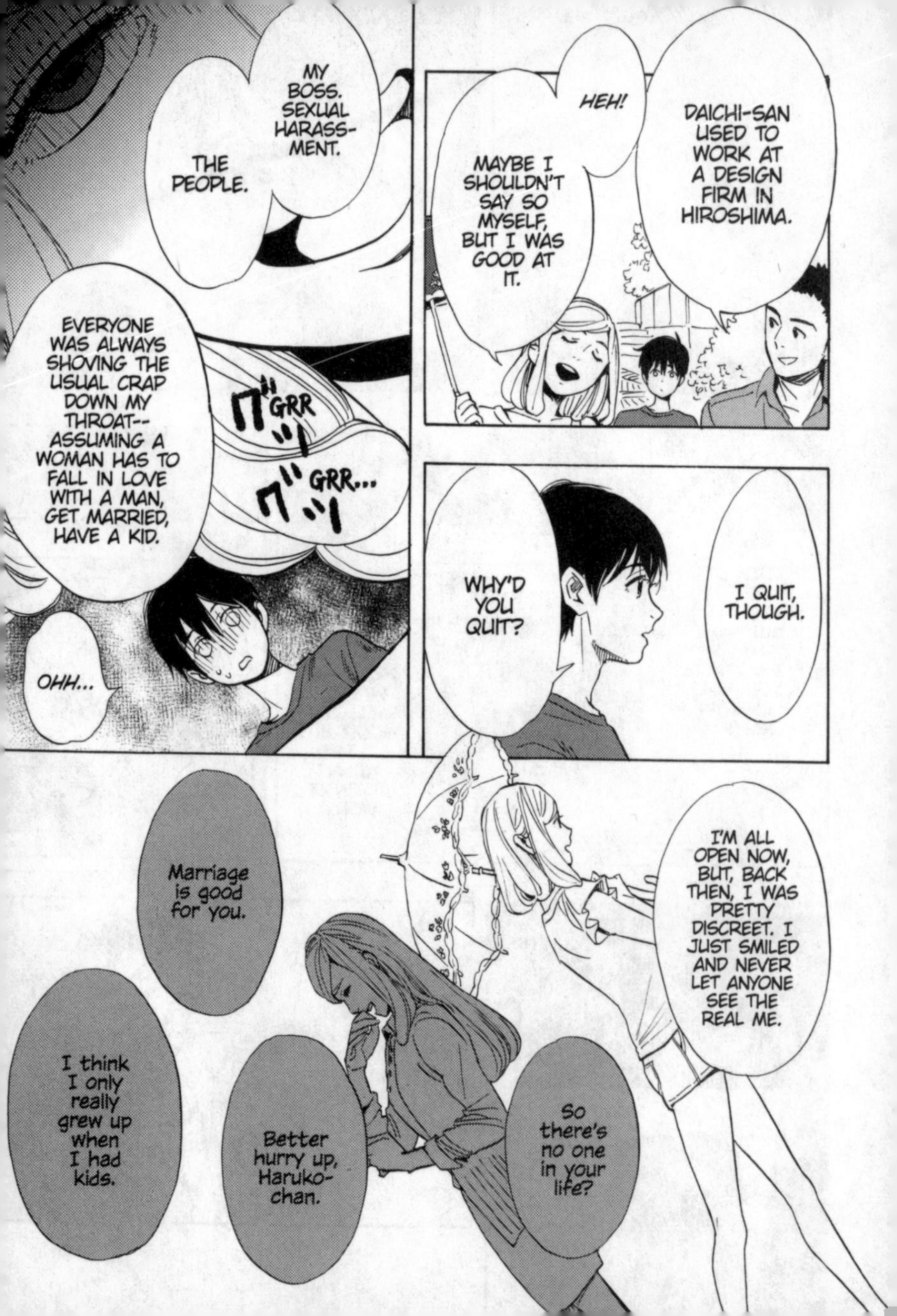
DAICHI-SAN USED TO WORK AT A DESIGN FIRM IN HIROSHIMA.
HEH!
MAYBE I SHOULDN'T SAY SO MYSELF, BUT I WAS GOOD AT IT.
I QUIT, THOUGH.
WHY'D YOU QUIT?
MY BOSS. SEXUAL HARASS-MENT.
THE PEOPLE.
EVERYONE WAS ALWAYS SHOVING THE USUAL CRAP DOWN MY THROAT-- ASSUMING A WOMAN HAS TO FALL IN LOVE WITH A MAN, GET MARRIED, HAVE A KID.
GRR
GRR...
OHH...
I'M ALL OPEN NOW, BUT, BACK THEN, I WAS PRETTY DISCREET. I JUST SMILED AND NEVER LET ANYONE SEE THE REAL ME.
Marriage is good for you.
So there's no one in your life?
Better hurry up, Haruko-chan.
I think I only really grew up when I had kids.

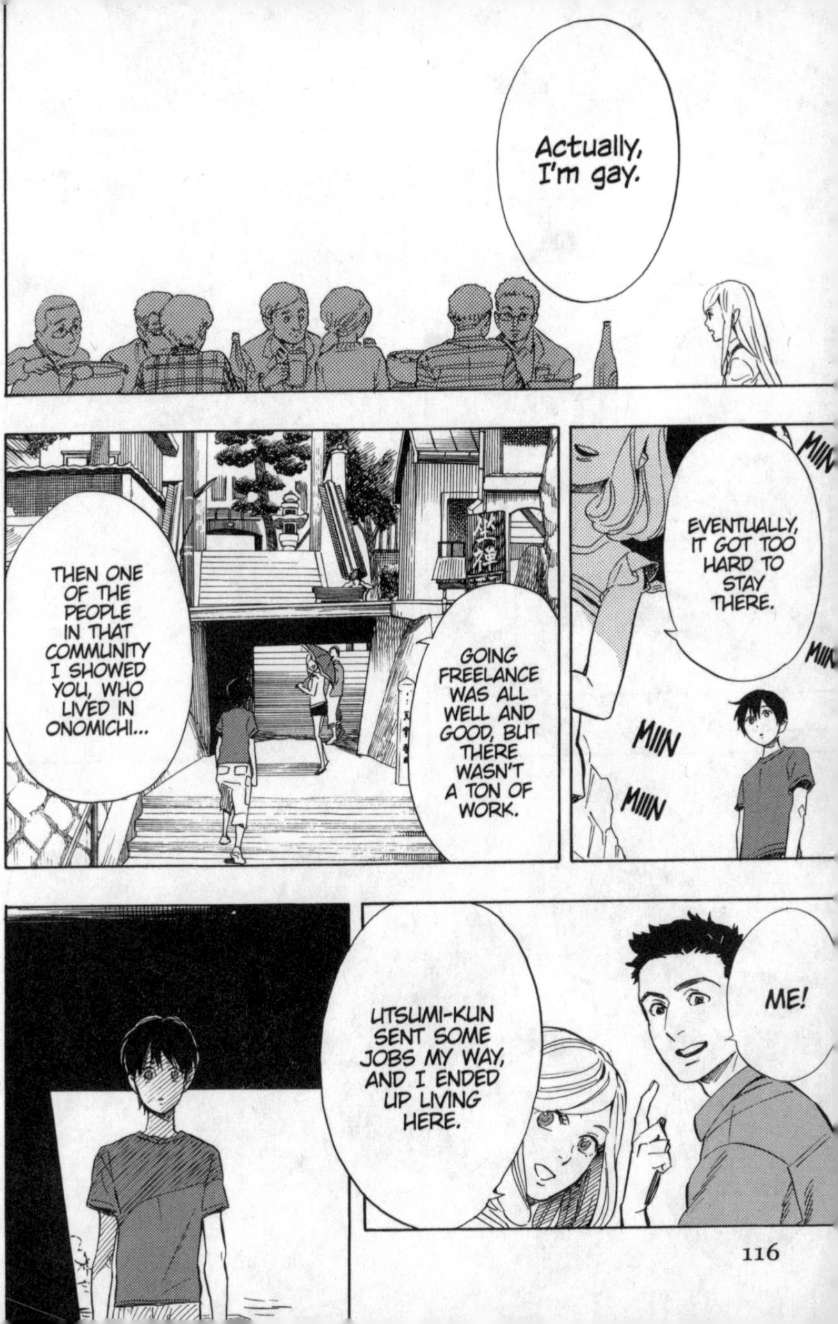
Actually, I'm gay.
MIIN
EVENTUALLY, IT GOT TOO HARD TO STAY THERE.
MIIN
MIIN
MIIN
GOING FREELANCE WAS ALL WELL AND GOOD, BUT THERE WASN'T A TON OF WORK.
THEN ONE OF THE PEOPLE IN THAT COMMUNITY I SHOWED YOU, WHO LIVED IN ONOMICHI...
UTSUMI-KUN SENT SOME JOBS MY WAY, AND I ENDED UP LIVING HERE.
ME!

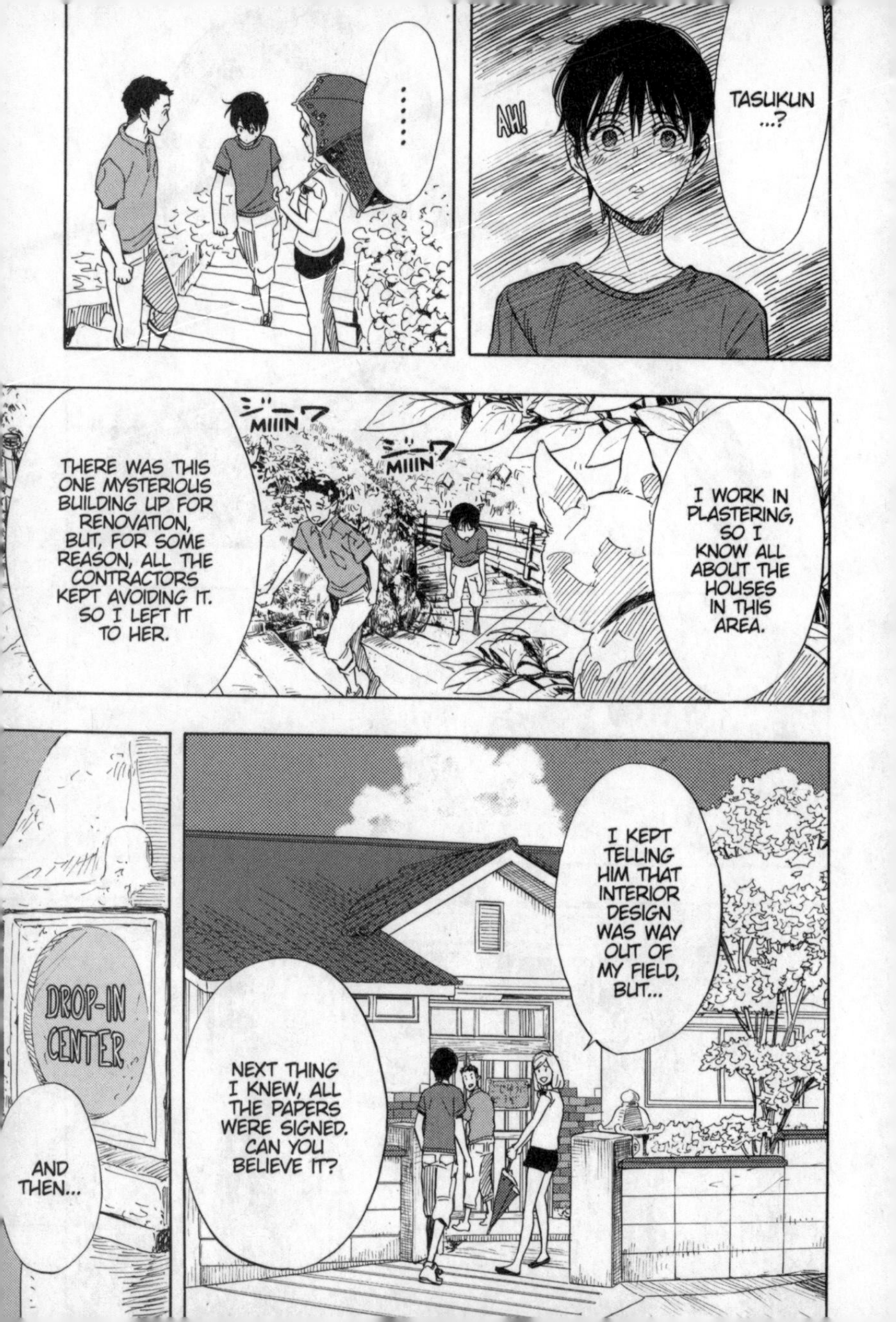
AH!
TASUKUN ...?
......
I WORK IN PLASTERING, SO I KNOW ALL ABOUT THE HOUSES IN THIS AREA.
ジーワ MIIIN
ジーワ MIIIN
THERE WAS THIS ONE MYSTERIOUS BUILDING UP FOR RENOVATION, BUT, FOR SOME REASON, ALL THE CONTRACTORS KEPT AVOIDING IT. SO I LEFT IT TO HER.
I KEPT TELLING HIM THAT INTERIOR DESIGN WAS WAY OUT OF MY FIELD, BUT...
NEXT THING I KNEW, ALL THE PAPERS WERE SIGNED. CAN YOU BELIEVE IT?
DROP-IN CENTER
AND THEN...

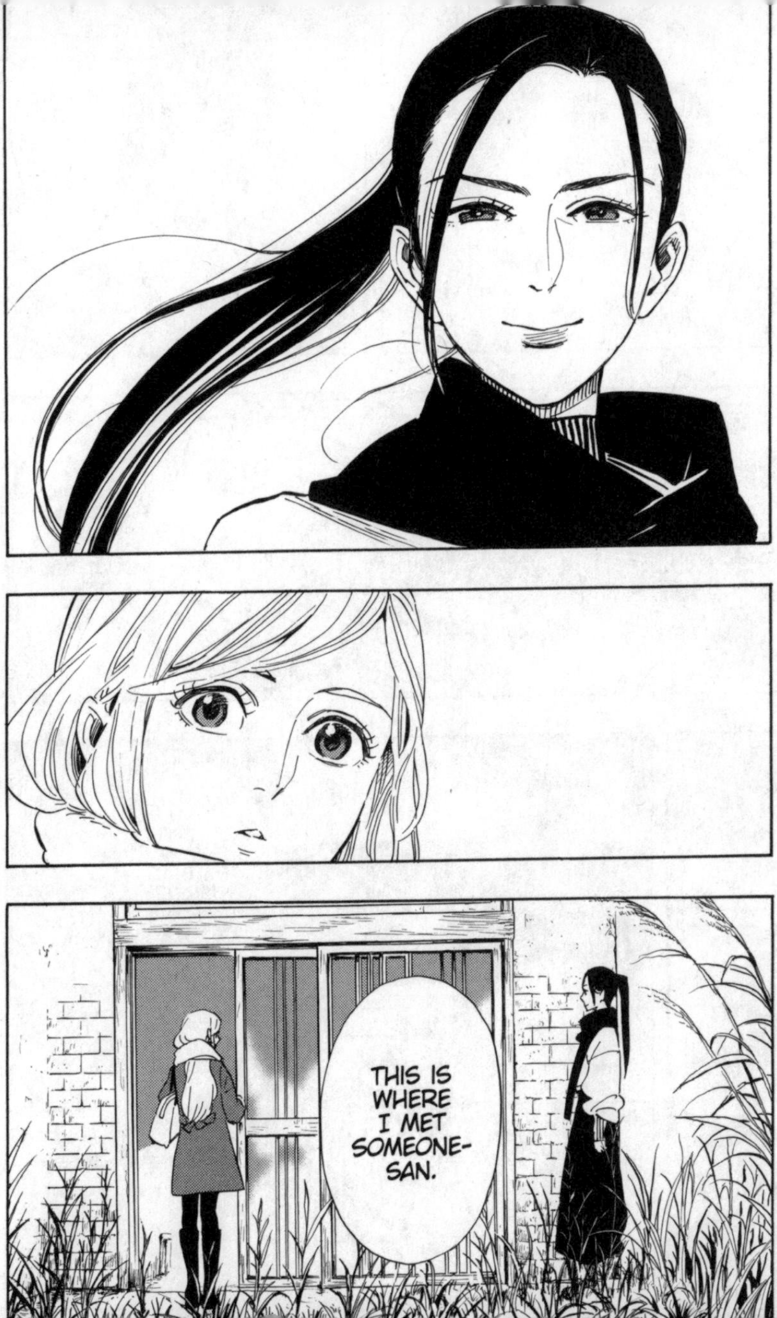
THIS IS WHERE I MET SOMEONE-SAN.

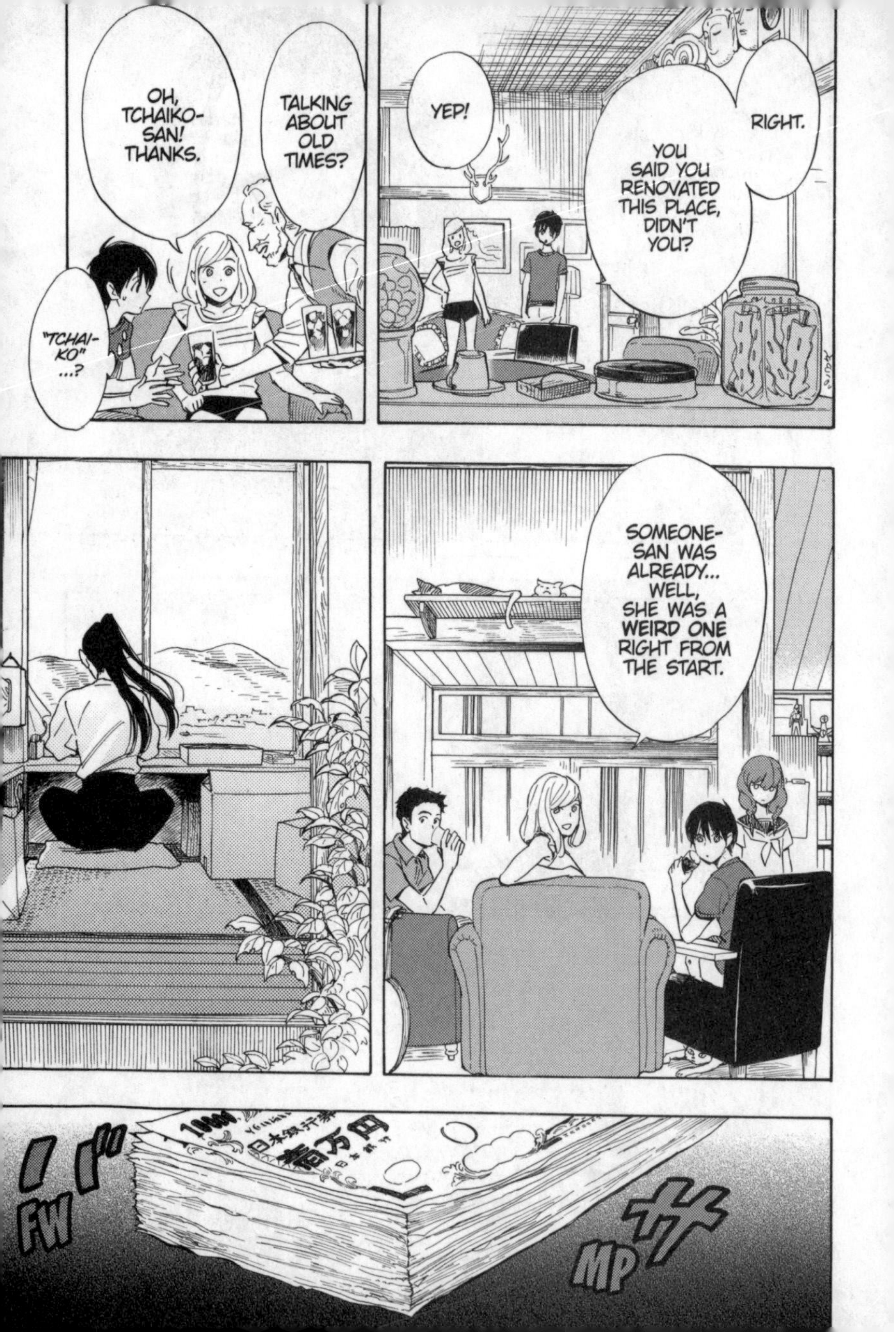
RIGHT.
YOU SAID YOU RENOVATED THIS PLACE, DIDN'T YOU?
YEP!
TALKING ABOUT OLD TIMES?
OH, TCHAIKO-SAN! THANKS.
"TCHAIKO" ...?
SOMEONE-SAN WAS ALREADY... WELL, SHE WAS A WEIRD ONE RIGHT FROM THE START.
FW
MP

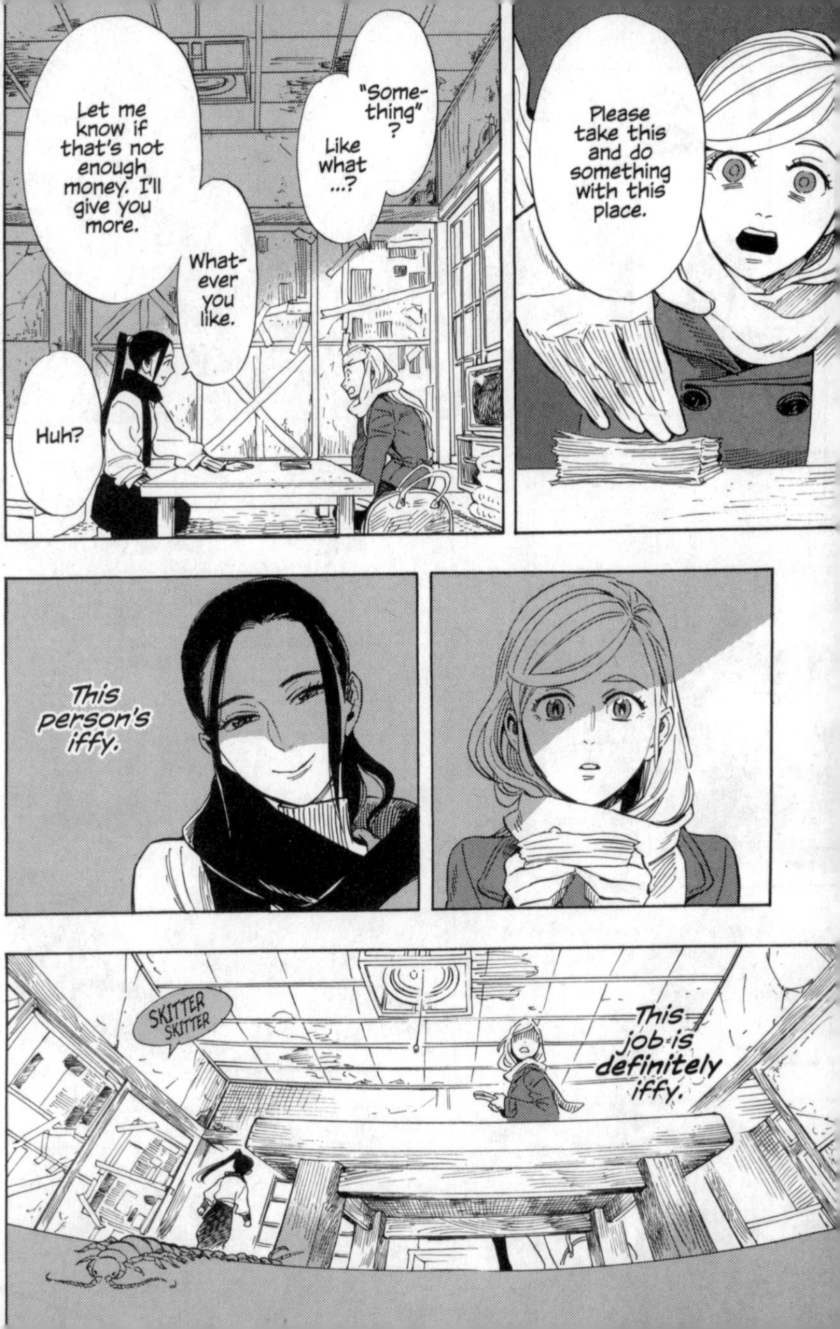
Please take this and do something with this place.
"Something"?
Like what ...?
Let me know if that's not enough money. I'll give you more.
Whatever you like.
Huh?
This person's iffy.
This job is definitely iffy.
SKITTER SKITTER

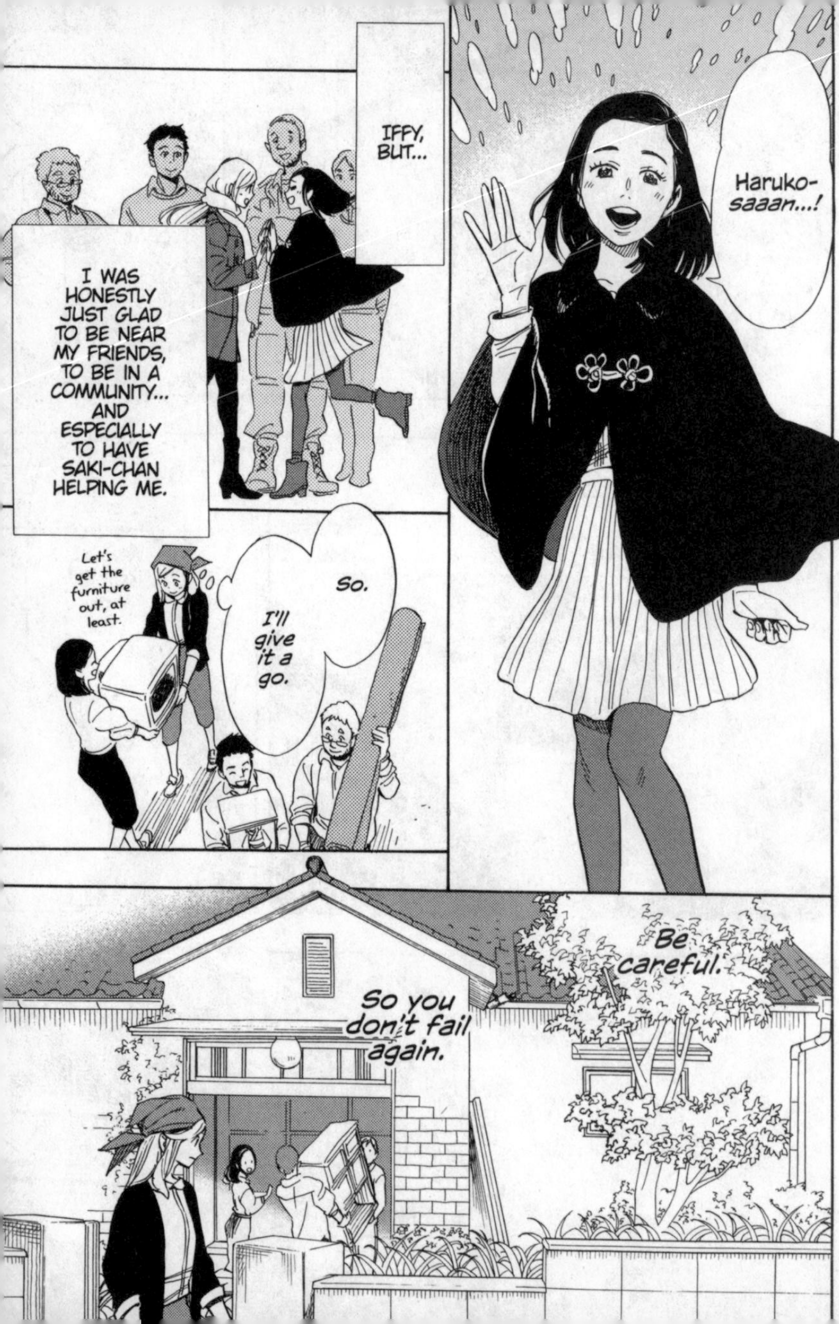
Haruko-saaan...!
IFFY, BUT...
I WAS HONESTLY JUST GLAD TO BE NEAR MY FRIENDS, TO BE IN A COMMUNITY... AND ESPECIALLY TO HAVE SAKI-CHAN HELPING ME.
So.
I'll give it a go.
Let's get the furniture out, at least.
Be careful.
So you don't fail again.

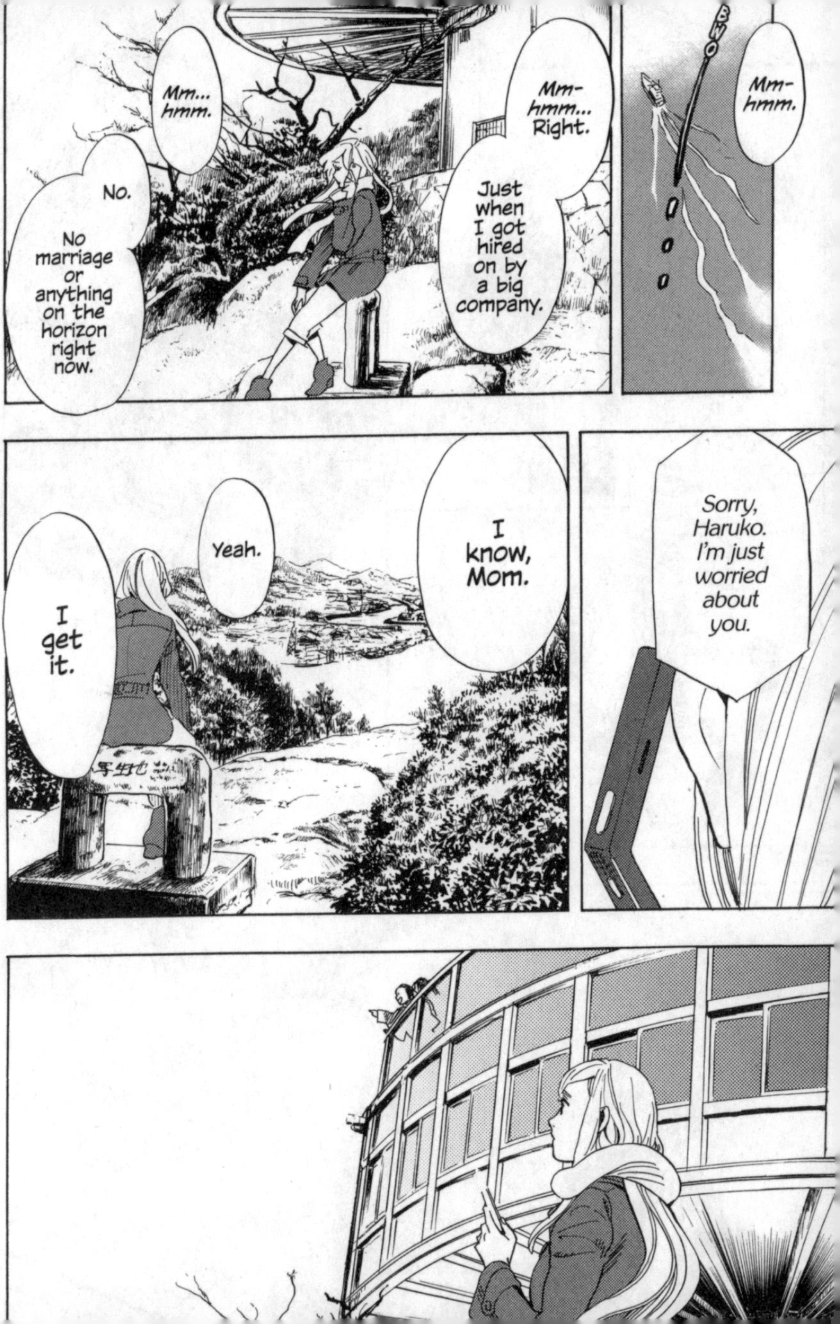
BWO
Mm-hmm.
Mm-hmm... Right.
Just when I got hired on by a big company.
Mm... hmm.
No.
No marriage or anything on the horizon right now.
Sorry, Haruko. I'm just worried about you.
I know, Mom.
Yeah.
I get it.

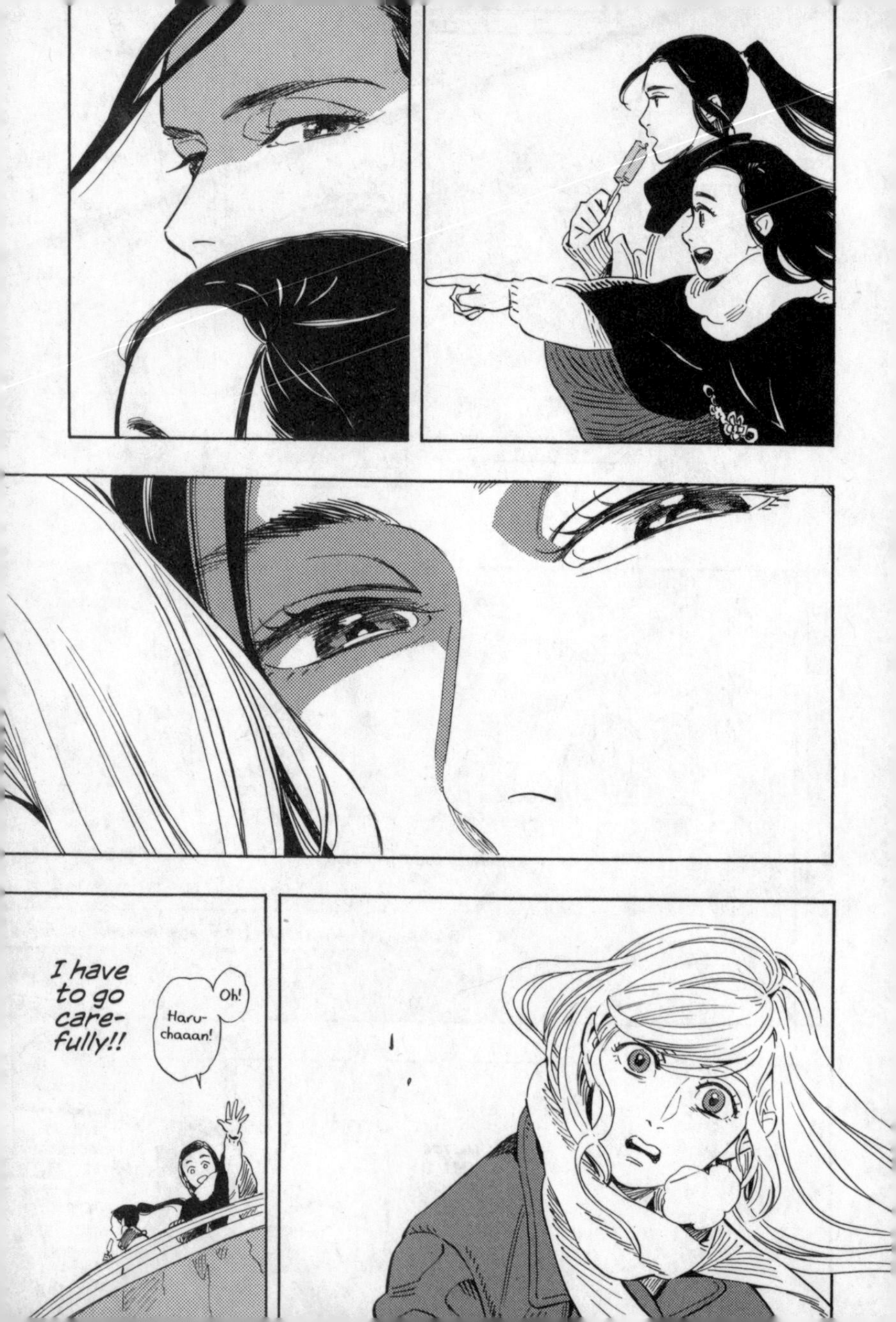
Oh! Haru-chaaan!
I have to go care-fully!!

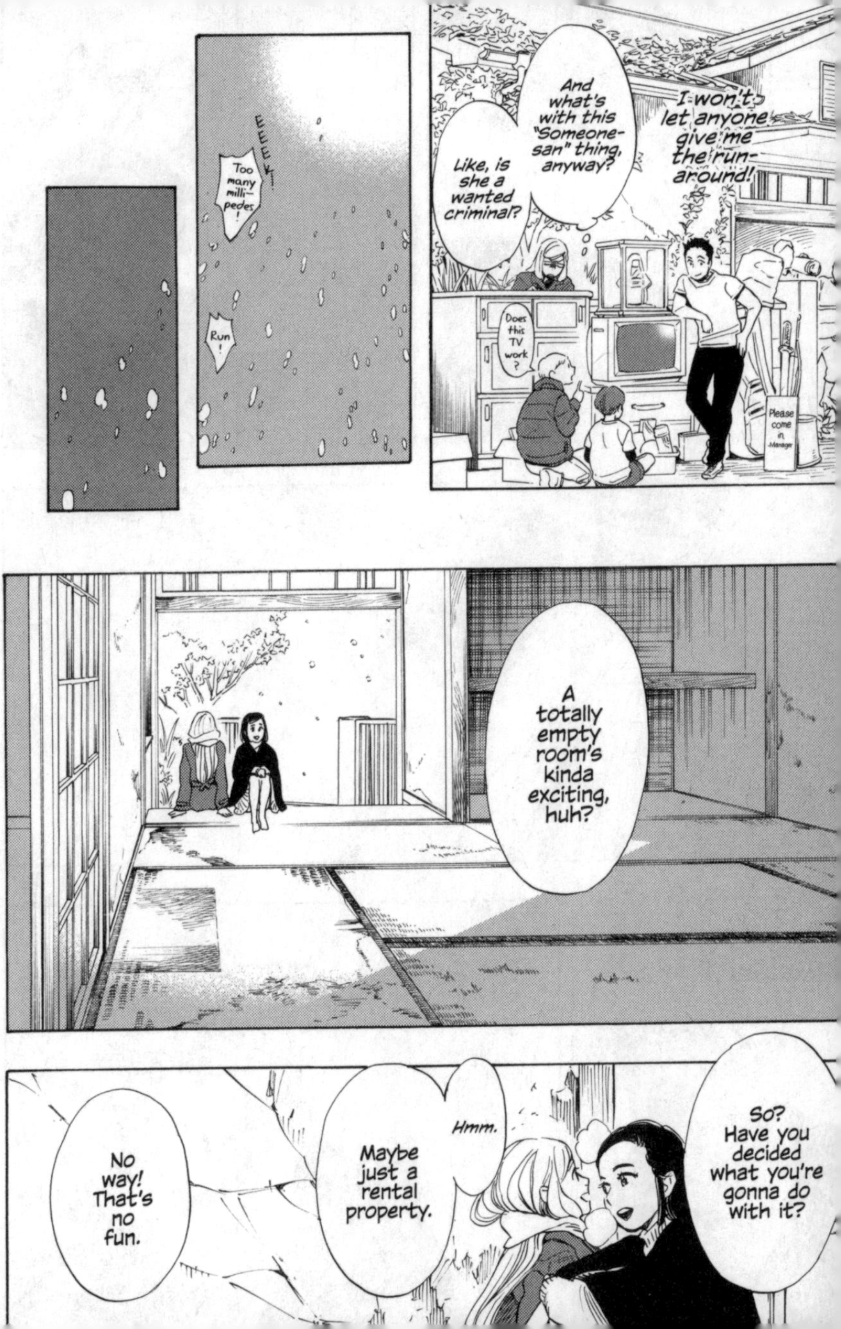
I won't let anyone give me the run-around!
And what's with this "Someone-san" thing, anyway?
Like, is she a wanted criminal?
Does this TV work?
Please come in. -Manager
EEEEK!
Too many milli-pedes!
Run!
A totally empty room's kinda exciting, huh?
So? Have you decided what you're gonna do with it?
Hmm.
Maybe just a rental property.
No way! That's no fun.

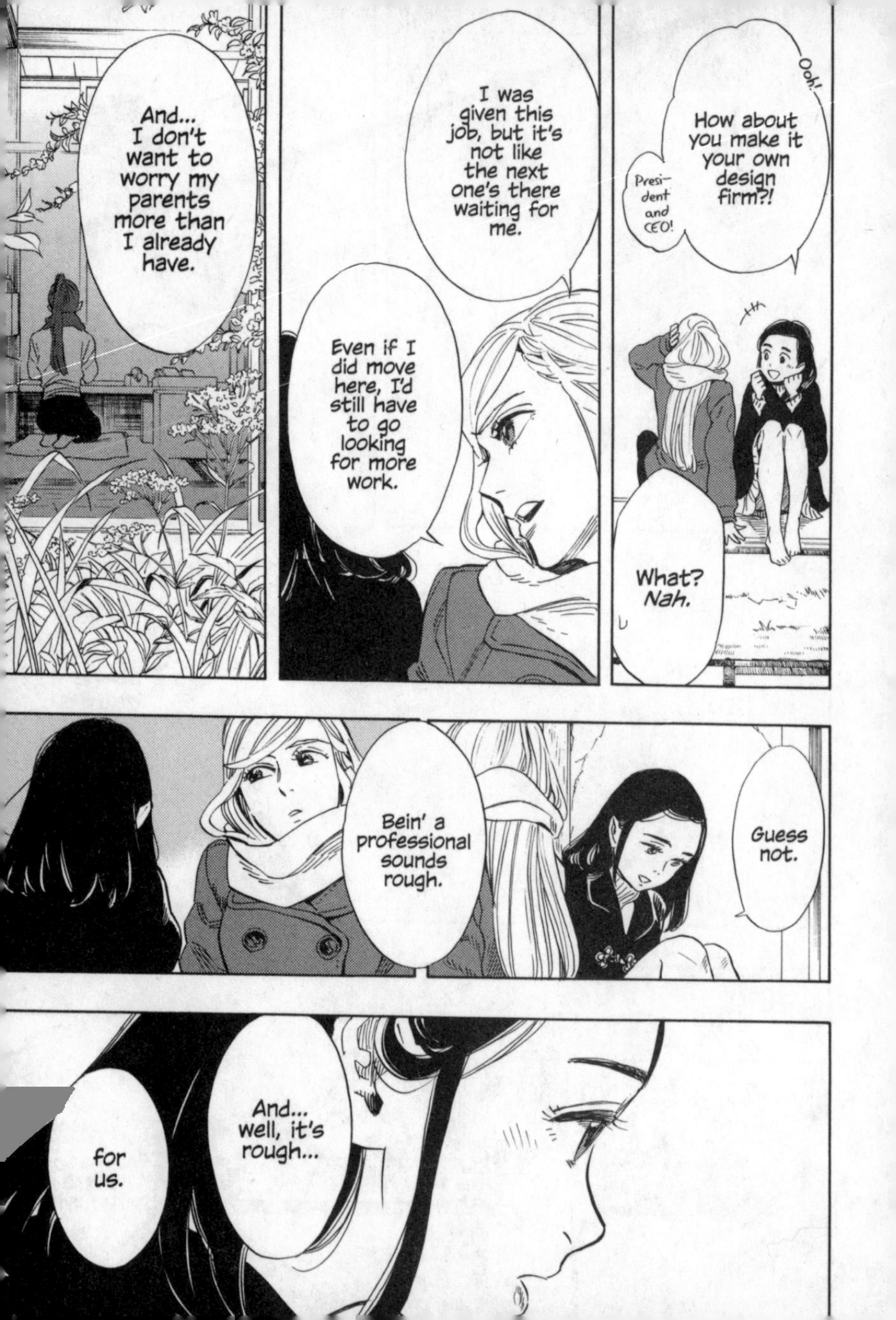
Ooh!
How about you make it your own design firm?!
President and CEO!
What? Nah.
I was given this job, but it's not like the next one's there waiting for me.
Even if I did move here, I'd still have to go looking for more work.
And... I don't want to worry my parents more than I already have.
Guess not.
Bein' a professional sounds rough.
And... well, it's rough...
for us.

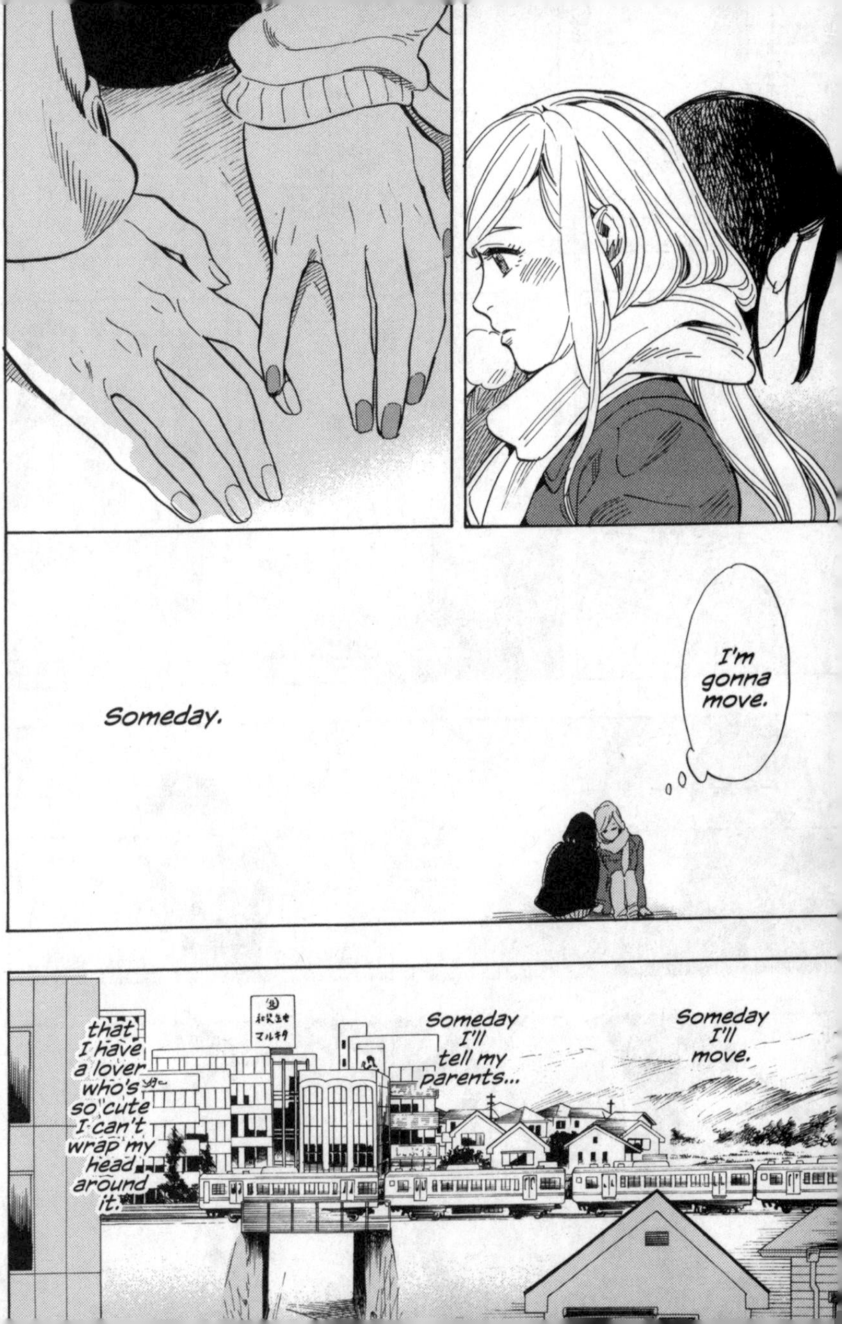
I'm gonna move.
Someday.
Someday I'll move.
Someday I'll tell my parents...
that I have a lover who's so cute I can't wrap my head around it.

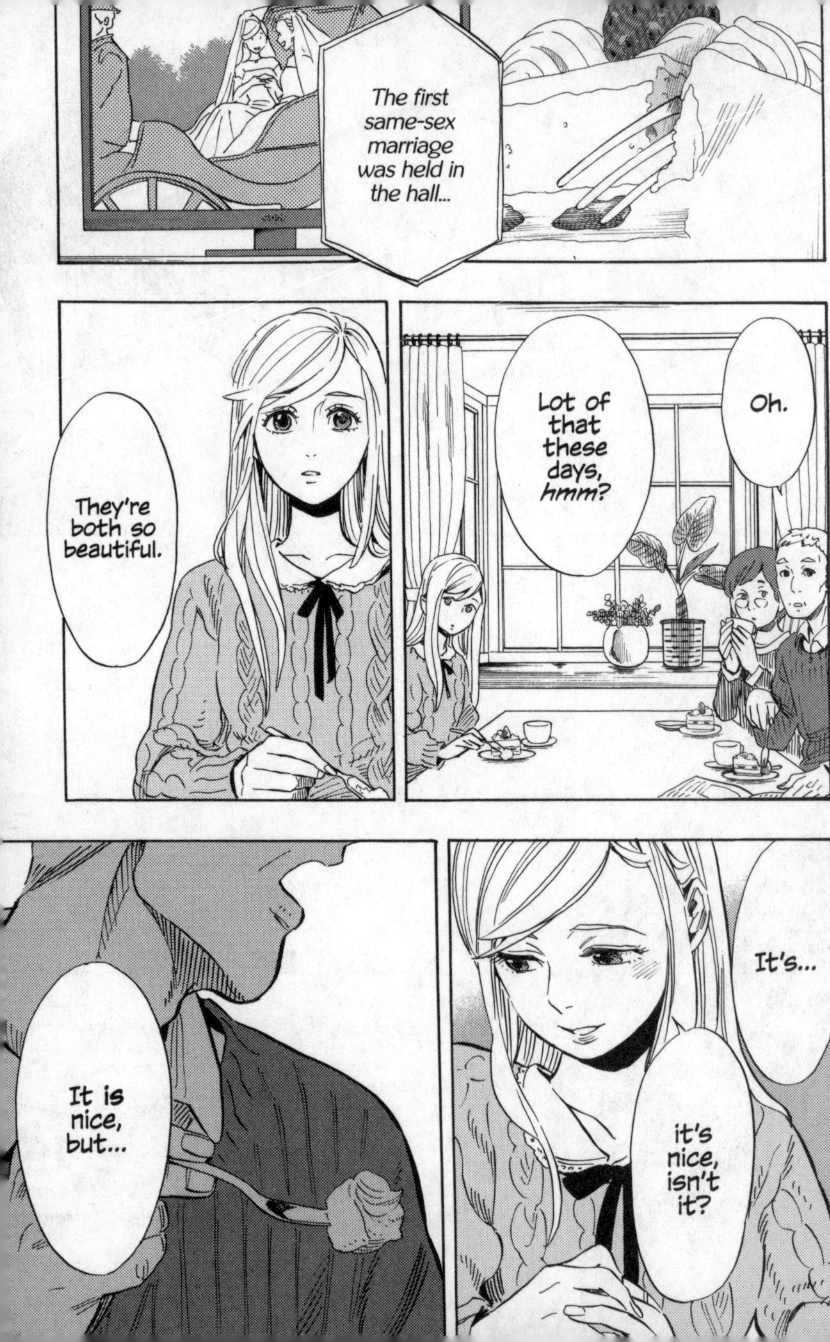
The first same-sex marriage was held in the hall...
Oh.
Lot of that these days, *hmm?*
They're both so beautiful.
It's...
it's nice, isn't it?
It is nice, but...

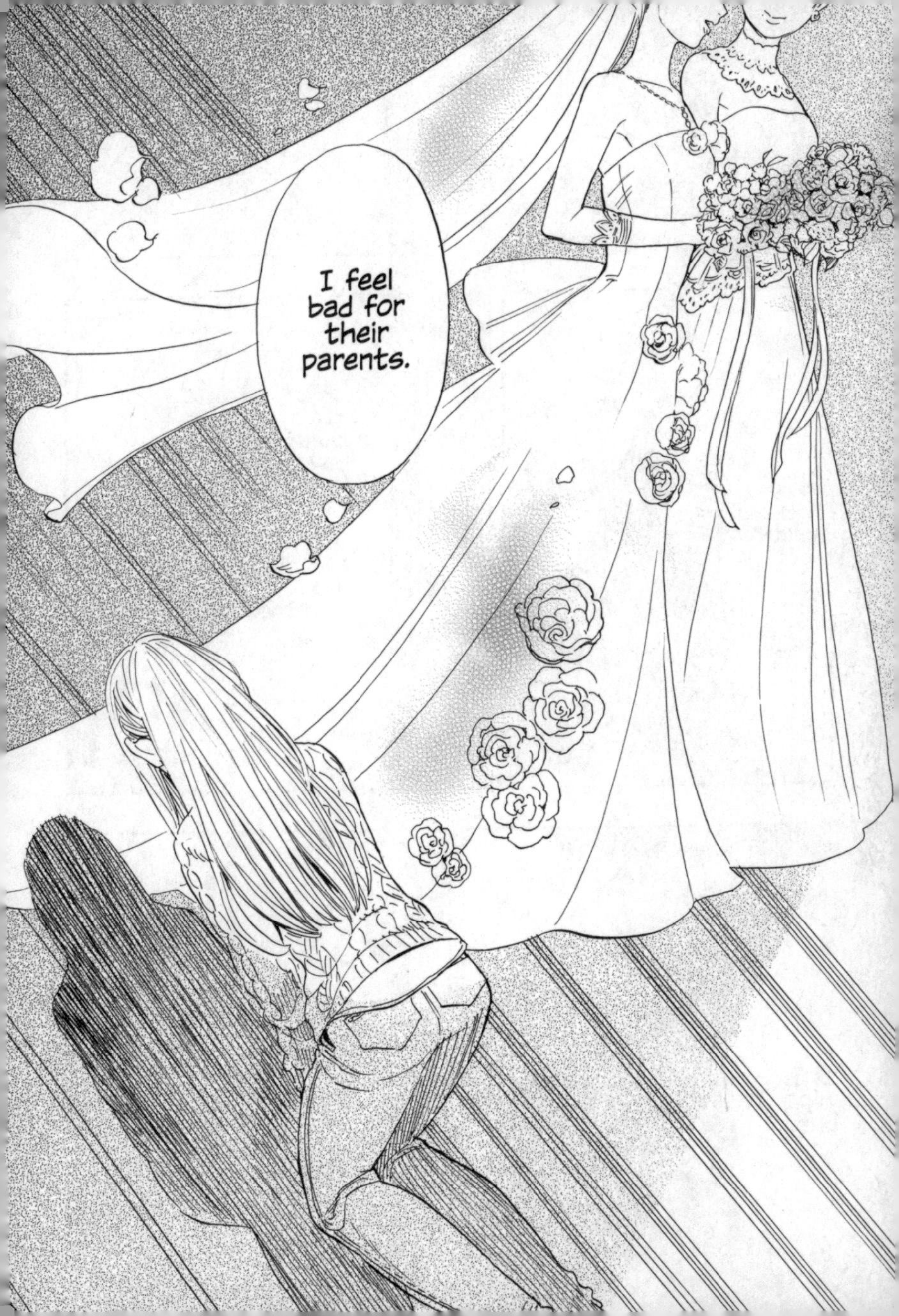
I feel bad for their parents.

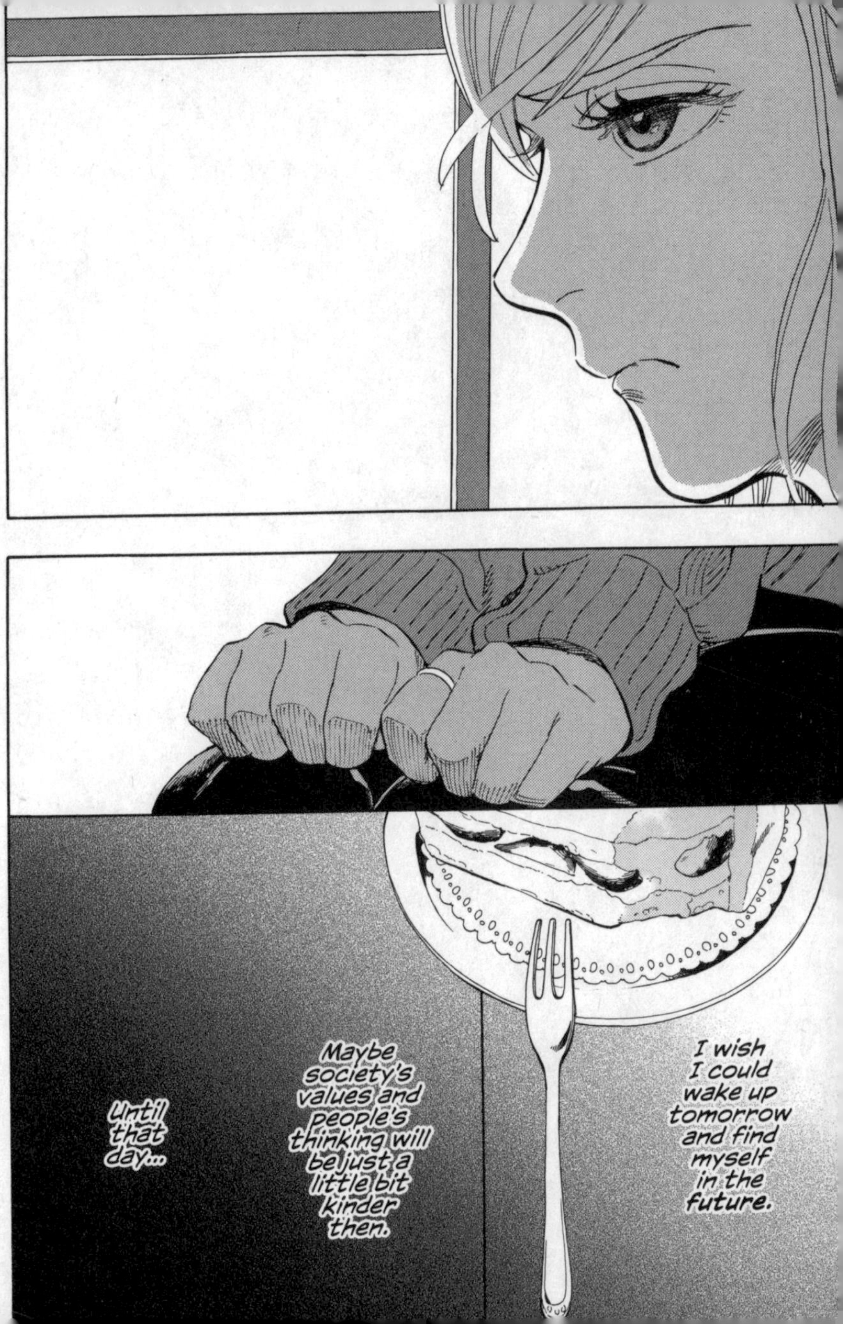
I wish I could wake up tomorrow and find myself in the future.
Maybe society's values and people's thinking will be just a little bit kinder then.
Until that day...

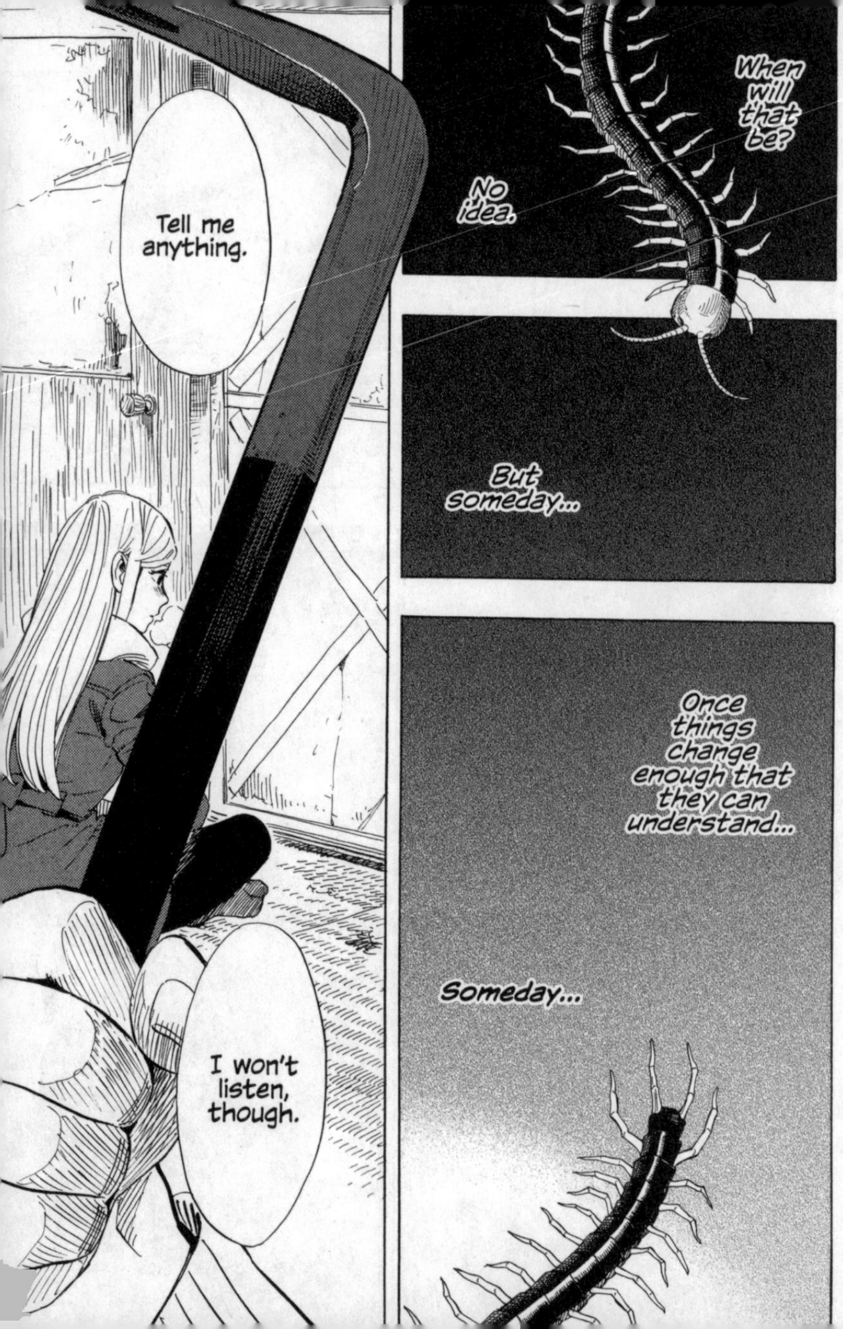

When will that be?
No idea.
But someday...
Once things change enough that they can understand...
Someday...
Tell me anything.
I won't listen, though.

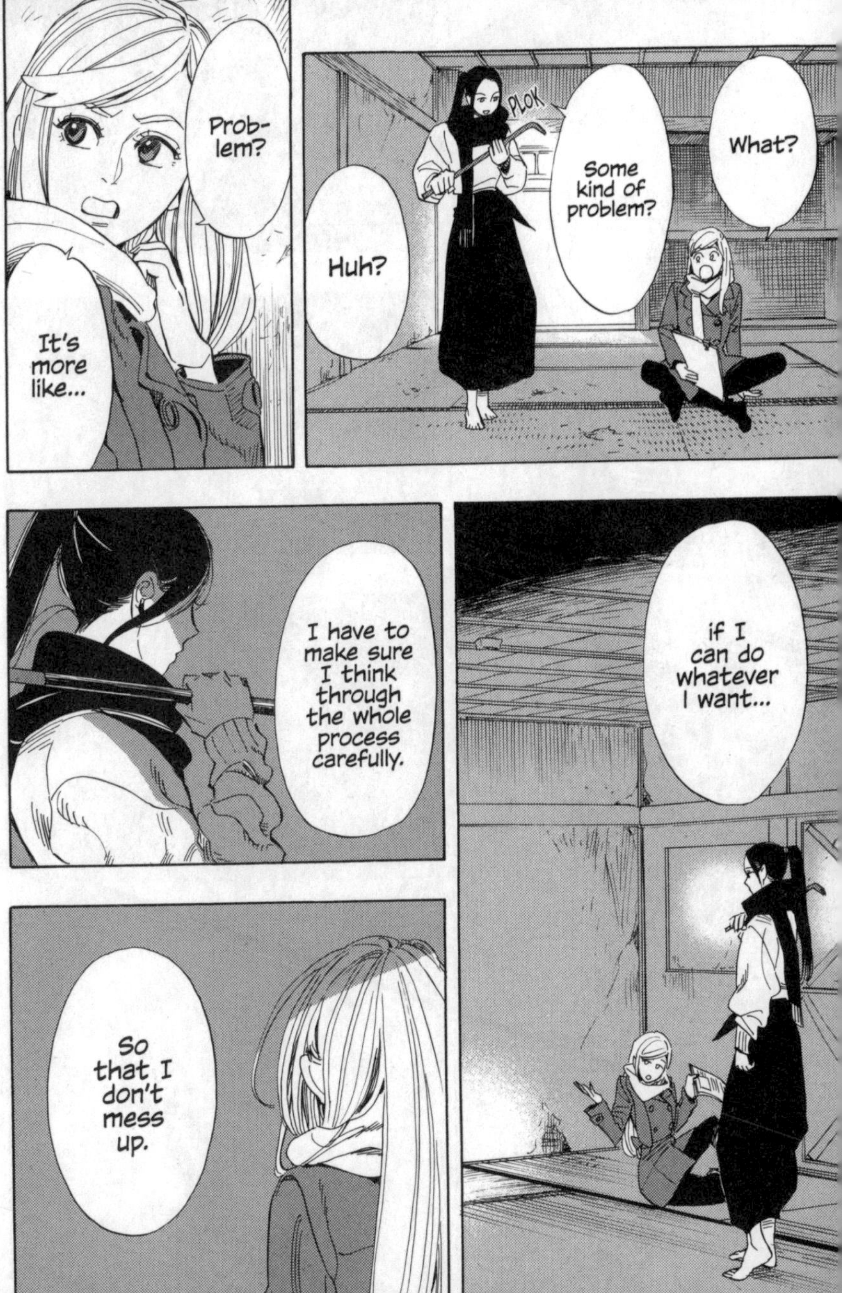
What?
Some kind of problem?
PLOK
Huh?
Prob-lem?
It's more like...
if I can do whatever I want...
I have to make sure I think through the whole process carefully.
So that I don't mess up.

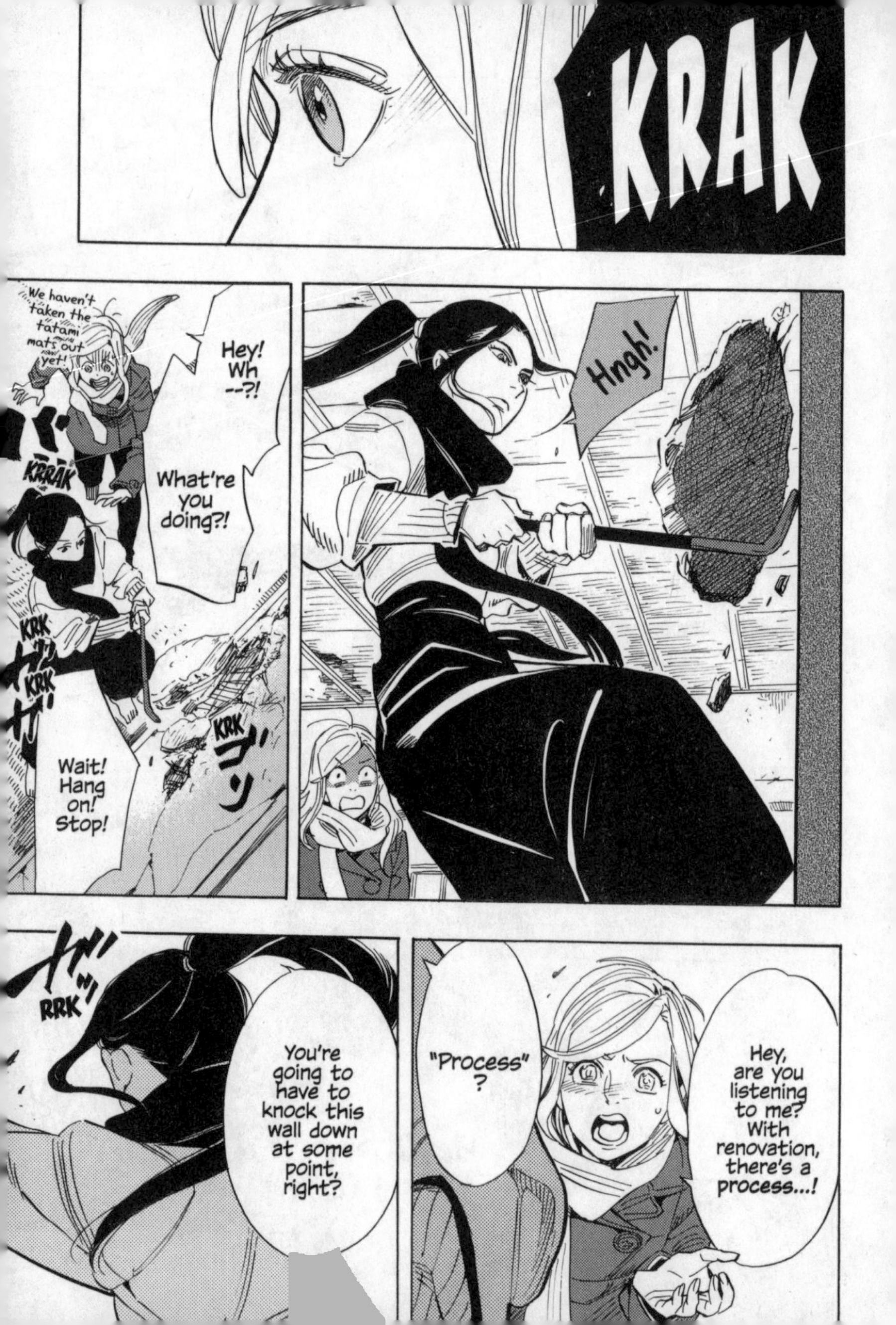
KRAK
Hngh!
Hey! Wh--?!
What're you doing?!
We haven't taken the tatami mats out yet!
KRRAK
KRK
KRK
KRK
Wait! Hang on! Stop!
Hey, are you listening to me? With renovation, there's a process...!
"Process"?
RRK
You're going to have to knock this wall down at some point, right?

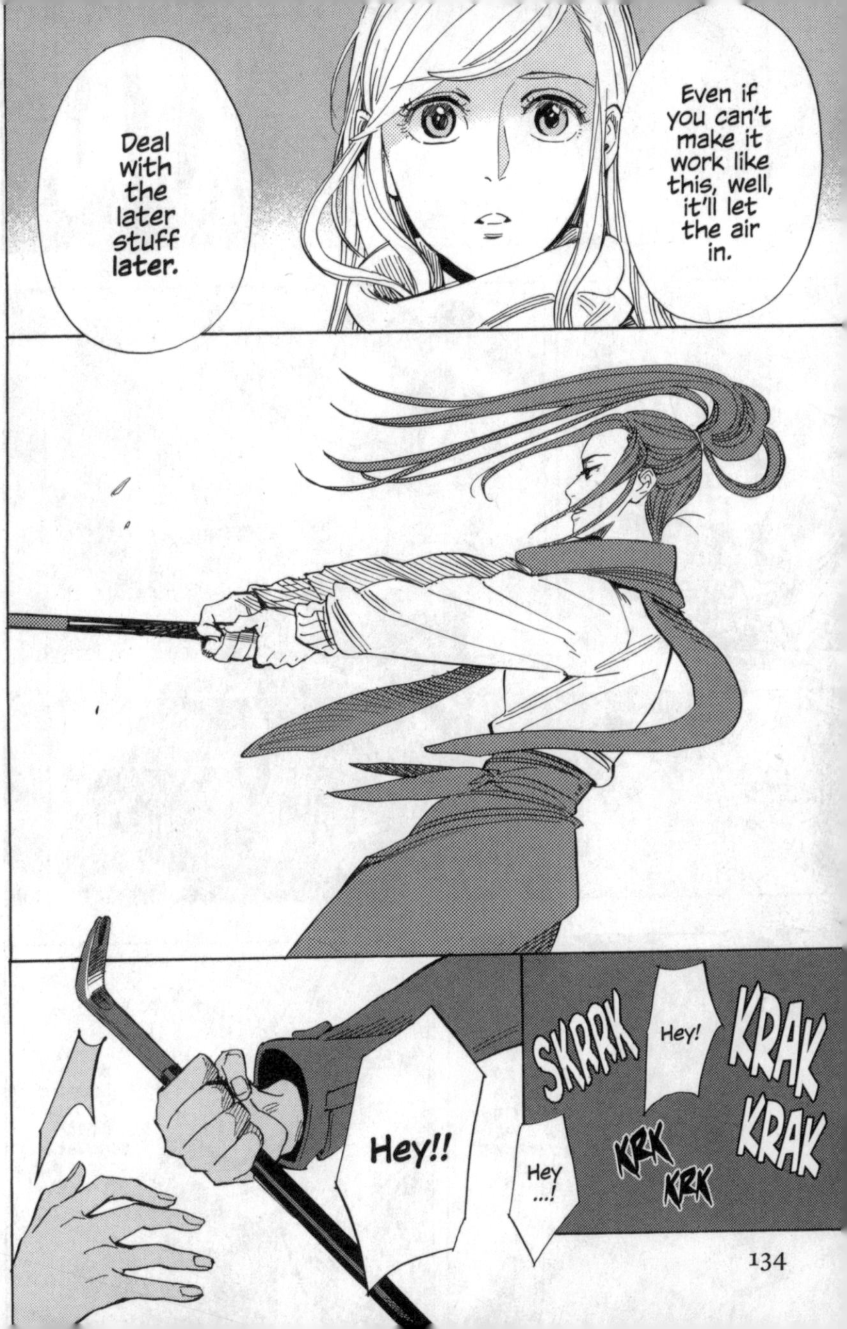
Even if you can't make it work like this, well, it'll let the air in.
Deal with the later stuff later.
KRAK KRAK
Hey!
SKRRK
KRK KRK
Hey ...!
Hey!!

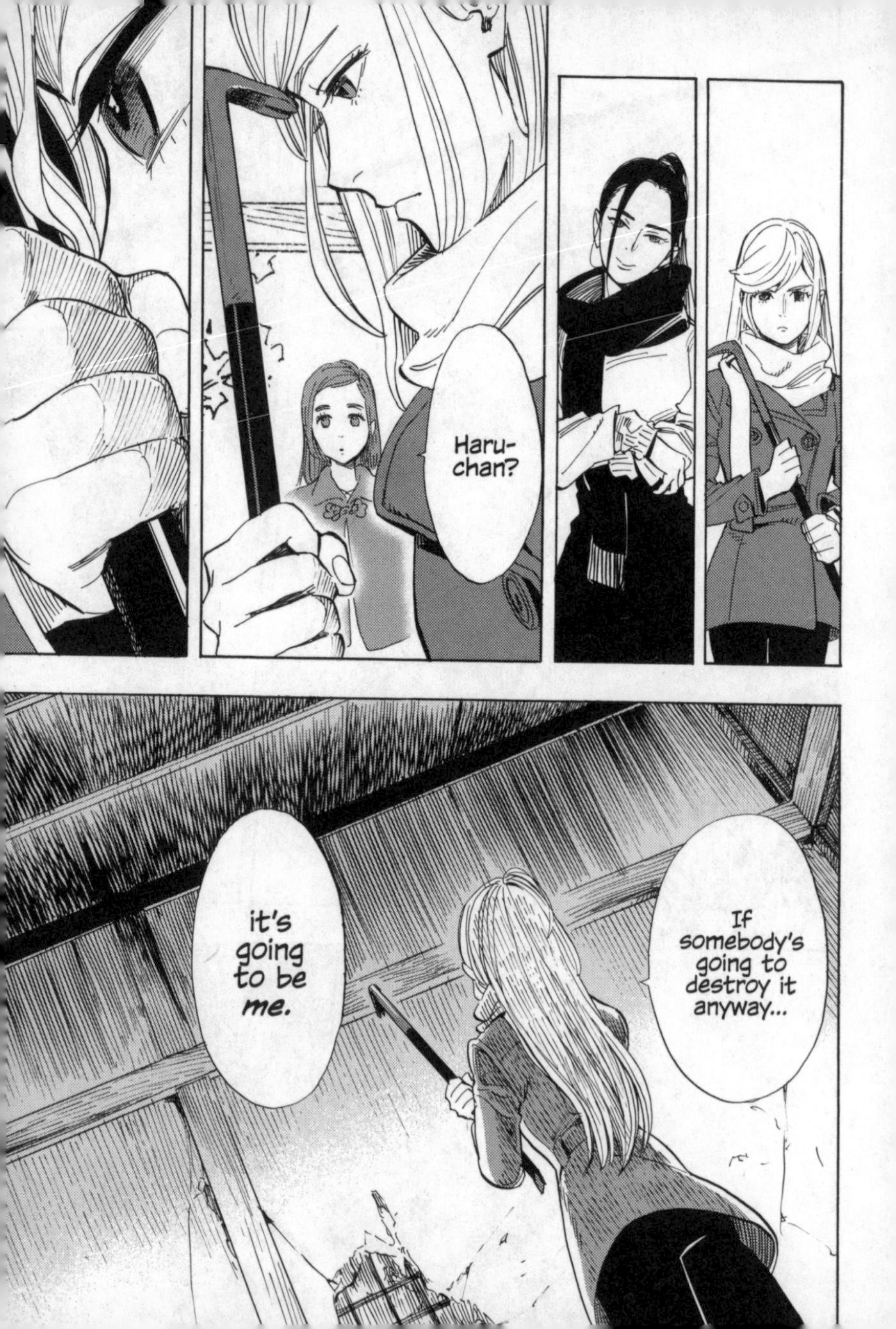
Haru-chan?
If somebody's going to destroy it anyway...
it's going to be *me.*

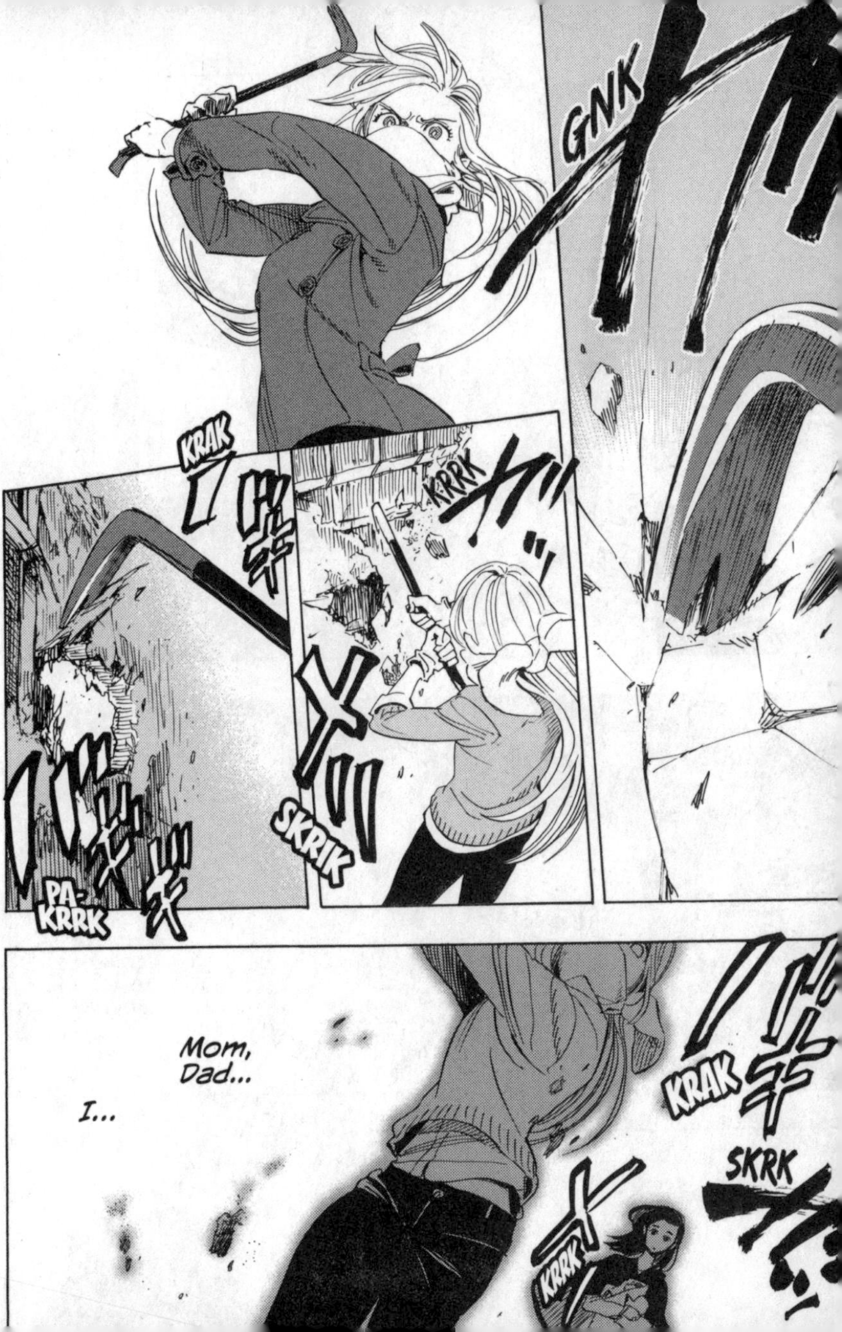
GNK
KRRK
SKRIK
KRAK
PA-KRRK
KRAK
SKRK
KRRK
Mom, Dad...
I...

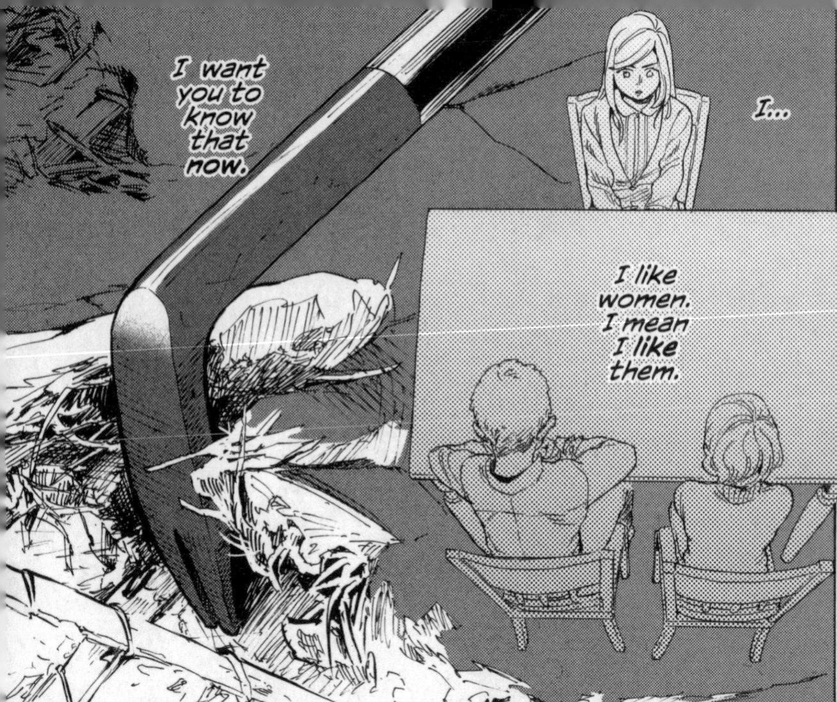
I...
I like women. I mean I like them.
Not tomorrow, not ten years from now...
but who I am right now.
I want you to know that now.

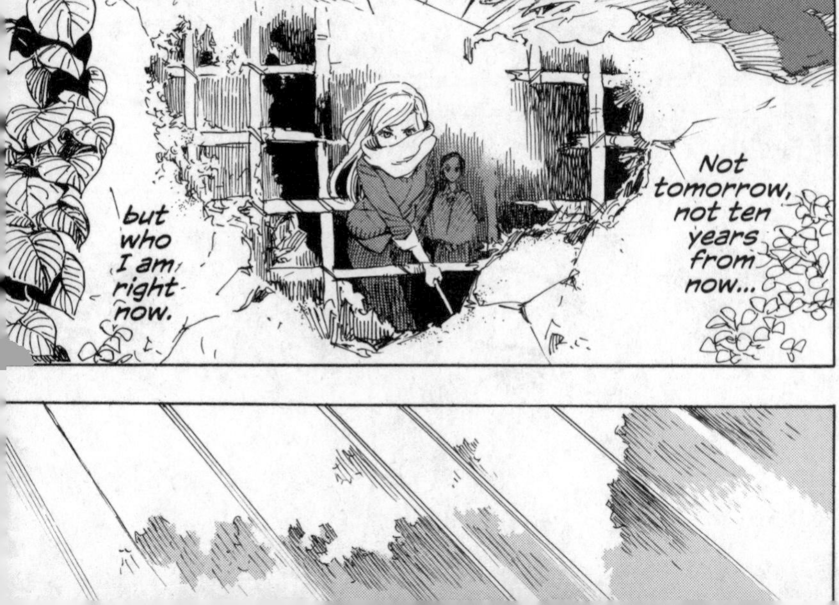

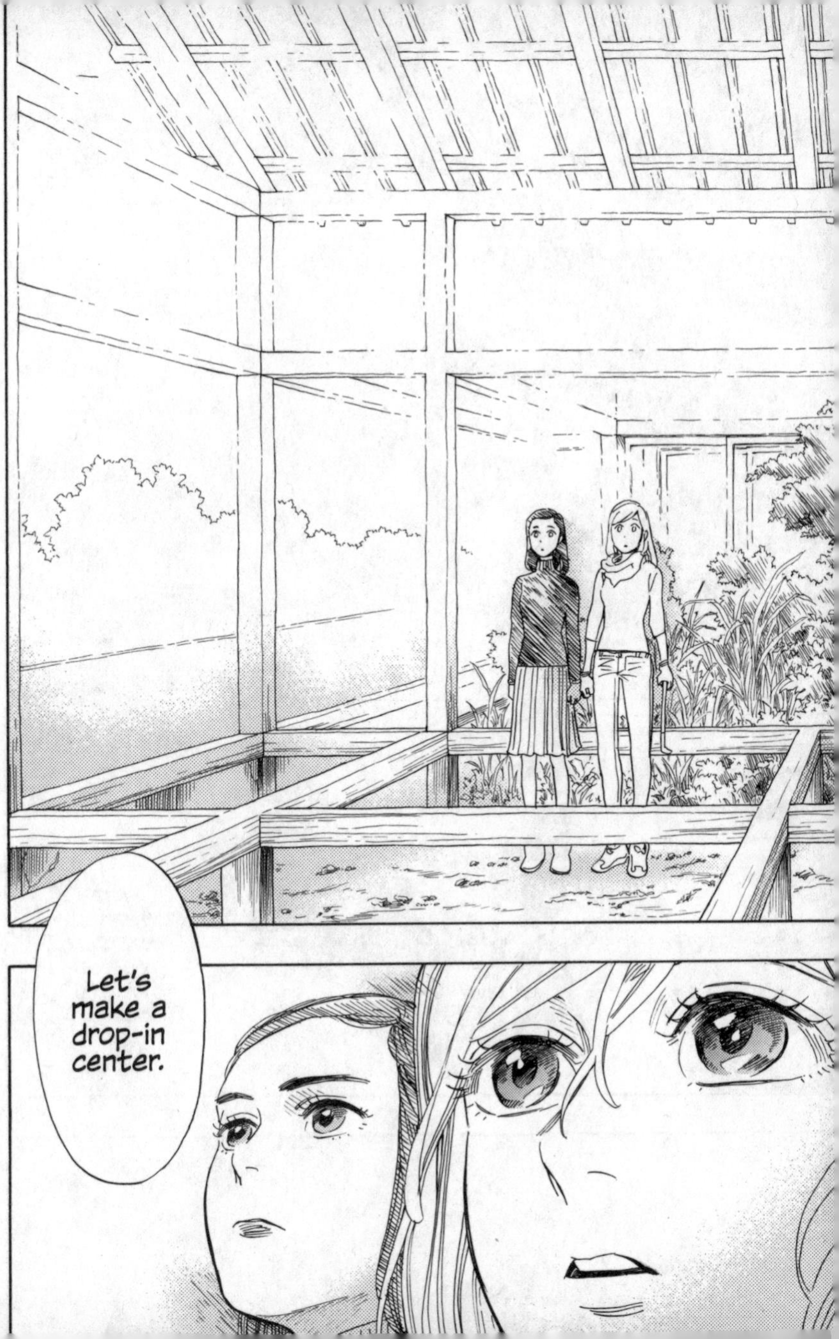
Let's make a drop-in center.

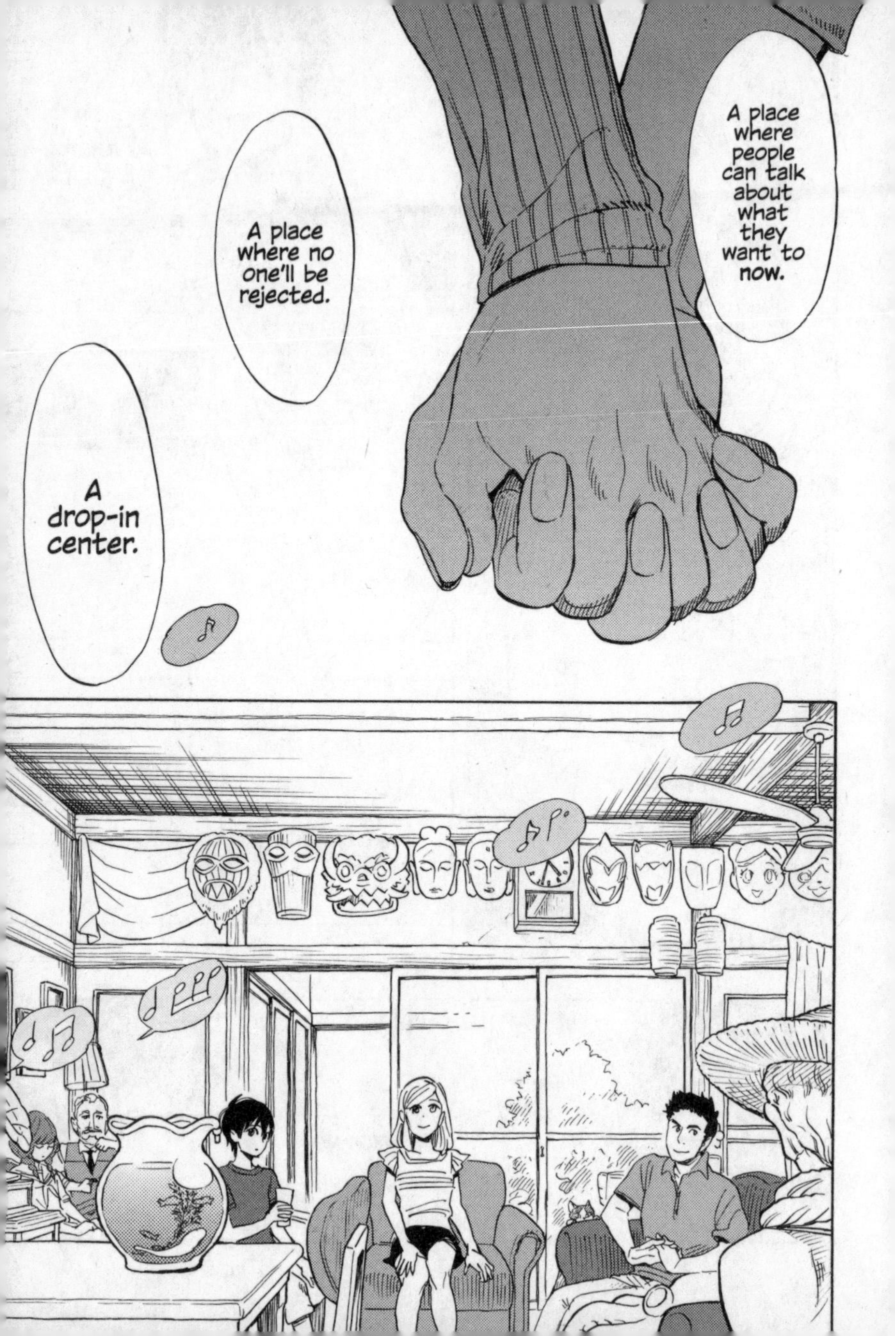
A place where people can talk about what they want to now.
A place where no one'll be rejected.
A drop-in center.

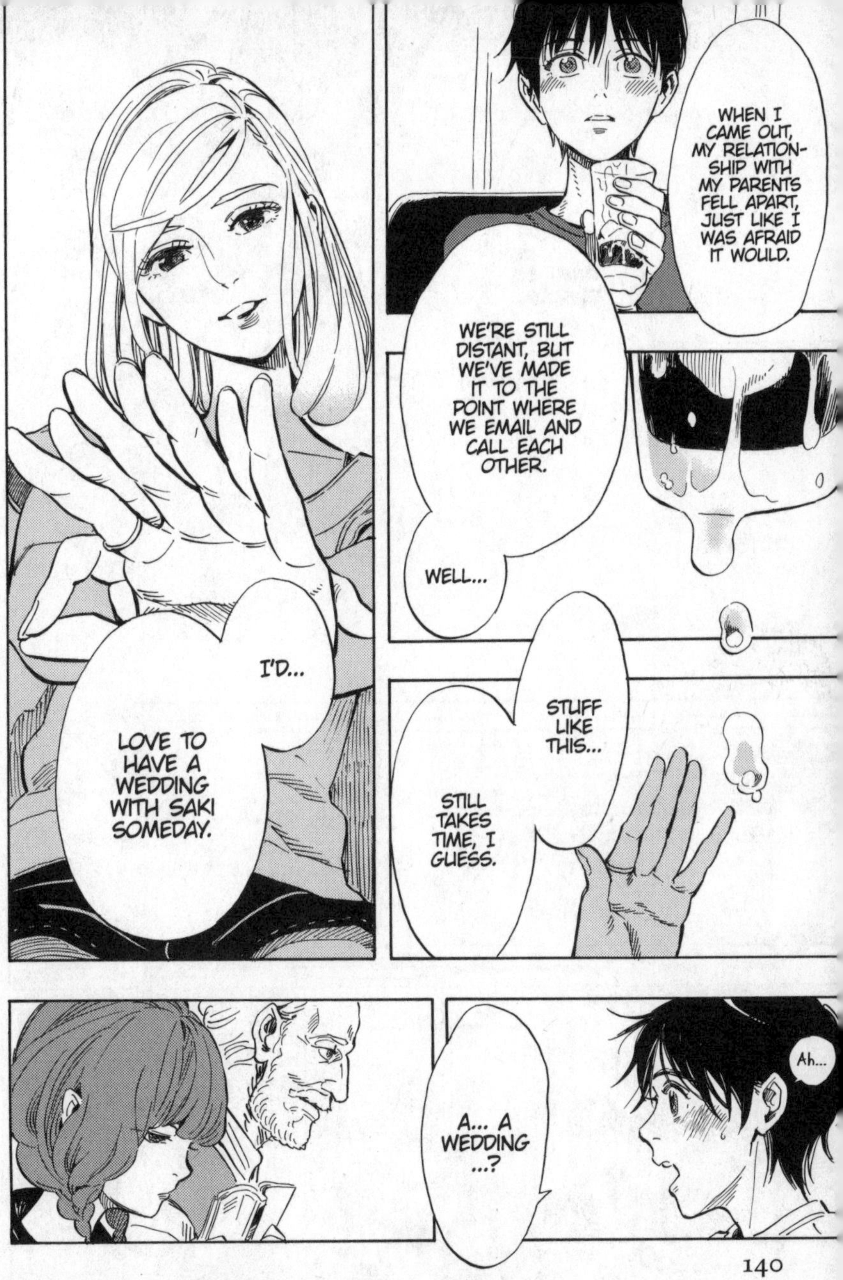
WHEN I CAME OUT, MY RELATION-SHIP WITH MY PARENTS FELL APART, JUST LIKE I WAS AFRAID IT WOULD.
WE'RE STILL DISTANT, BUT WE'VE MADE IT TO THE POINT WHERE WE EMAIL AND CALL EACH OTHER.
WELL...
STUFF LIKE THIS...
STILL TAKES TIME, I GUESS.
I'D...
LOVE TO HAVE A WEDDING WITH SAKI SOMEDAY.
Ah...
A... A WEDDING ...?

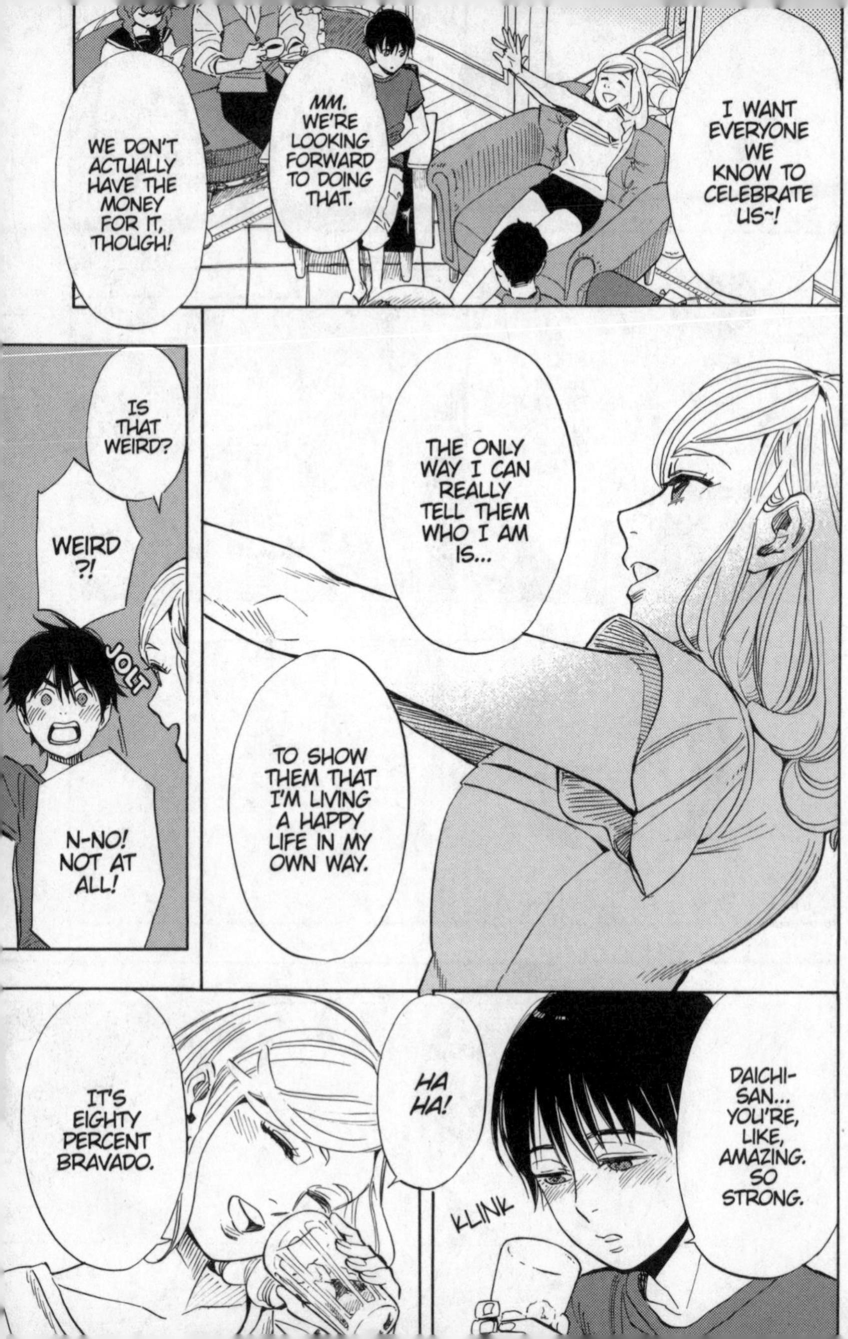
I WANT EVERYONE WE KNOW TO CELEBRATE US~!
MM. WE'RE LOOKING FORWARD TO DOING THAT.
WE DON'T ACTUALLY HAVE THE MONEY FOR IT, THOUGH!
THE ONLY WAY I CAN REALLY TELL THEM WHO I AM IS...
TO SHOW THEM THAT I'M LIVING A HAPPY LIFE IN MY OWN WAY.
IS THAT WEIRD?
WEIRD?!
JOLT
N-NO! NOT AT ALL!
DAICHI-SAN... YOU'RE, LIKE, AMAZING. SO STRONG.
KLINK
HA HA!
IT'S EIGHTY PERCENT BRAVADO.

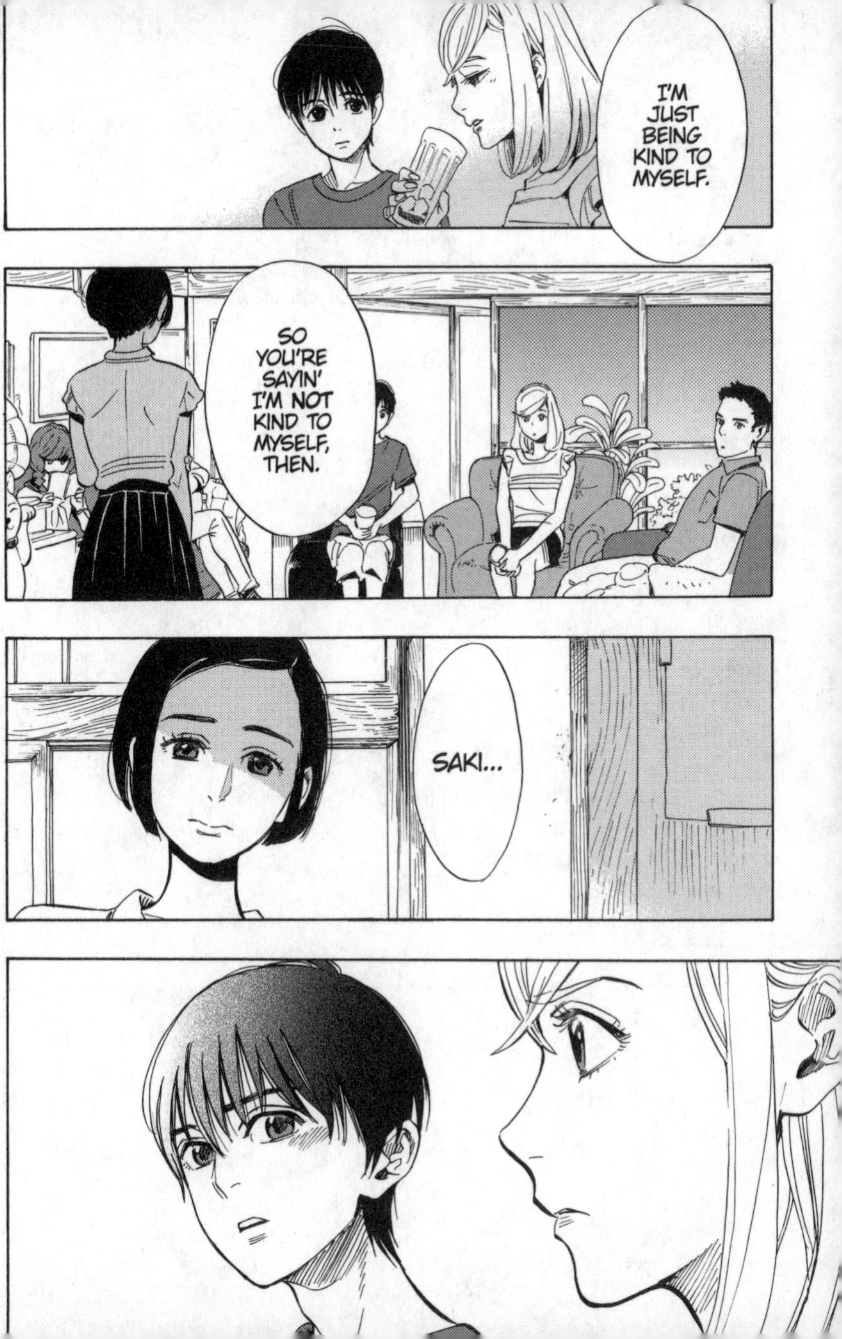
I'M JUST BEING KIND TO MYSELF.
SO YOU'RE SAYIN' I'M NOT KIND TO MYSELF, THEN.
SAKI...

Our Dreams at Dusk

SHIMANAMI TASOGARE

Onomichi is all about hilly streets and alleys and temples and cats.

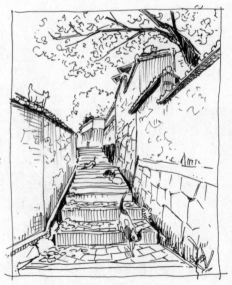

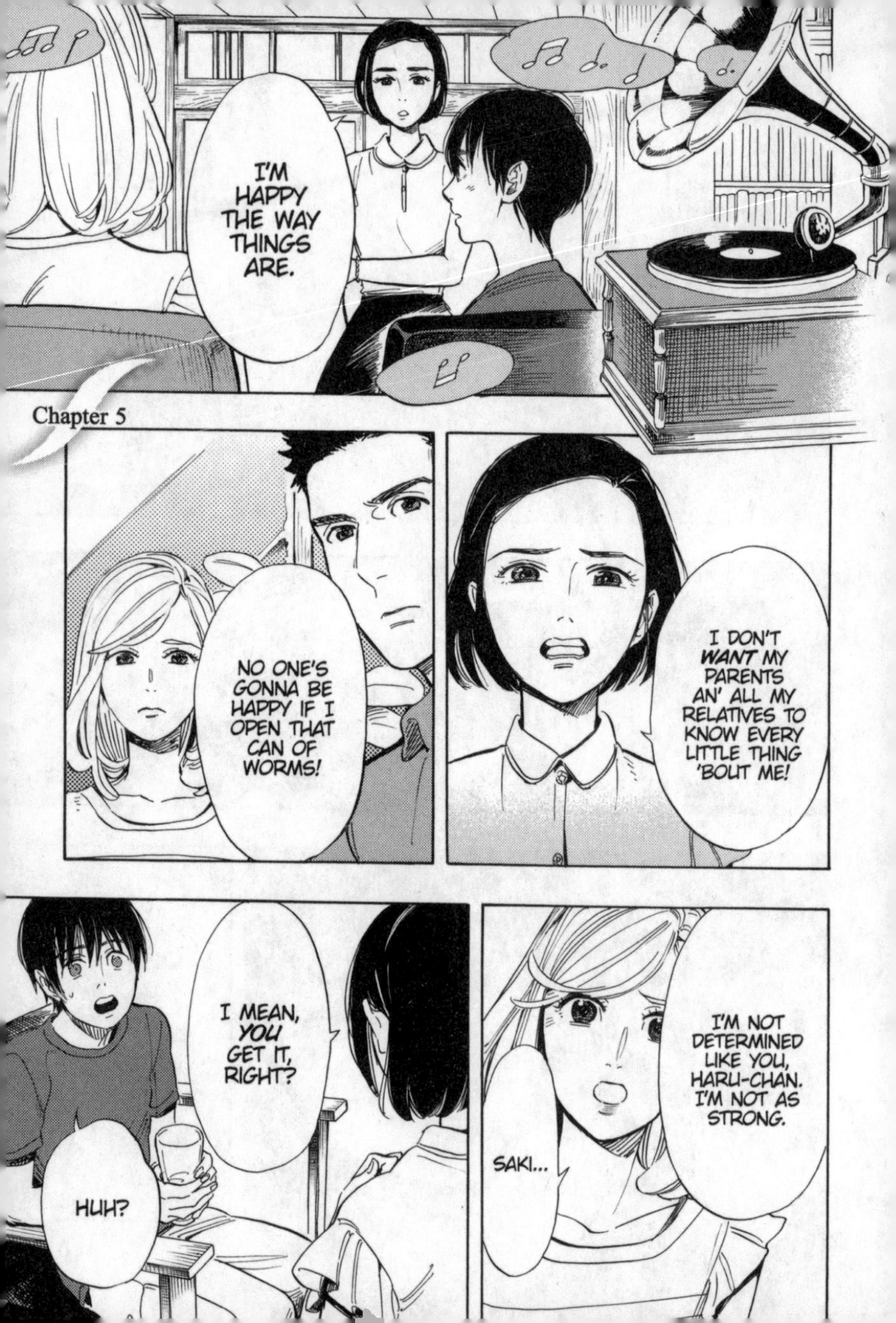
Chapter 5
I'M HAPPY THE WAY THINGS ARE.
I DON'T *WANT* MY PARENTS AN' ALL MY RELATIVES TO KNOW EVERY LITTLE THING 'BOUT ME!
NO ONE'S GONNA BE HAPPY IF I OPEN THAT CAN OF WORMS!
I'M NOT DETERMINED LIKE YOU, HARU-CHAN. I'M NOT AS STRONG.
SAKI...
I MEAN, *YOU* GET IT, RIGHT?
HUH?

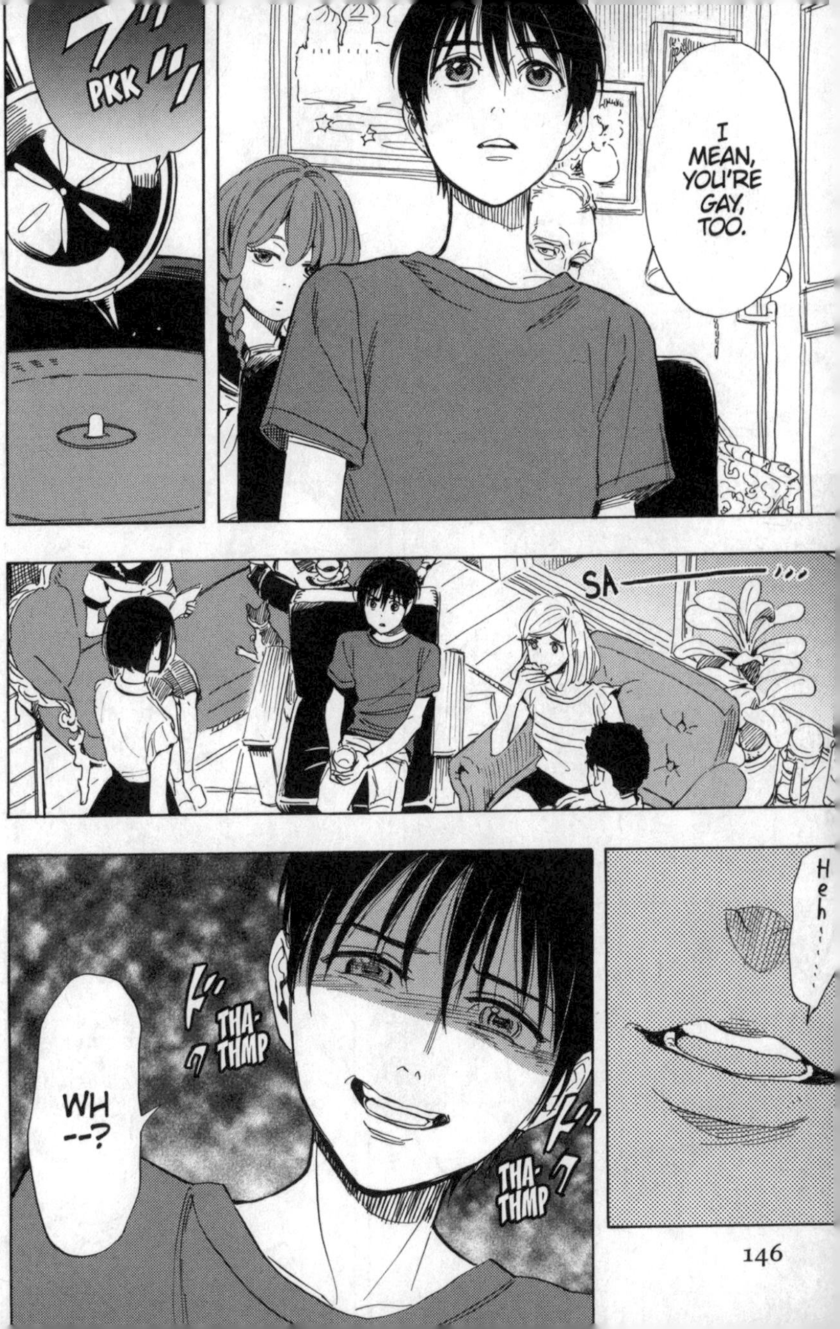
I MEAN, YOU'RE GAY, TOO.
PKK
SA———...
Heh......
THA-THMP
WH--?
THA-THMP

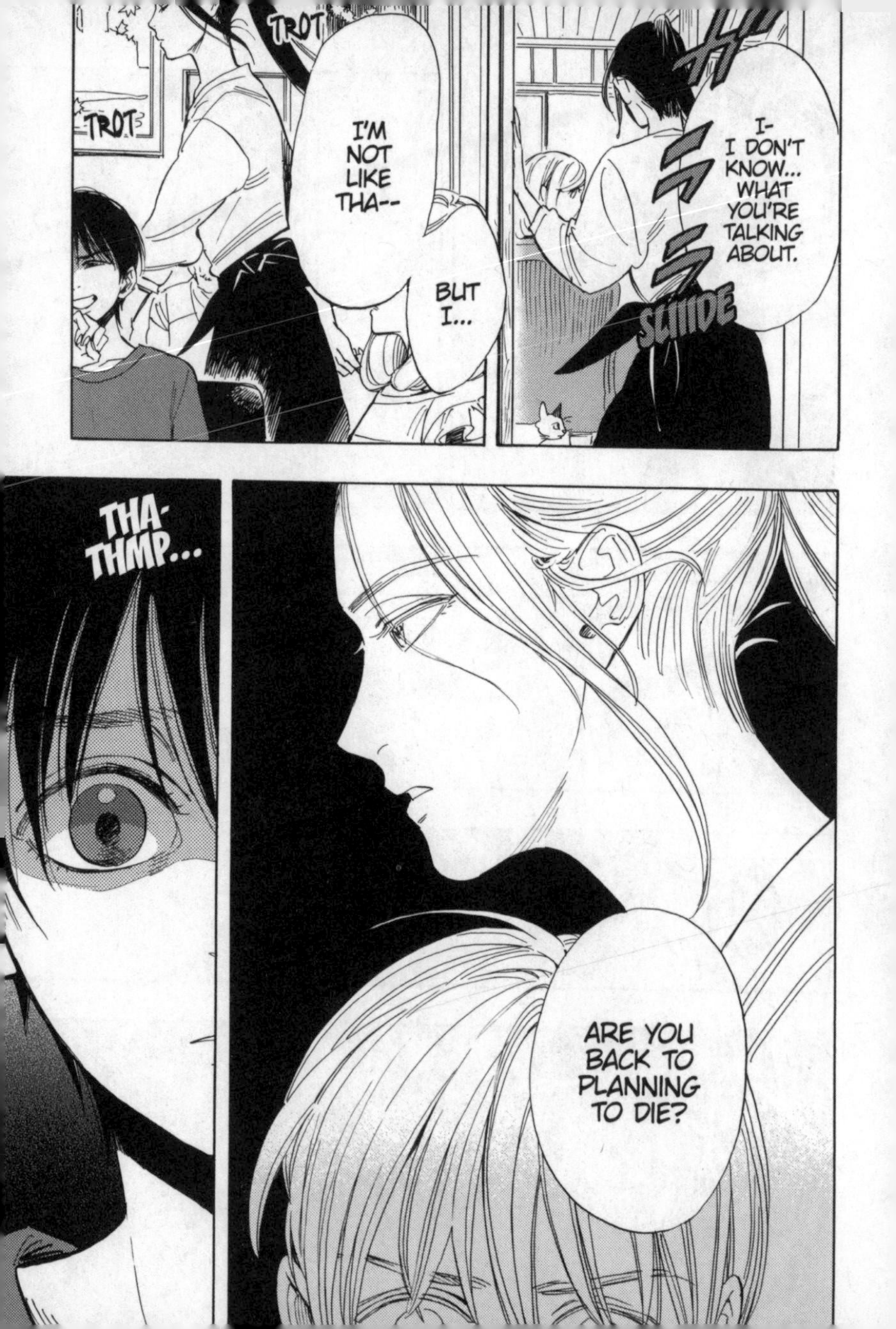
I- I DON'T KNOW... WHAT YOU'RE TALKING ABOUT.
SLIIIDE
TROT
TROT
I'M NOT LIKE THA--
BUT I...
ARE YOU BACK TO PLANNING TO DIE?
THA-THMP...

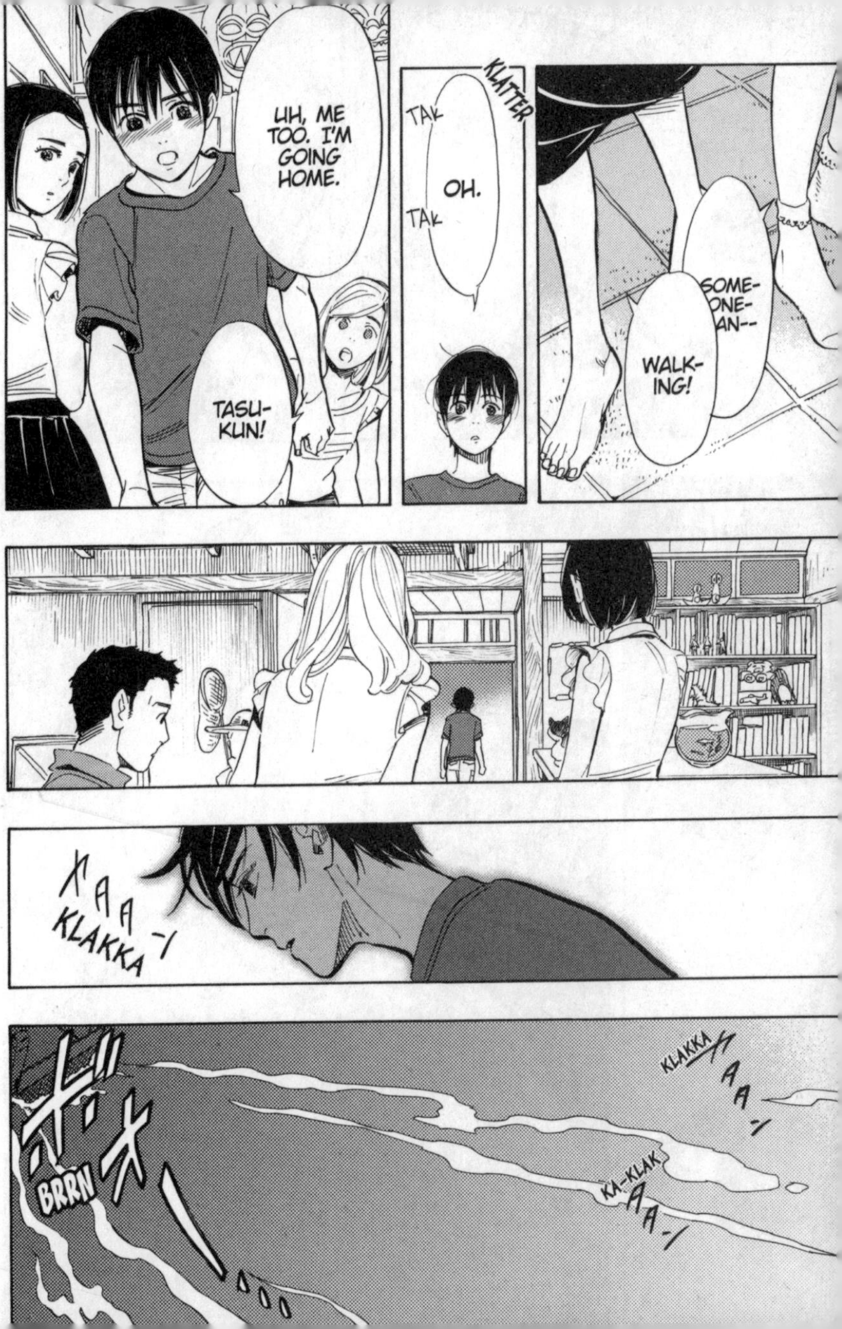
SOME-ONE-SAN--
WALKING!
KLATTER
TAK
TAK
OH.
UH, ME TOO. I'M GOING HOME.
TASU-KUN!
KLAKKA
KLAKKA
KA-KLAK
BRRN

Chapter 5

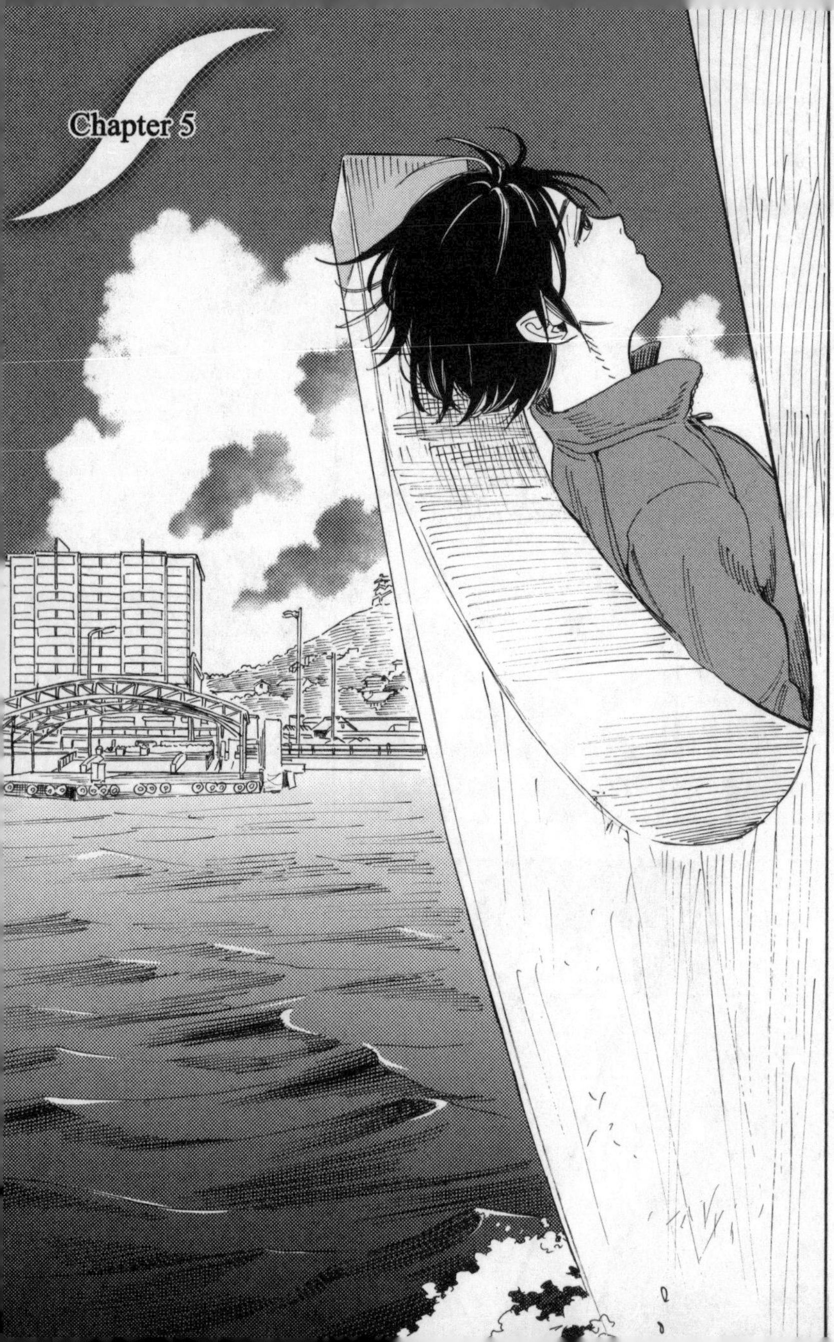

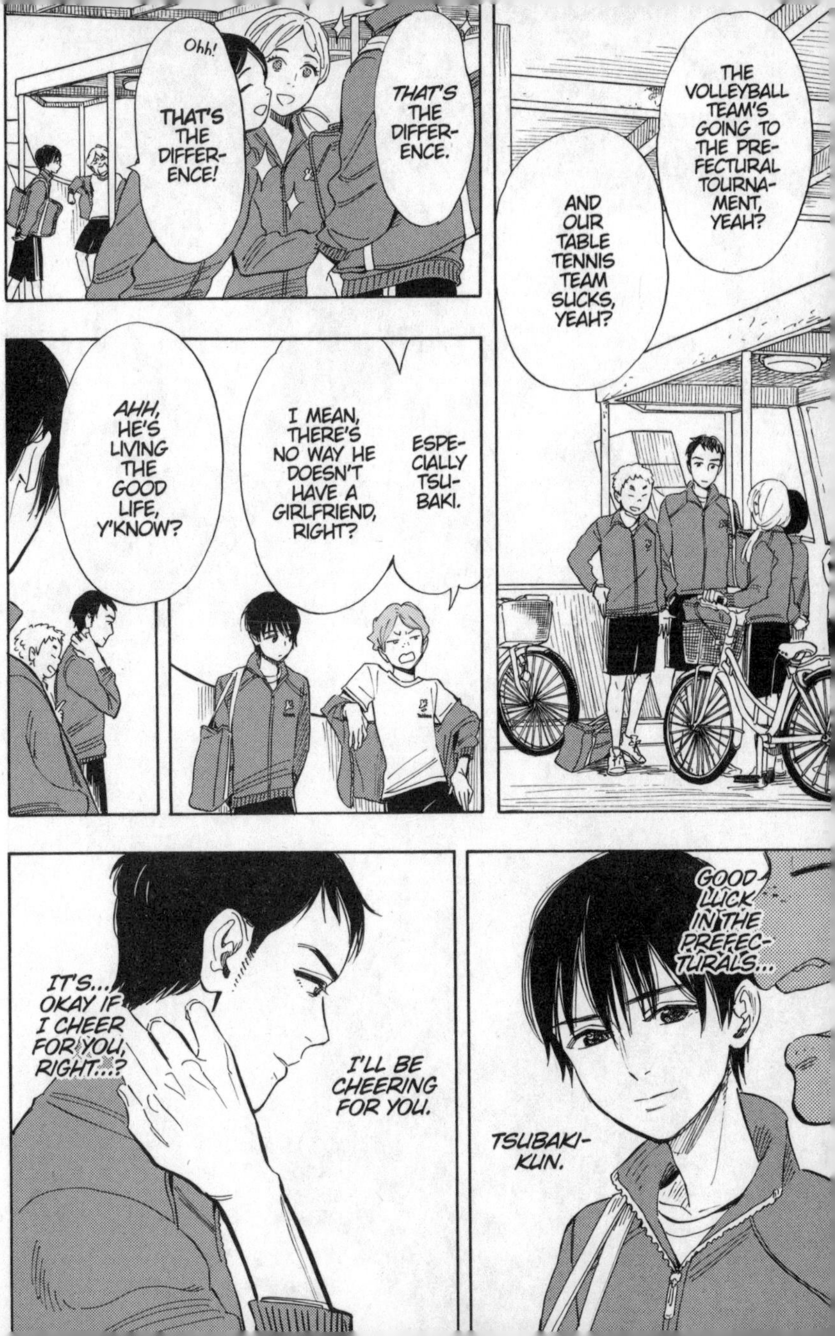
THE VOLLEYBALL TEAM'S GOING TO THE PREFECTURAL TOURNAMENT, YEAH?
AND OUR TABLE TENNIS TEAM SUCKS, YEAH?
THAT'S THE DIFFERENCE.
Ohh!
THAT'S THE DIFFERENCE!
ESPECIALLY TSUBAKI.
I MEAN, THERE'S NO WAY HE DOESN'T HAVE A GIRLFRIEND, RIGHT?
AHH, HE'S LIVING THE GOOD LIFE, Y'KNOW?
GOOD LUCK IN THE PREFECTURALS...
TSUBAKI-KUN.
I'LL BE CHEERING FOR YOU.
IT'S... OKAY IF I CHEER FOR YOU, RIGHT...?

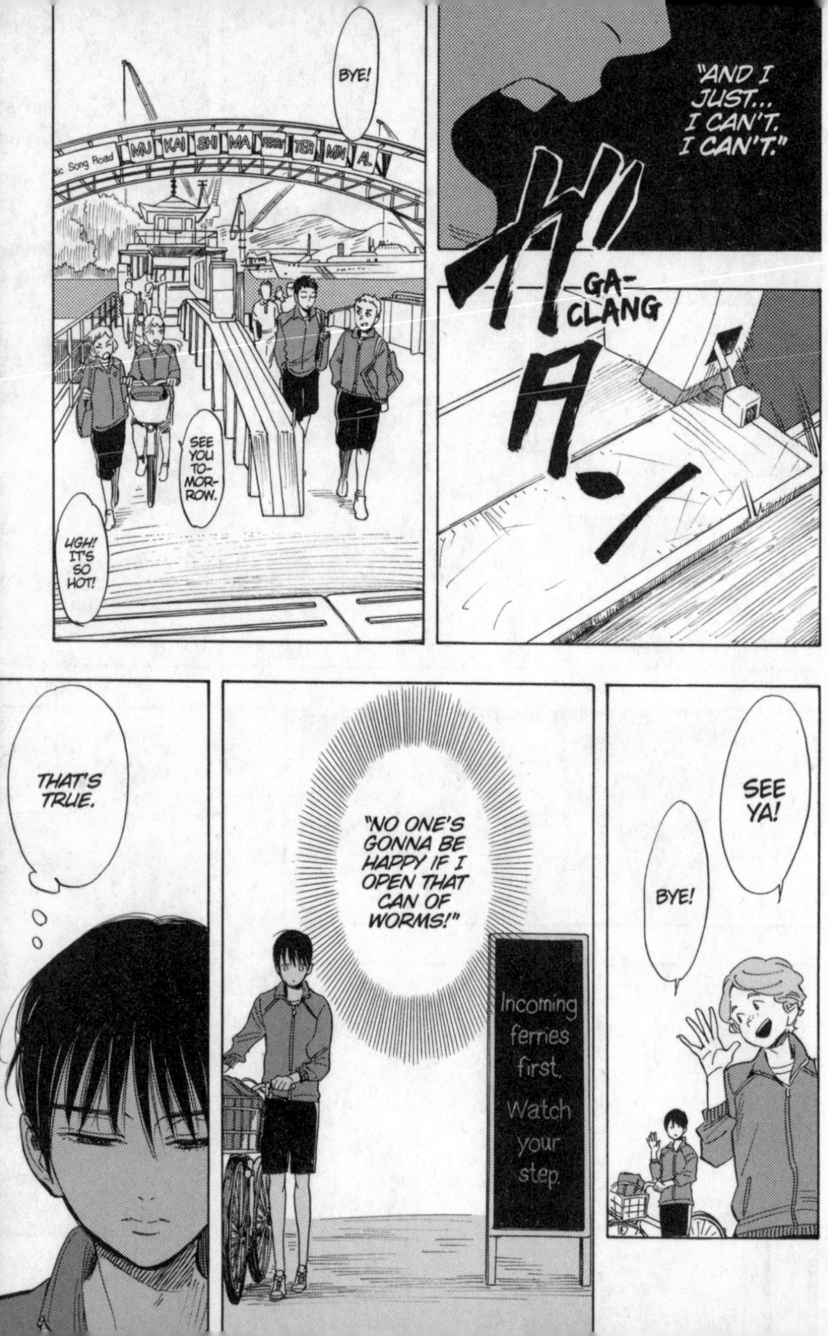

"AND I JUST... I CAN'T. I CAN'T."
GA-CLANG
BYE!
MU KAI SHI MA FERRY TER MIN AL
SEE YOU TO-MOR-ROW.
UGH! IT'S SO HOT!
SEE YA!
BYE!
"NO ONE'S GONNA BE HAPPY IF I OPEN THAT CAN OF WORMS!"
Incoming ferries first. Watch your step.
THAT'S TRUE.

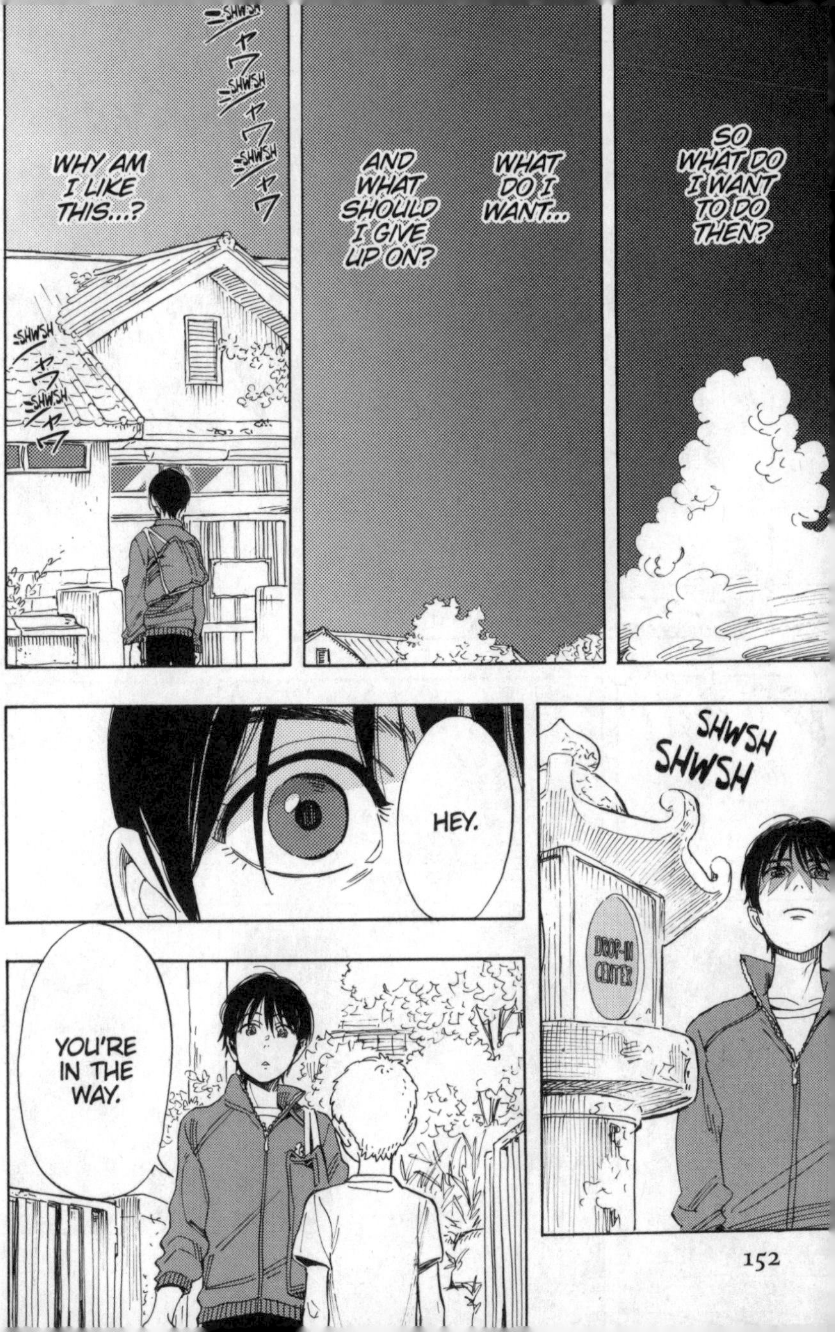
SO WHAT DO I WANT TO DO THEN?
WHAT DO I WANT...
AND WHAT SHOULD I GIVE UP ON?
SHWSH ヤワ
SHWSH ヤワ
SHWSH ヤワ
WHY AM I LIKE THIS...?
SHWSH ヤワ
SHWSH ヤワ
SHWSH SHWSH
DROP-IN CENTER
HEY.
YOU'RE IN THE WAY.

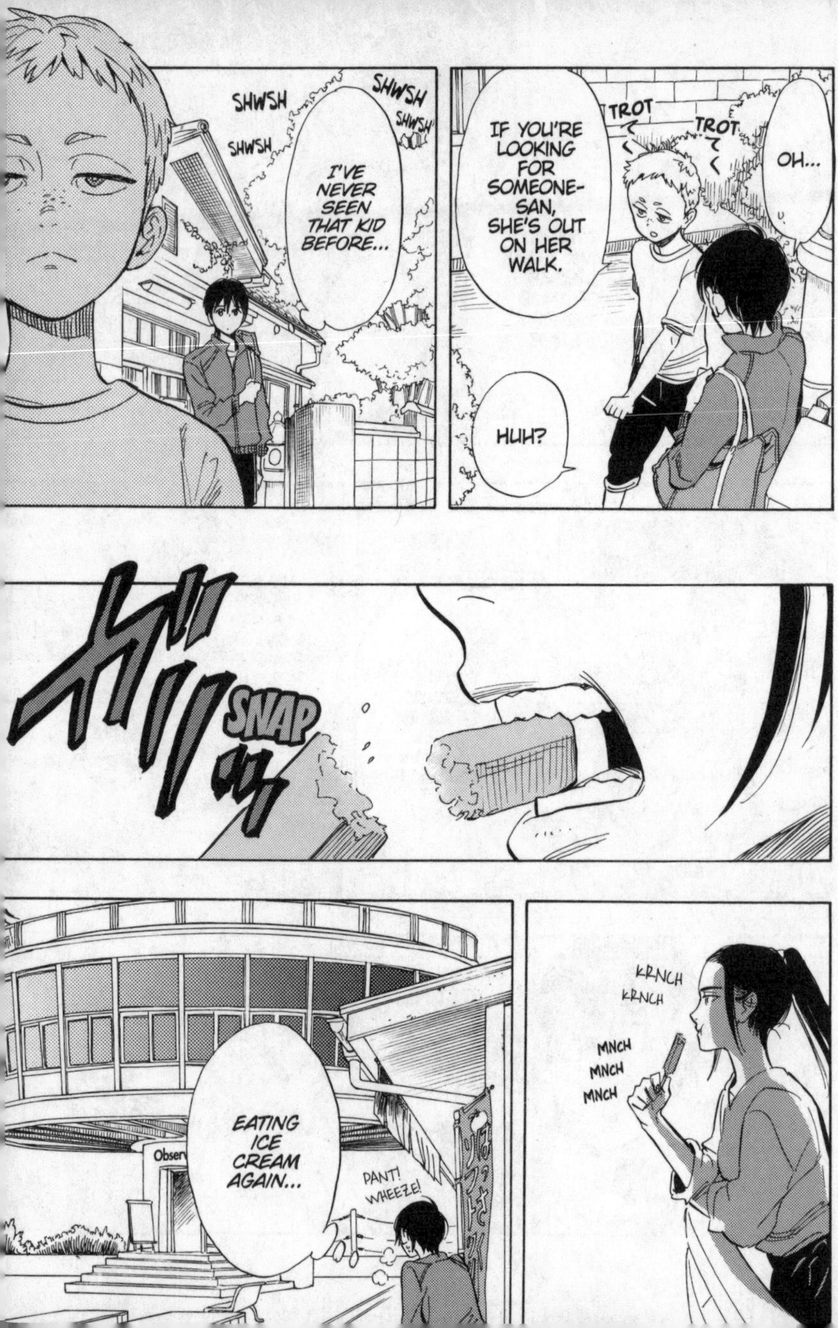
OH...
TROT TROT
IF YOU'RE LOOKING FOR SOMEONE-SAN, SHE'S OUT ON HER WALK.
HUH?
SHWSH SHWSH
I'VE NEVER SEEN THAT KID BEFORE...
SHWSH SHWSH
SNAP
KRNCH KRNCH
MNCH MNCH MNCH
EATING ICE CREAM AGAIN...
PANT! WHEEZE!

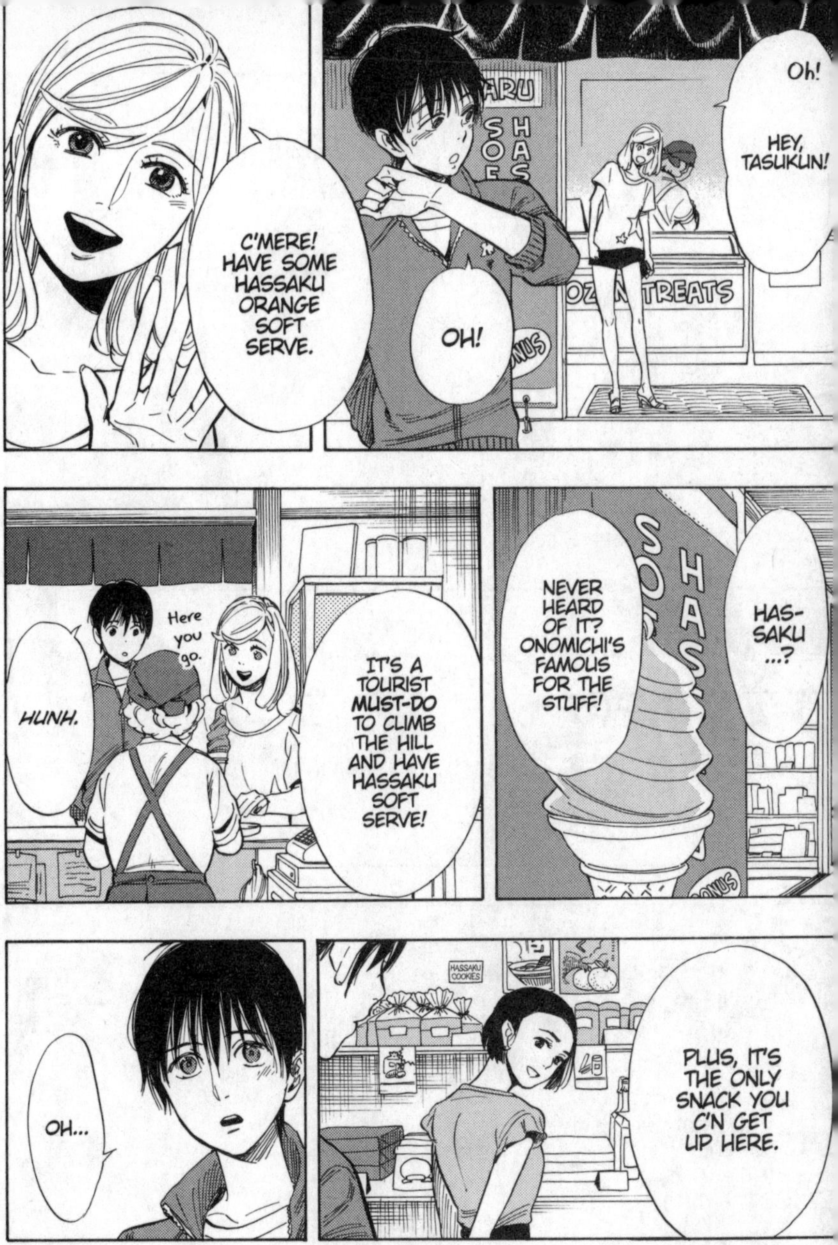
Oh!
HEY, TASUKUN!
OH!
C'MERE! HAVE SOME HASSAKU ORANGE SOFT SERVE.
HAS-SAKU ...?
NEVER HEARD OF IT? ONOMICHI'S FAMOUS FOR THE STUFF!
IT'S A TOURIST MUST-DO TO CLIMB THE HILL AND HAVE HASSAKU SOFT SERVE!
Here you go.
HUNH.
HASSAKU COOKIES
PLUS, IT'S THE ONLY SNACK YOU C'N GET UP HERE.
OH...

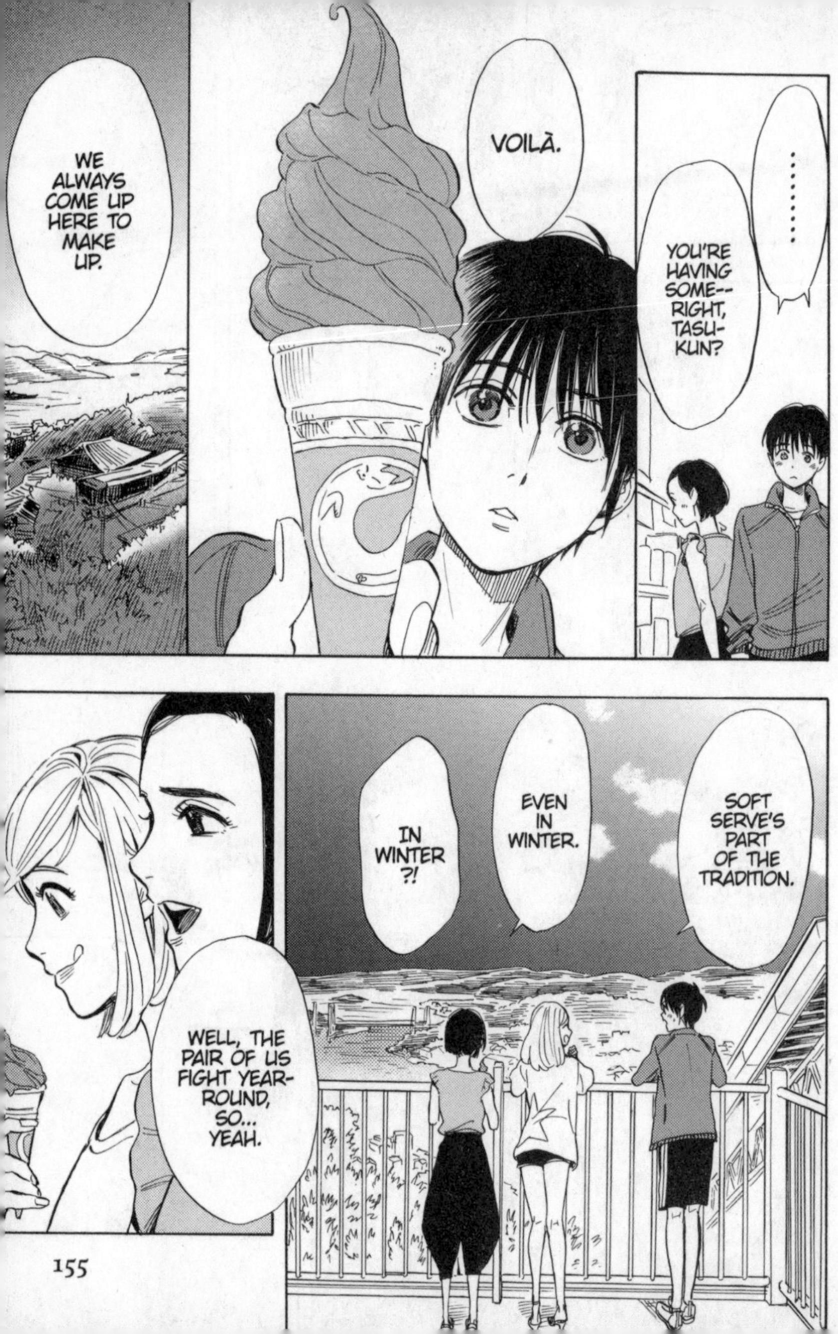
......
YOU'RE HAVING SOME-- RIGHT, TASU-KUN?
VOILÀ.
WE ALWAYS COME UP HERE TO MAKE UP.
SOFT SERVE'S PART OF THE TRADITION.
EVEN IN WINTER.
IN WINTER?!
WELL, THE PAIR OF US FIGHT YEAR-ROUND, SO... YEAH.

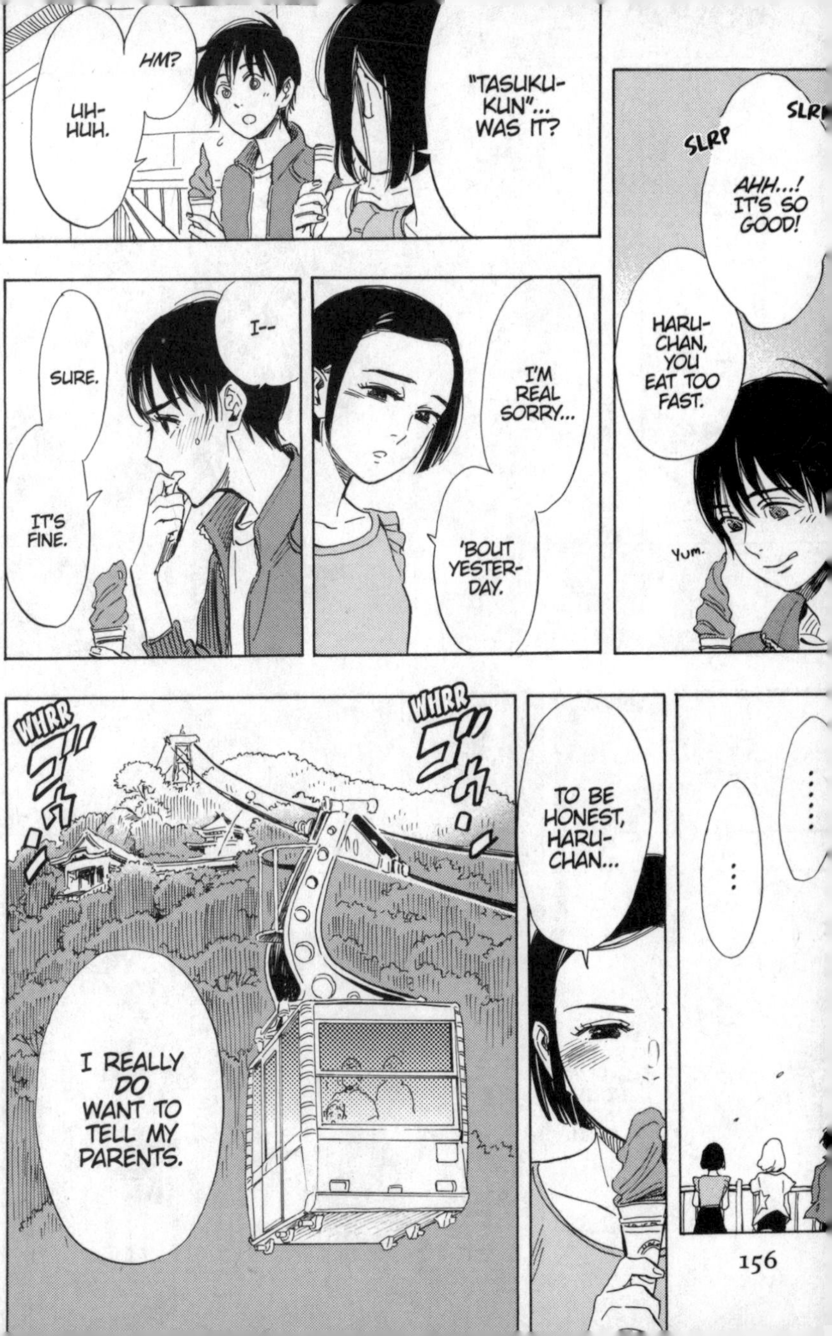
SLRP
SLR
AHH...! IT'S SO GOOD!
HARU-CHAN, YOU EAT TOO FAST.
Yum.
"TASUKU-KUN"... WAS IT?
HM?
UH-HUH.
I'M REAL SORRY...
'BOUT YESTER-DAY.
I--
SURE.
IT'S FINE.
......
...
TO BE HONEST, HARU-CHAN...
WHRR
WHRR
I REALLY DO WANT TO TELL MY PARENTS.

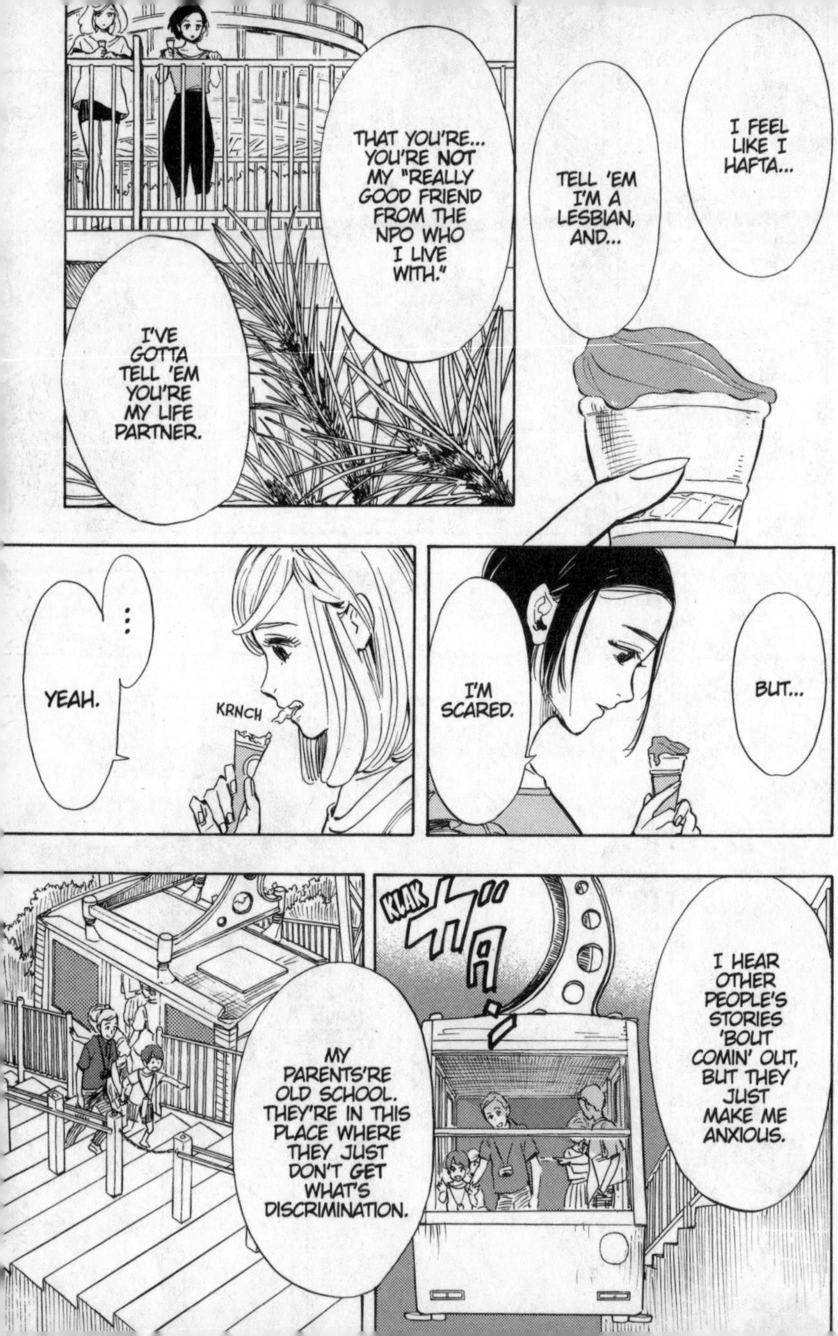
I FEEL LIKE I HAFTA...
TELL 'EM I'M A LESBIAN, AND...
THAT YOU'RE... YOU'RE NOT MY "REALLY GOOD FRIEND FROM THE NPO WHO I LIVE WITH."
I'VE GOTTA TELL 'EM YOU'RE MY LIFE PARTNER.
BUT...
I'M SCARED.
...
YEAH.
KRNCH
KLAK
I HEAR OTHER PEOPLE'S STORIES 'BOUT COMIN' OUT, BUT THEY JUST MAKE ME ANXIOUS.
MY PARENTS'RE OLD SCHOOL. THEY'RE IN THIS PLACE WHERE THEY JUST DON'T GET WHAT'S DISCRIMINATION.

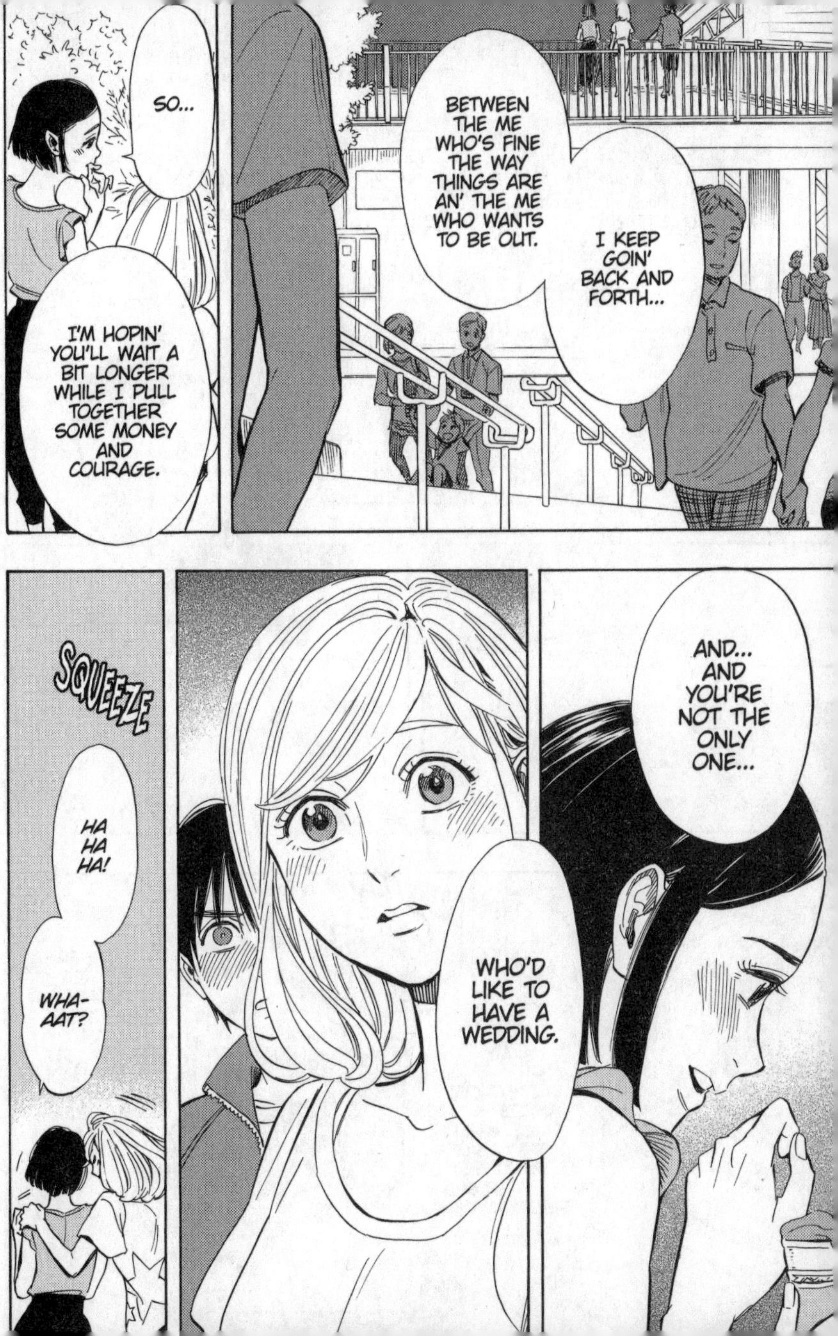
BETWEEN THE ME WHO'S FINE THE WAY THINGS ARE AN' THE ME WHO WANTS TO BE OUT.
I KEEP GOIN' BACK AND FORTH...
SO...
I'M HOPIN' YOU'LL WAIT A BIT LONGER WHILE I PULL TOGETHER SOME MONEY AND COURAGE.
AND... AND YOU'RE NOT THE ONLY ONE...
WHO'D LIKE TO HAVE A WEDDING.
SQUEEZE
HA HA HA!
WHA-AAT?

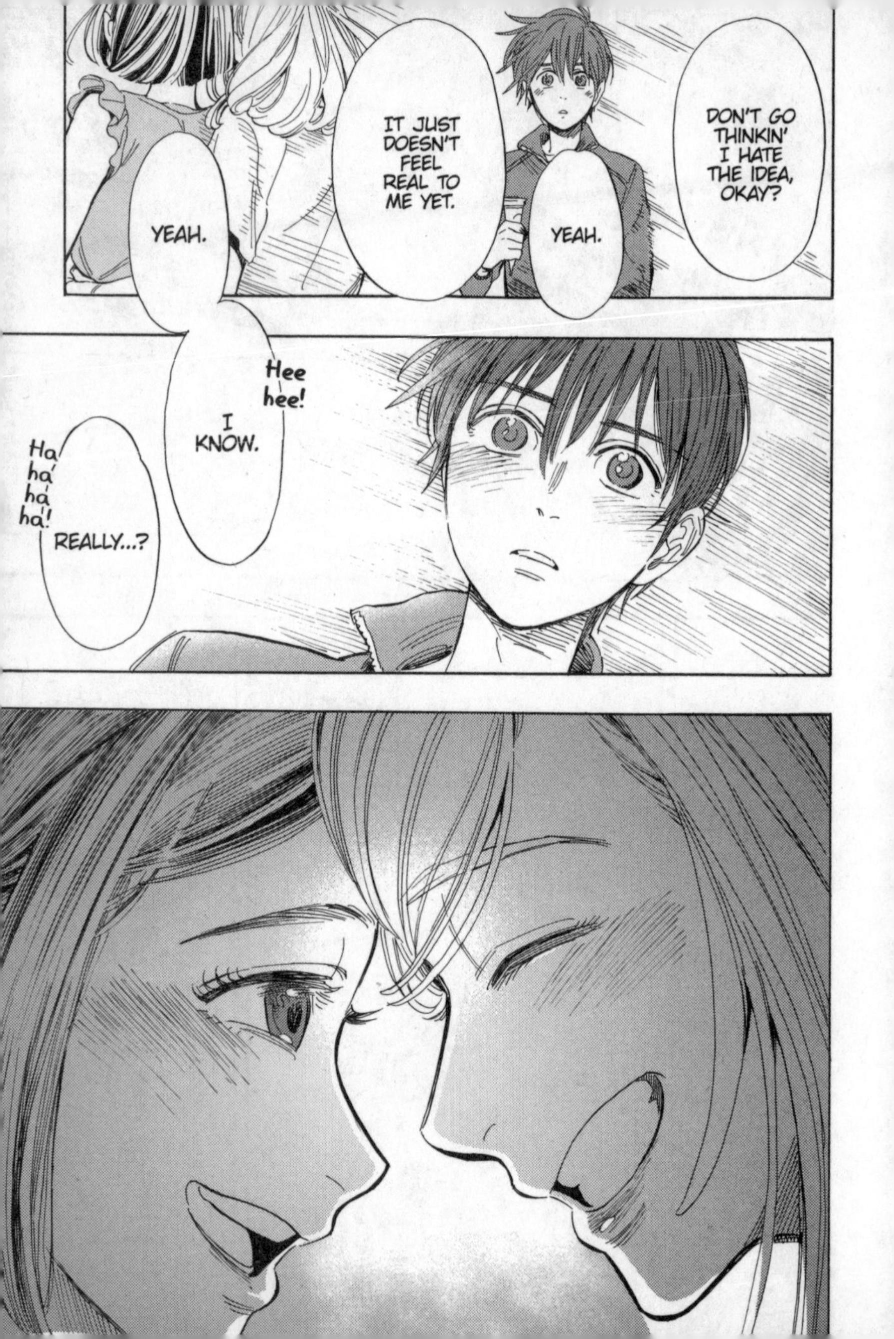
DON'T GO THINKIN' I HATE THE IDEA, OKAY?
YEAH.
IT JUST DOESN'T FEEL REAL TO ME YET.
YEAH.
I KNOW.
Hee hee!
Ha ha ha ha!
REALLY...?

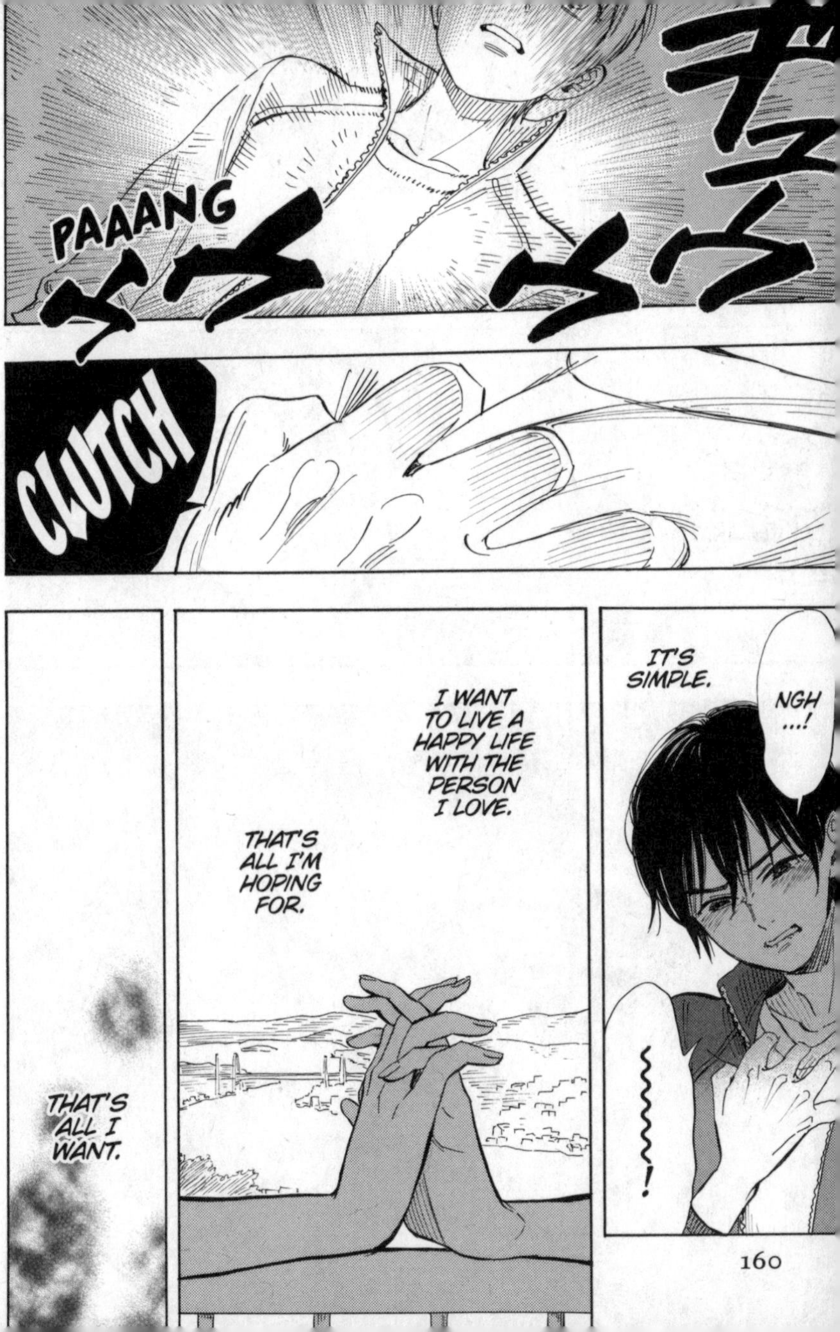
PAAANG
CLUTCH
NGH ...!
IT'S SIMPLE.
I WANT TO LIVE A HAPPY LIFE WITH THE PERSON I LOVE.
THAT'S ALL I'M HOPING FOR.
THAT'S ALL I WANT.

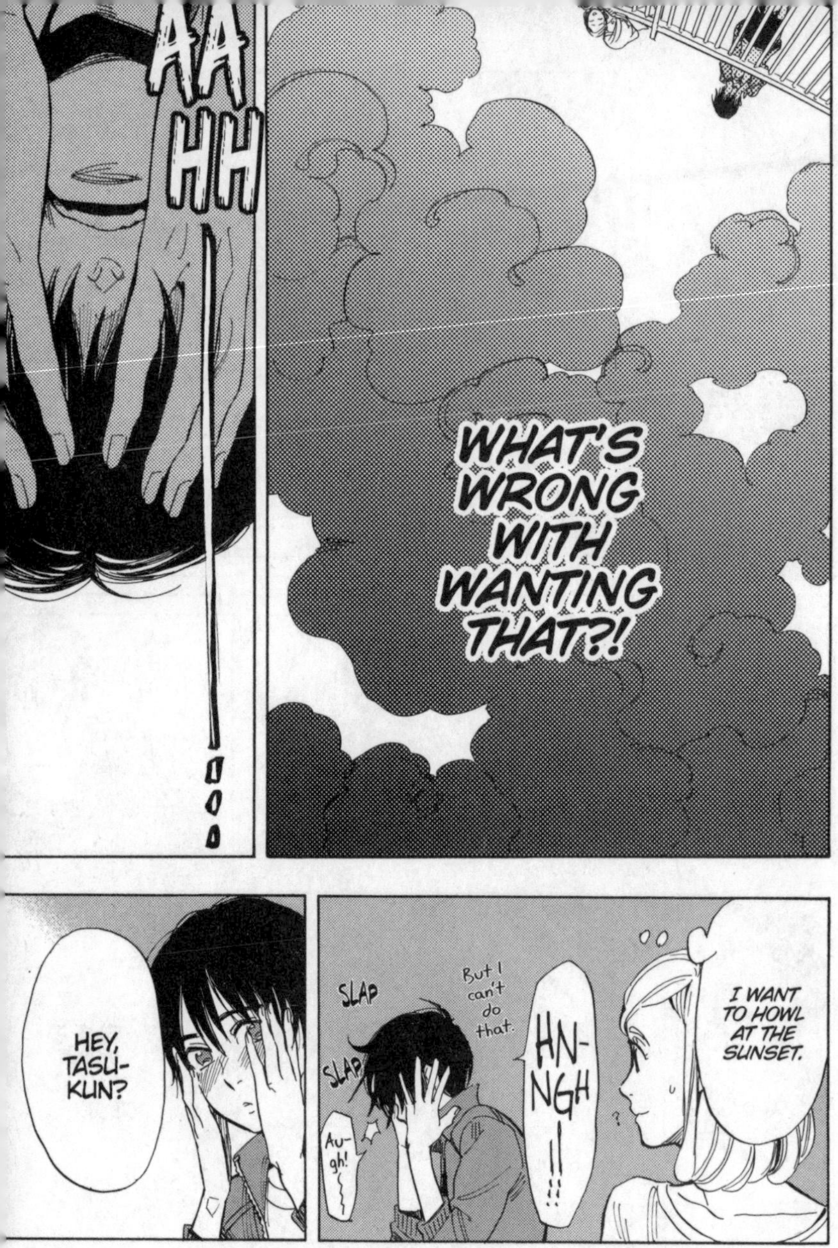
WHAT'S WRONG WITH WANTING THAT?!
AAHH—!!!
I WANT TO HOWL AT THE SUNSET.
HN-NGH!!!!
But I can't do that.
SLAP
SLAP
Augh!
HEY, TASU-KUN?

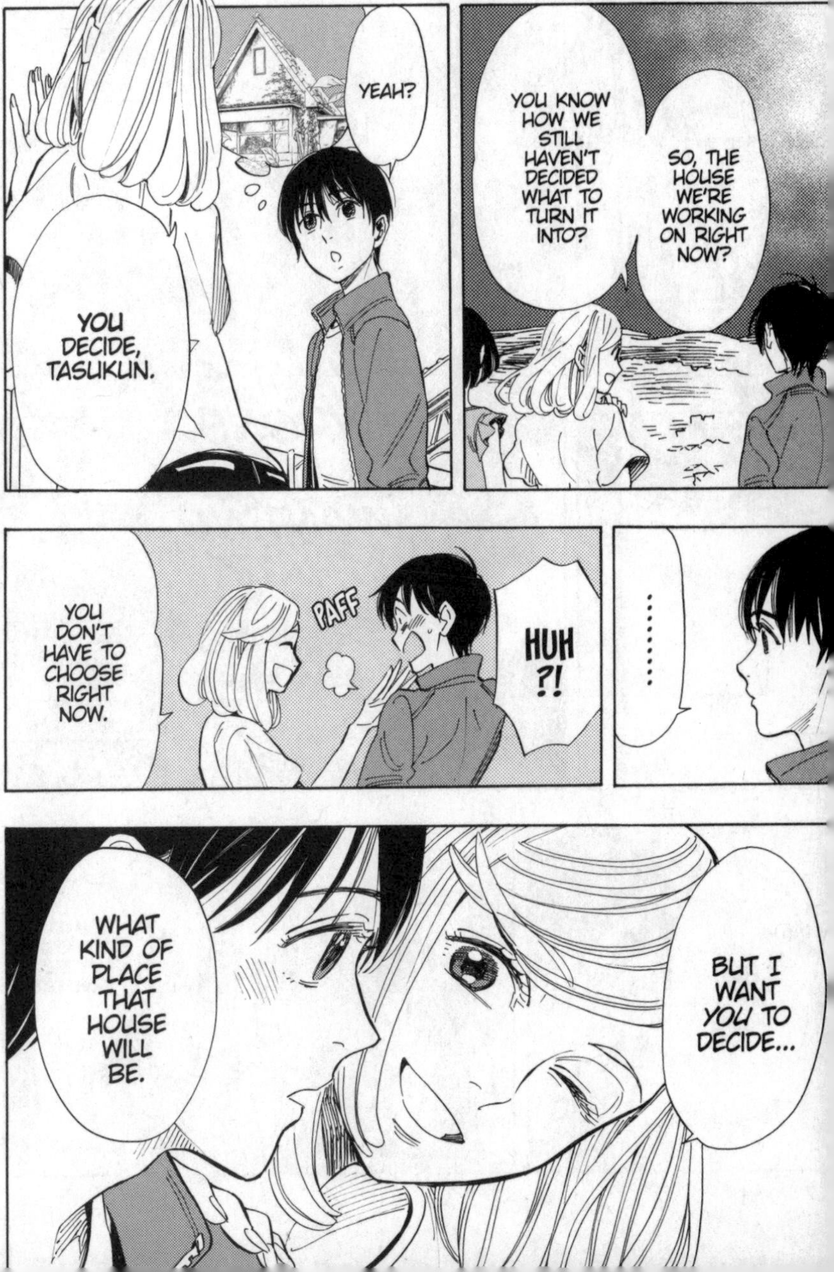
SO, THE HOUSE WE'RE WORKING ON RIGHT NOW?
YOU KNOW HOW WE STILL HAVEN'T DECIDED WHAT TO TURN IT INTO?
YEAH?
YOU DECIDE, TASUKUN.
......
HUH?!
PAFF
YOU DON'T HAVE TO CHOOSE RIGHT NOW.
BUT I WANT *YOU* TO DECIDE...
WHAT KIND OF PLACE THAT HOUSE WILL BE.

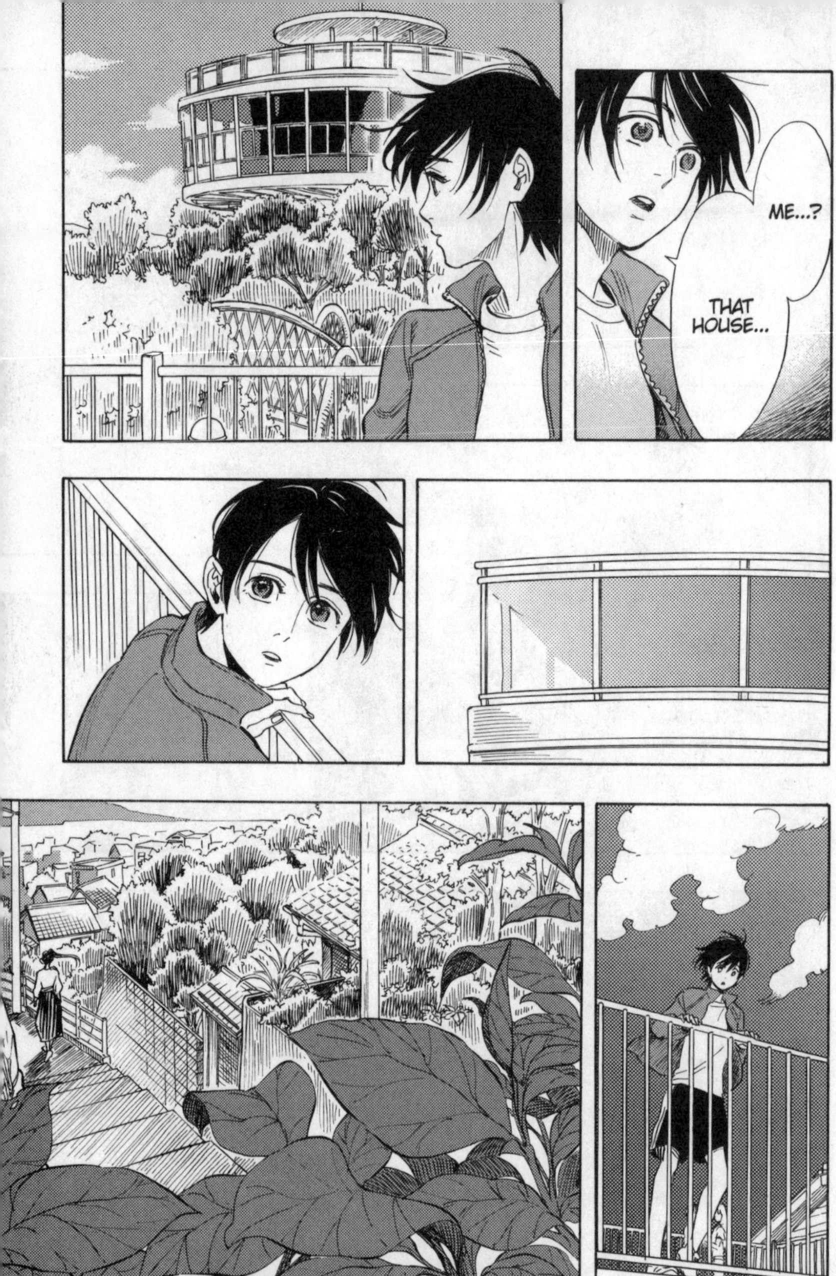
ME...?
THAT HOUSE...

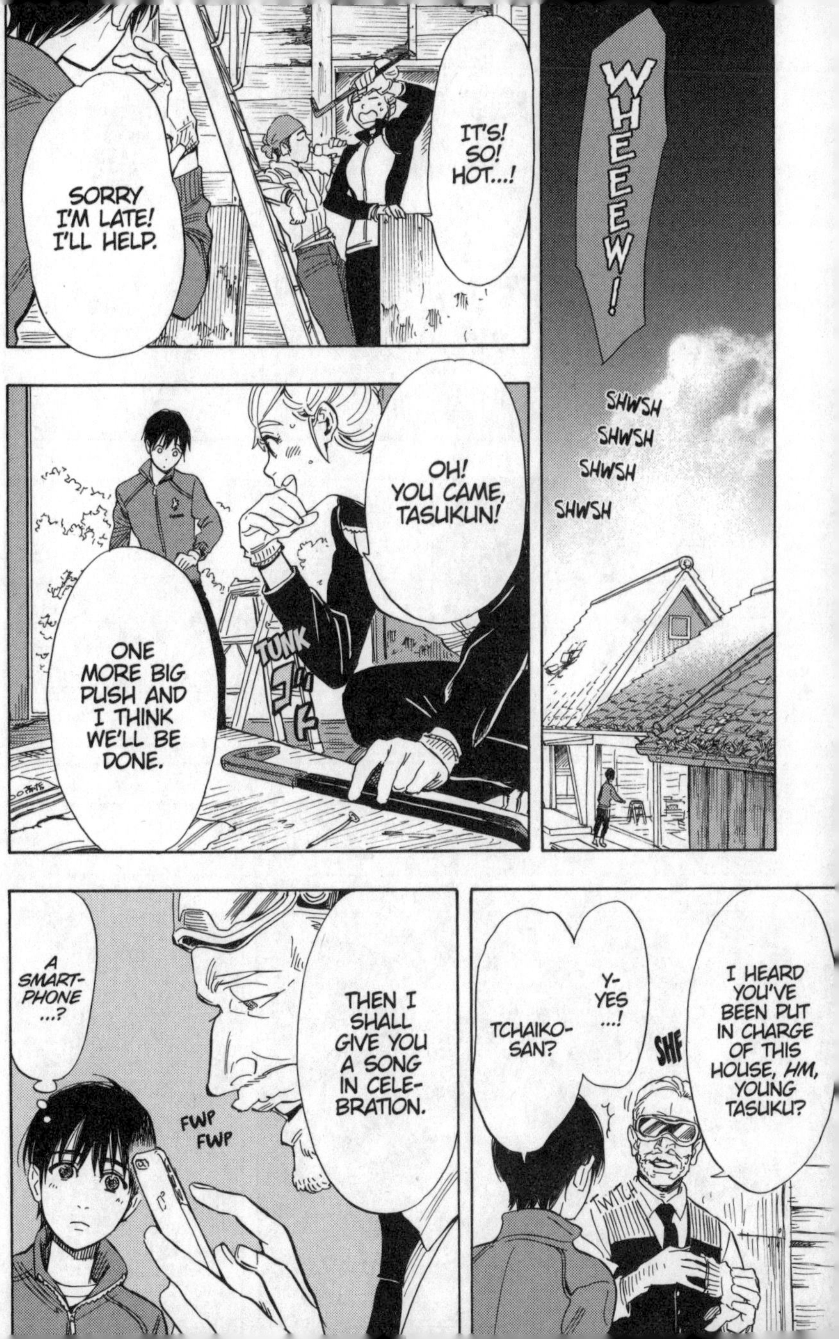
WHEEEW!
SHWSH
SHWSH
SHWSH
SHWSH
IT'S! SO! HOT...!
SORRY I'M LATE! I'LL HELP.
OH! YOU CAME, TASUKUN!
TUNK
ONE MORE BIG PUSH AND I THINK WE'LL BE DONE.
I HEARD YOU'VE BEEN PUT IN CHARGE OF THIS HOUSE, *HM*, YOUNG TASUKU?
SHF
Y-YES ...!
TCHAIKO-SAN?
TWITCH
THEN I SHALL GIVE YOU A SONG IN CELE-BRATION.
FWP FWP
A SMART-PHONE ...?

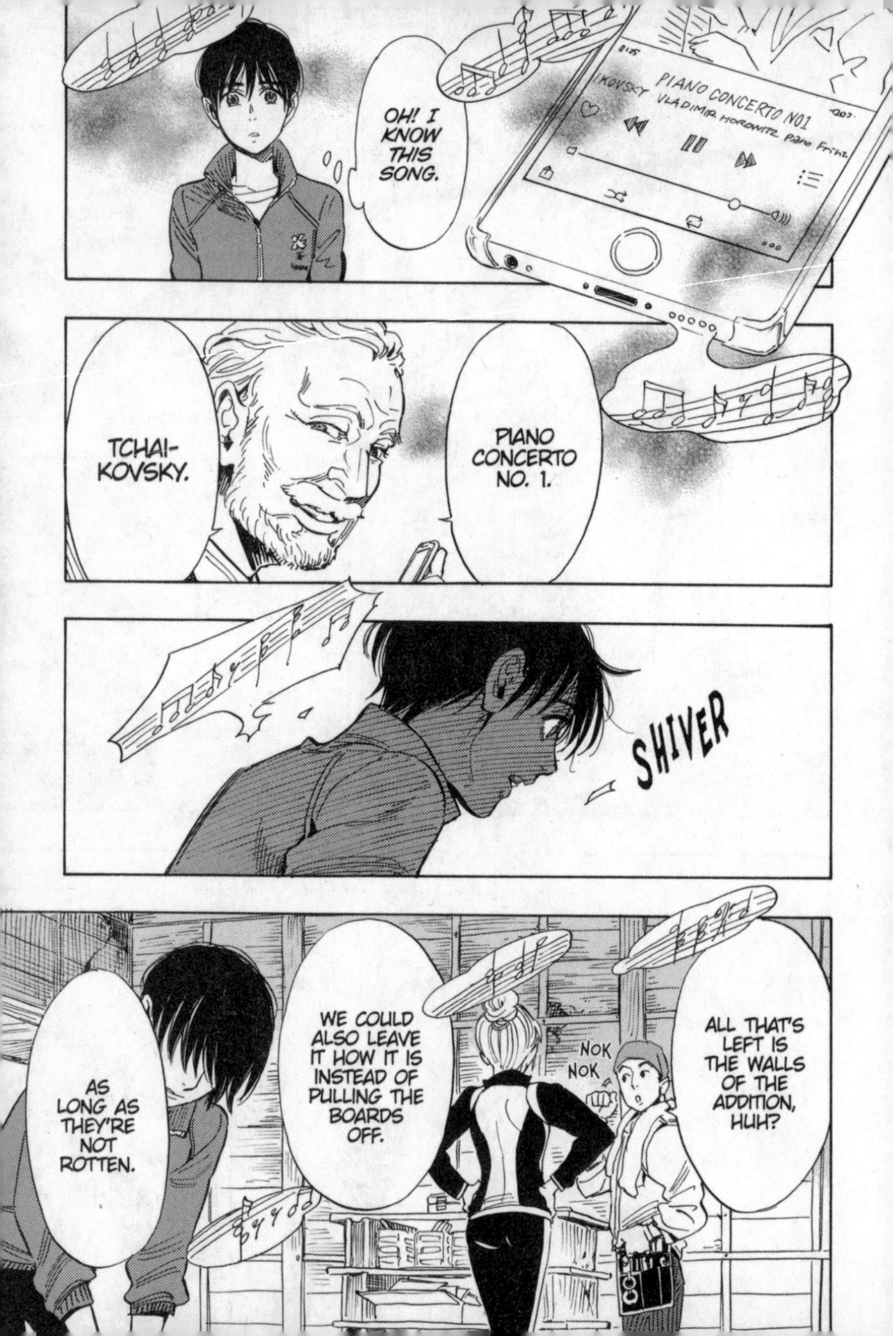
PIANO CONCERTO NO1
IKOVSKY VLADIMIR HOROWITZ Piano
OH! I KNOW THIS SONG.
PIANO CONCERTO NO. 1.
TCHAI-KOVSKY.
SHIVER
ALL THAT'S LEFT IS THE WALLS OF THE ADDITION, HUH?
NOK NOK
WE COULD ALSO LEAVE IT HOW IT IS INSTEAD OF PULLING THE BOARDS OFF.
AS LONG AS THEY'RE NOT ROTTEN.

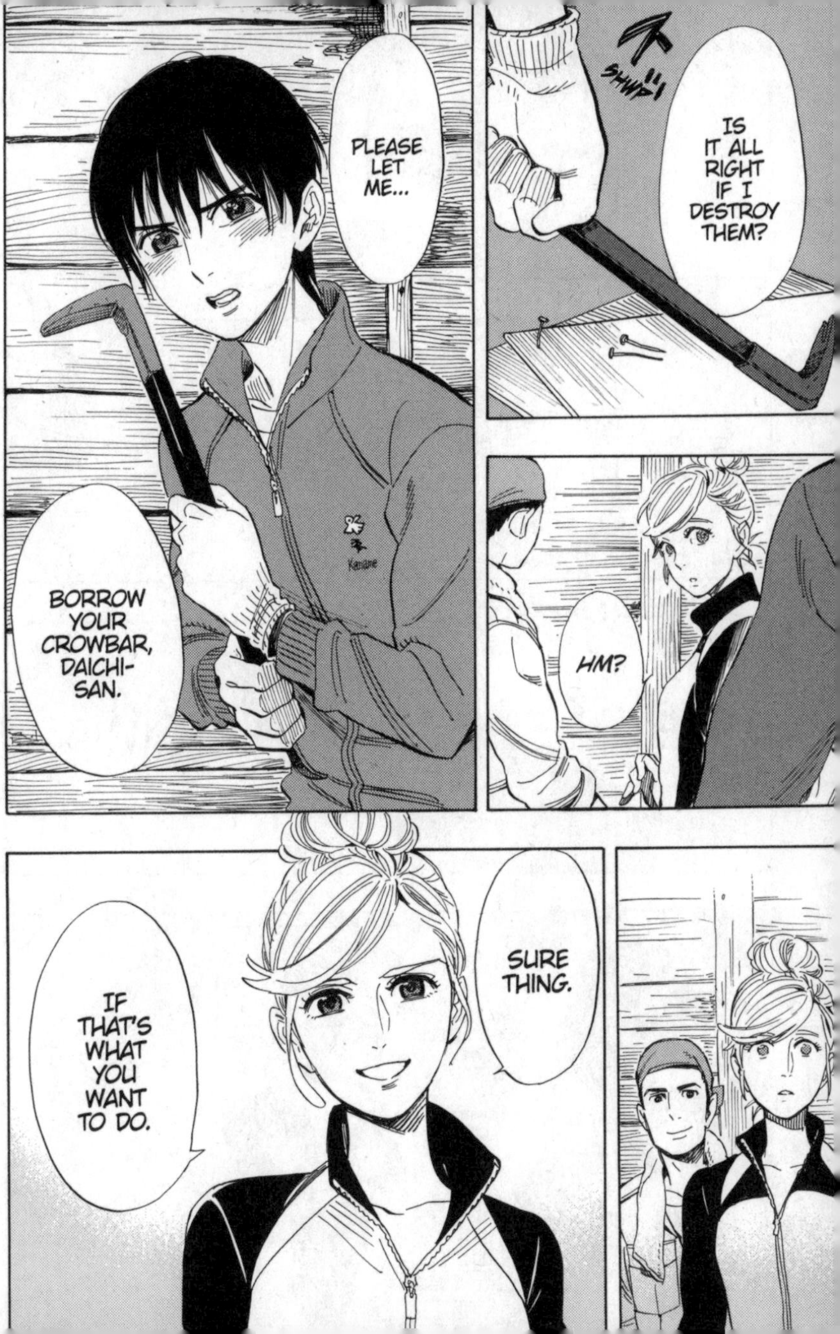
SHWP!
IS IT ALL RIGHT IF I DESTROY THEM?
HM?
PLEASE LET ME...
BORROW YOUR CROWBAR, DAICHI-SAN.
SURE THING.
IF THAT'S WHAT YOU WANT TO DO.

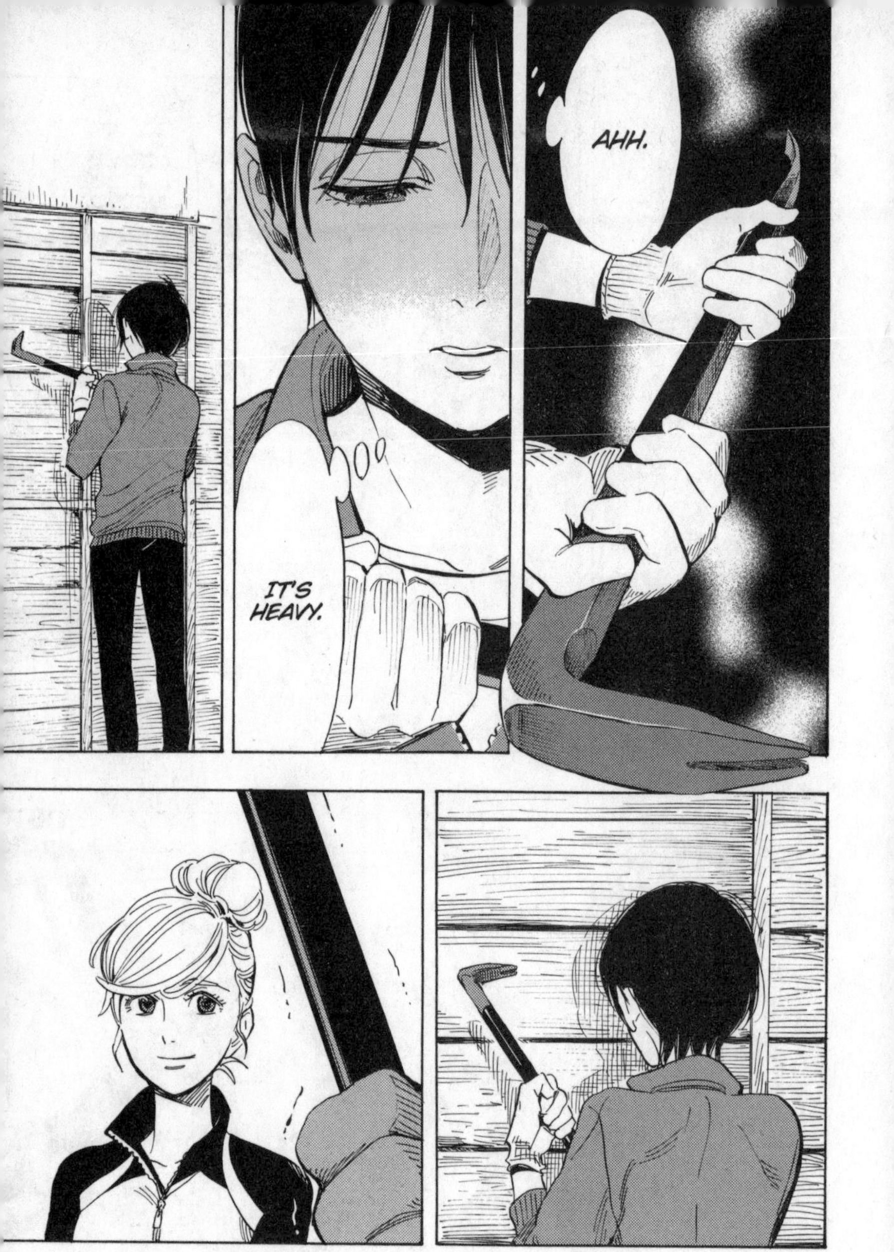
AHH.
IT'S HEAVY.

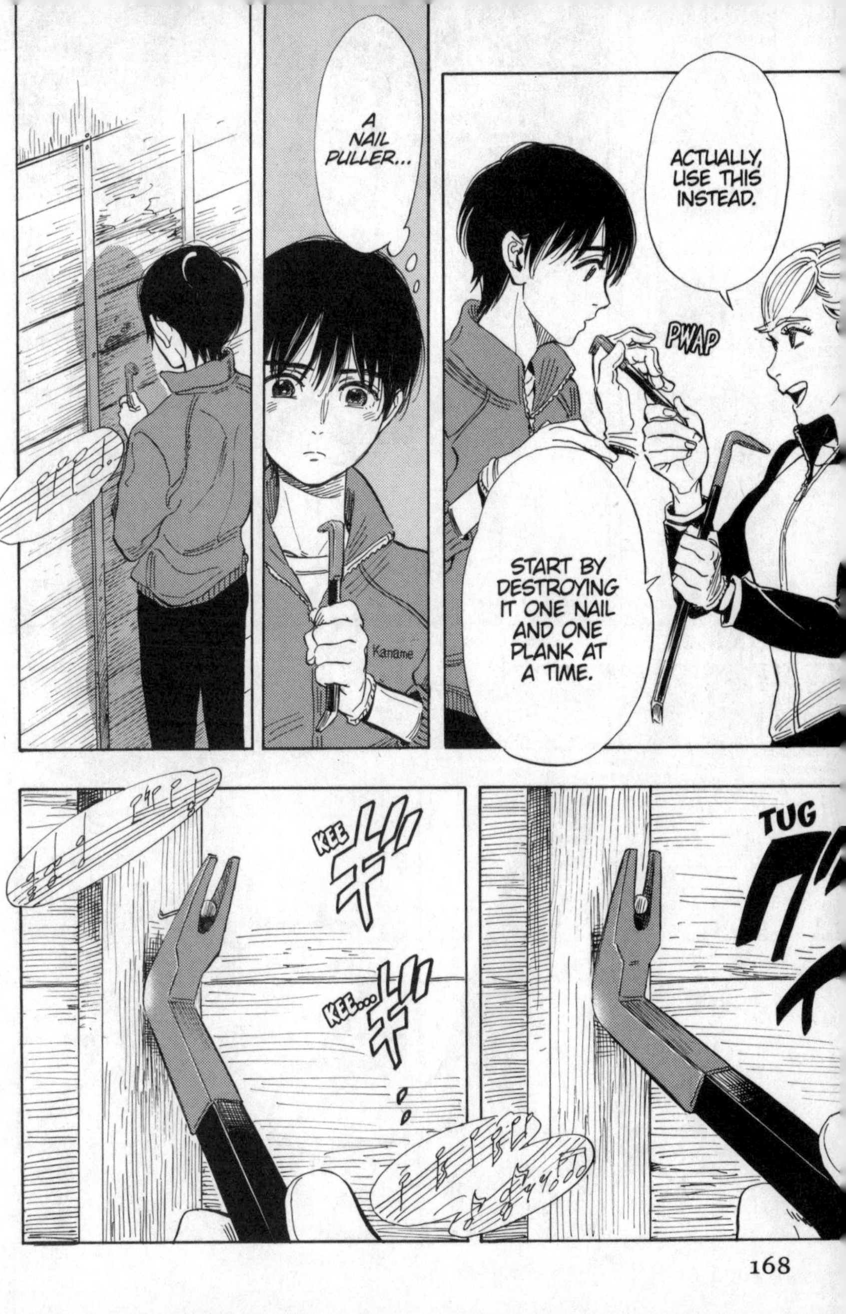
ACTUALLY, USE THIS INSTEAD.
PWAP
START BY DESTROYING IT ONE NAIL AND ONE PLANK AT A TIME.
A NAIL PULLER...
Kaname
TUG
KEE
KEE...

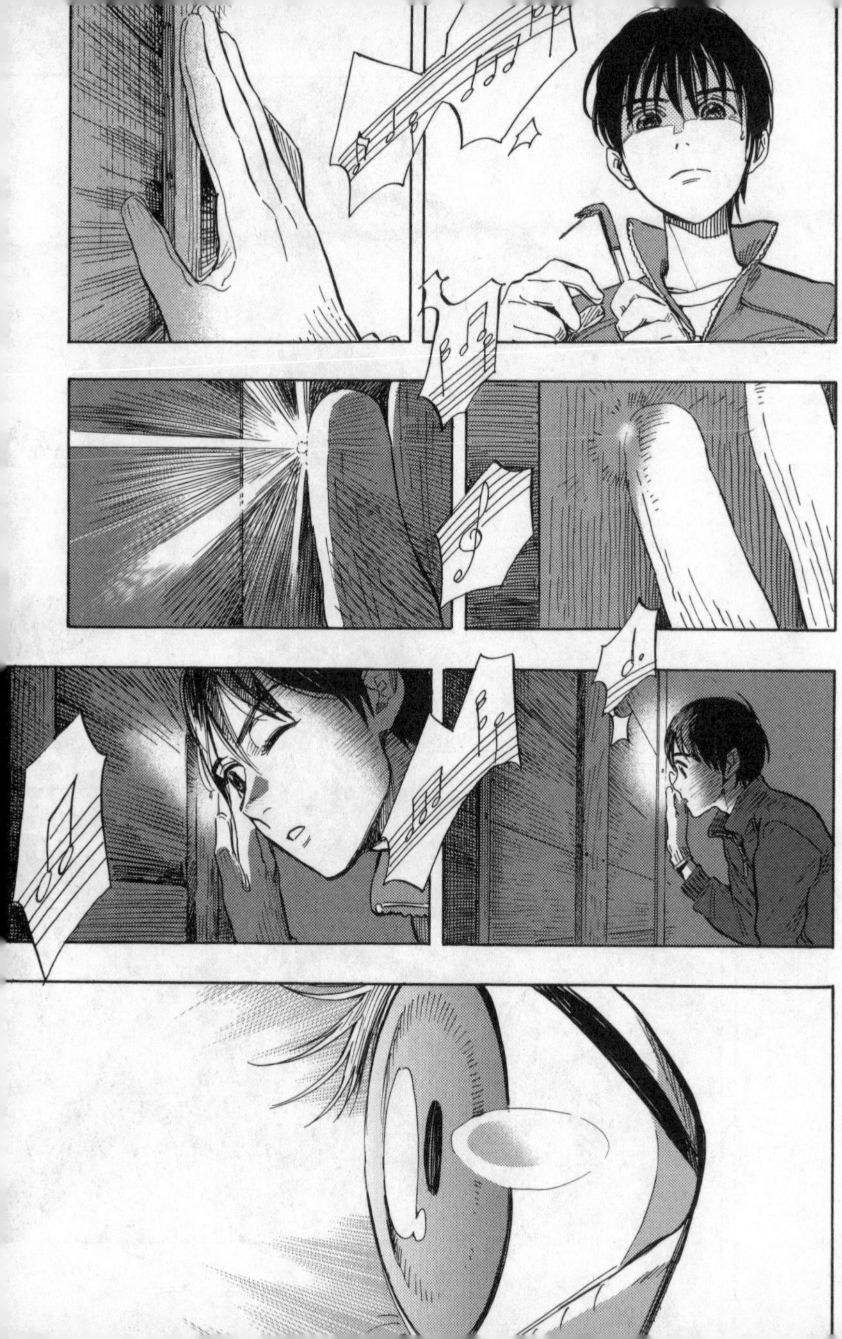

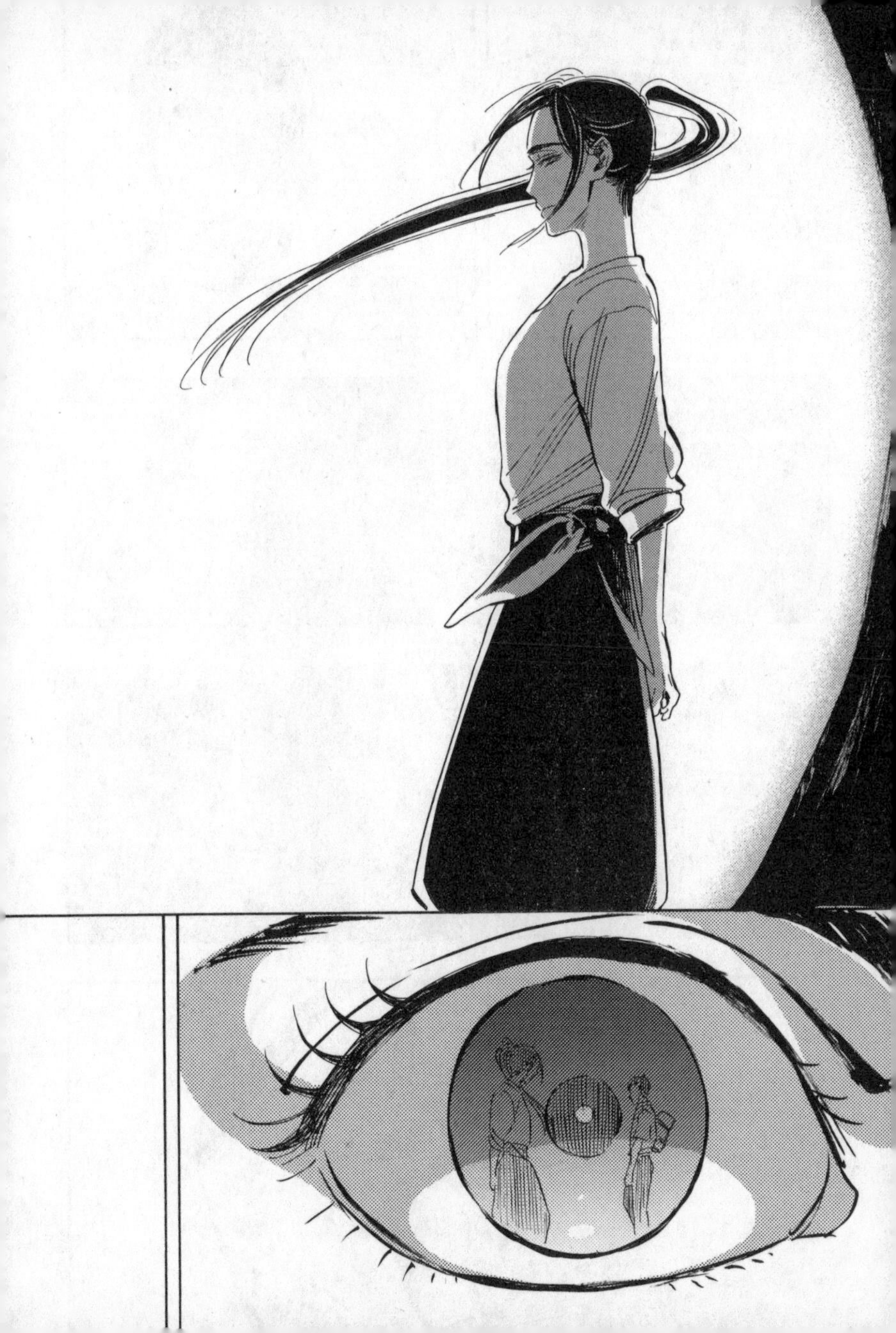

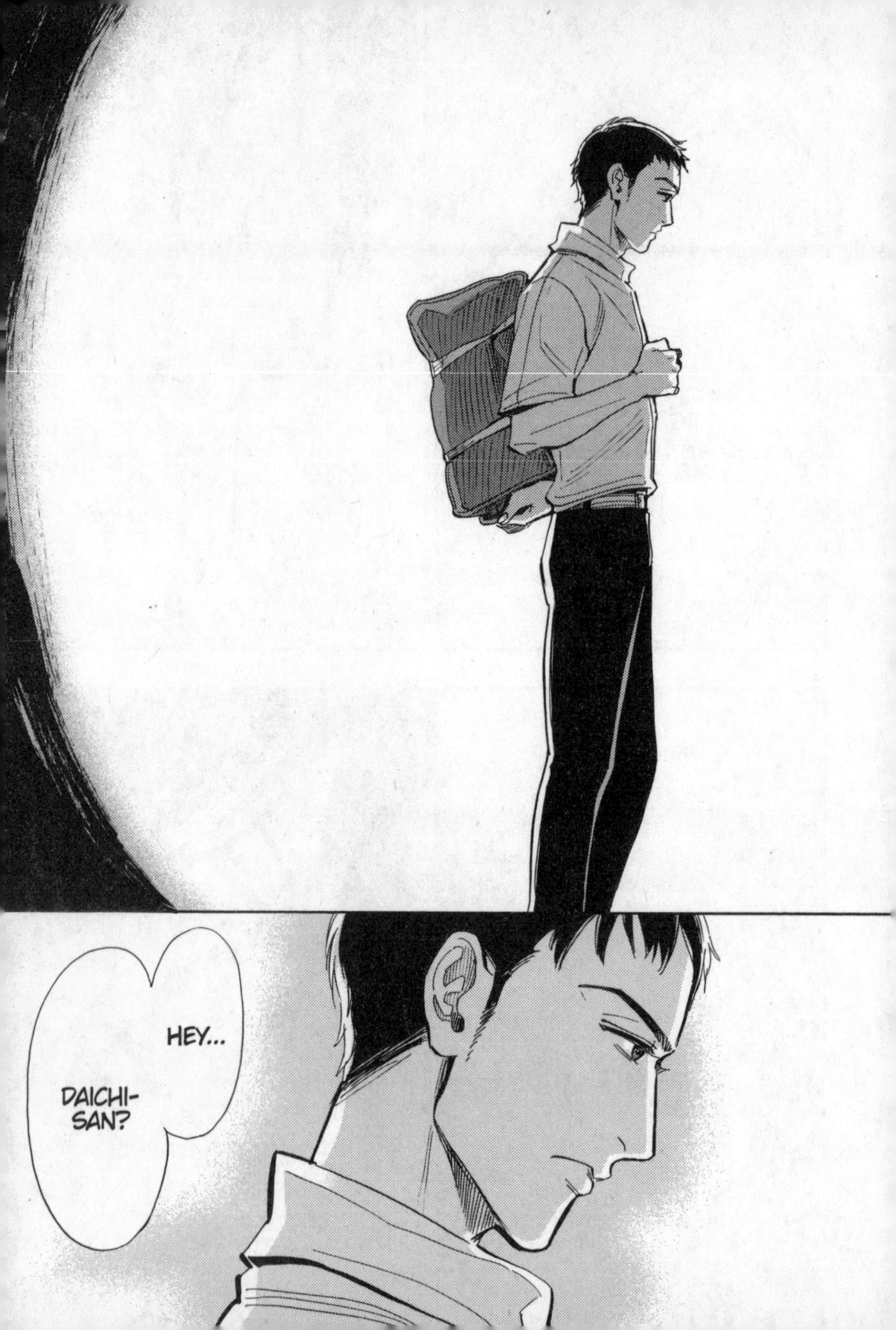
HEY...
DAICHI-SAN?

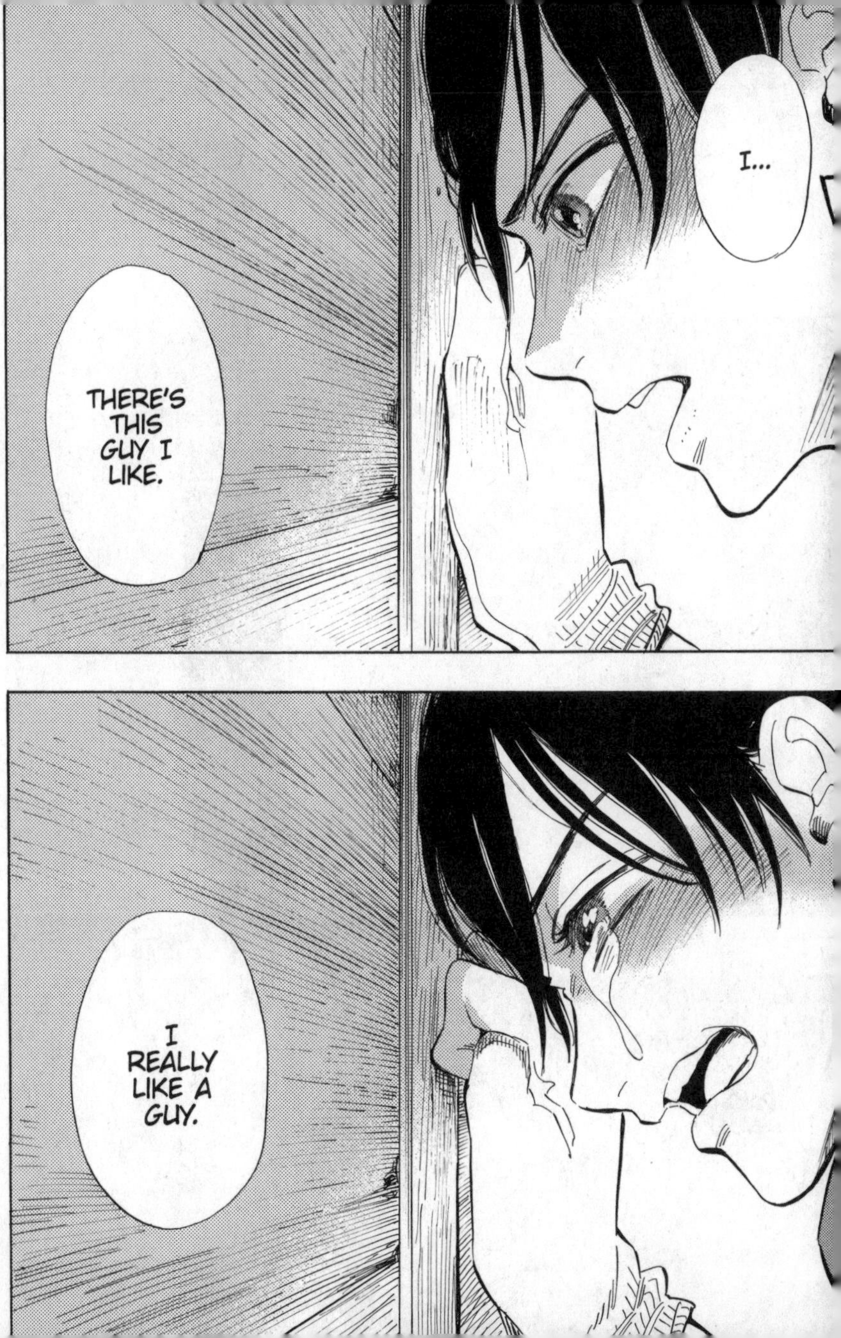
I...
THERE'S THIS GUY I LIKE.
I REALLY LIKE A GUY.

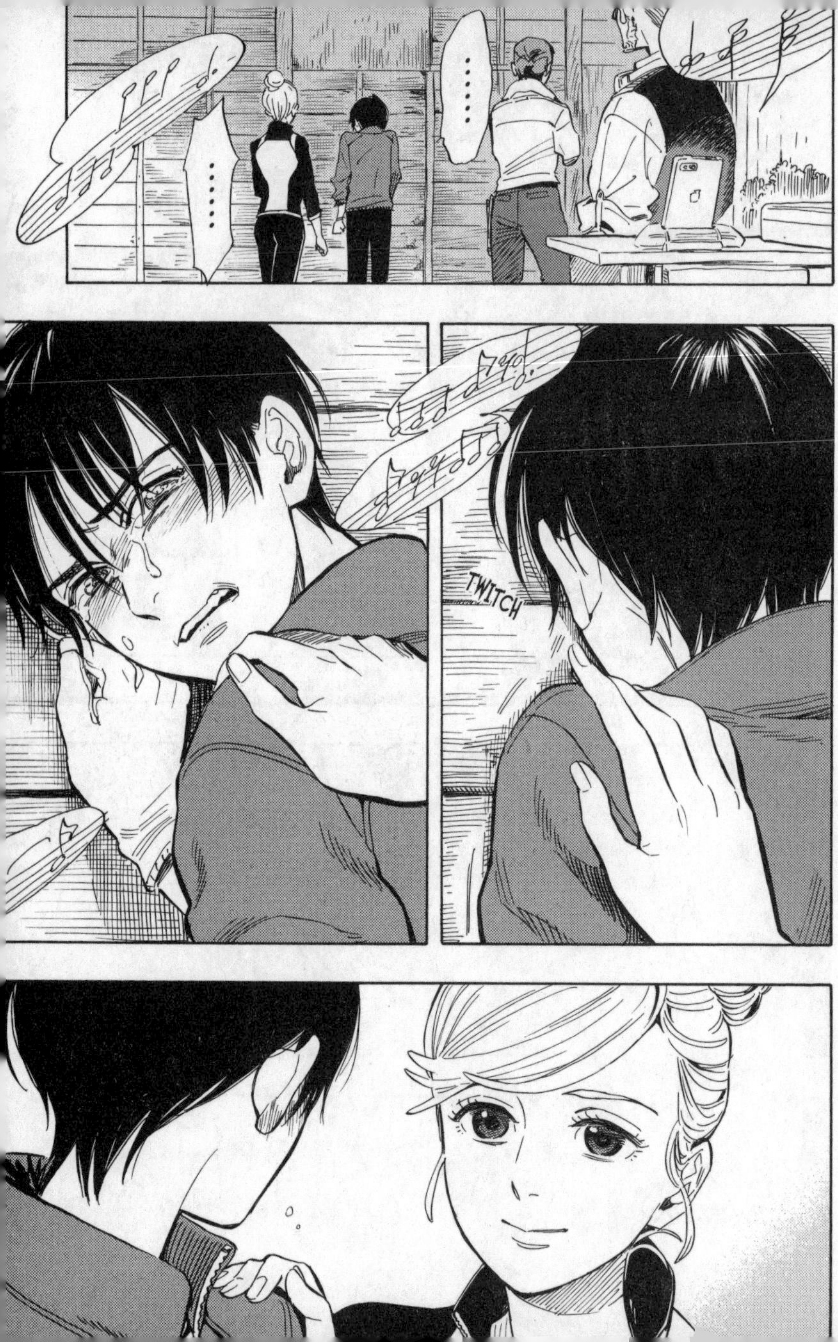
......
......
TWITCH

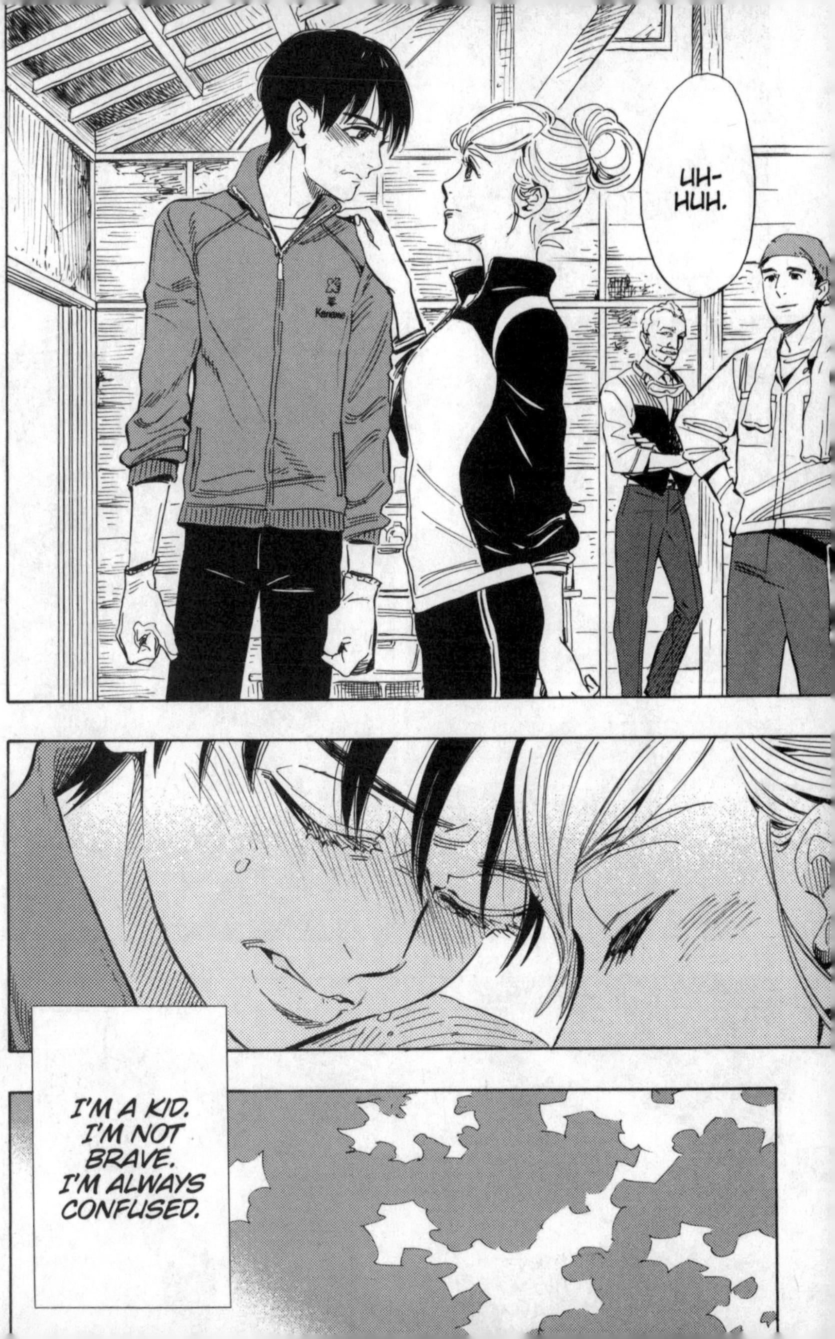
UH-HUH.
I'M A KID. I'M NOT BRAVE. I'M ALWAYS CONFUSED.

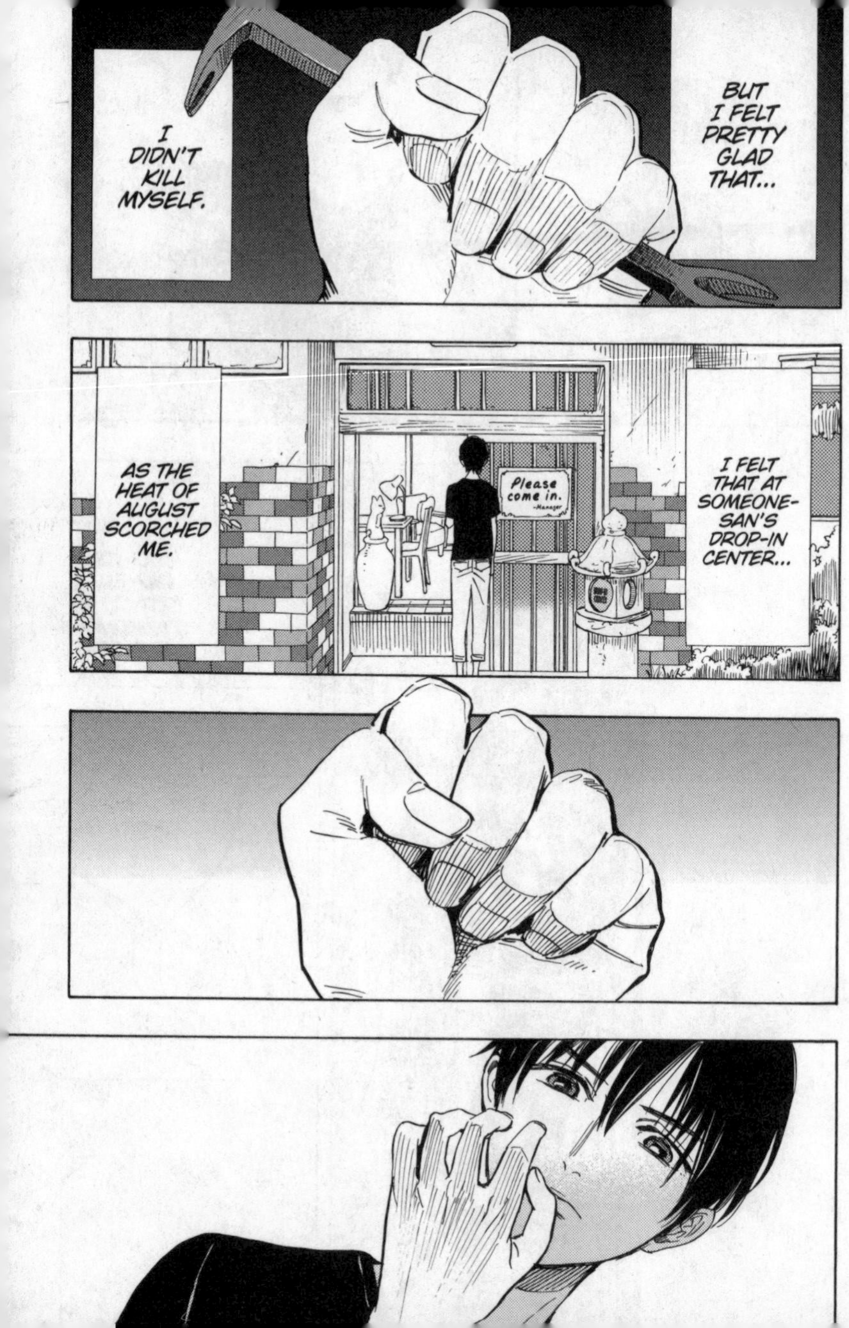
BUT I FELT PRETTY GLAD THAT...
I DIDN'T KILL MYSELF.
I FELT THAT AT SOMEONE-SAN'S DROP-IN CENTER...
Please come in. -Manager
AS THE HEAT OF AUGUST SCORCHED ME.

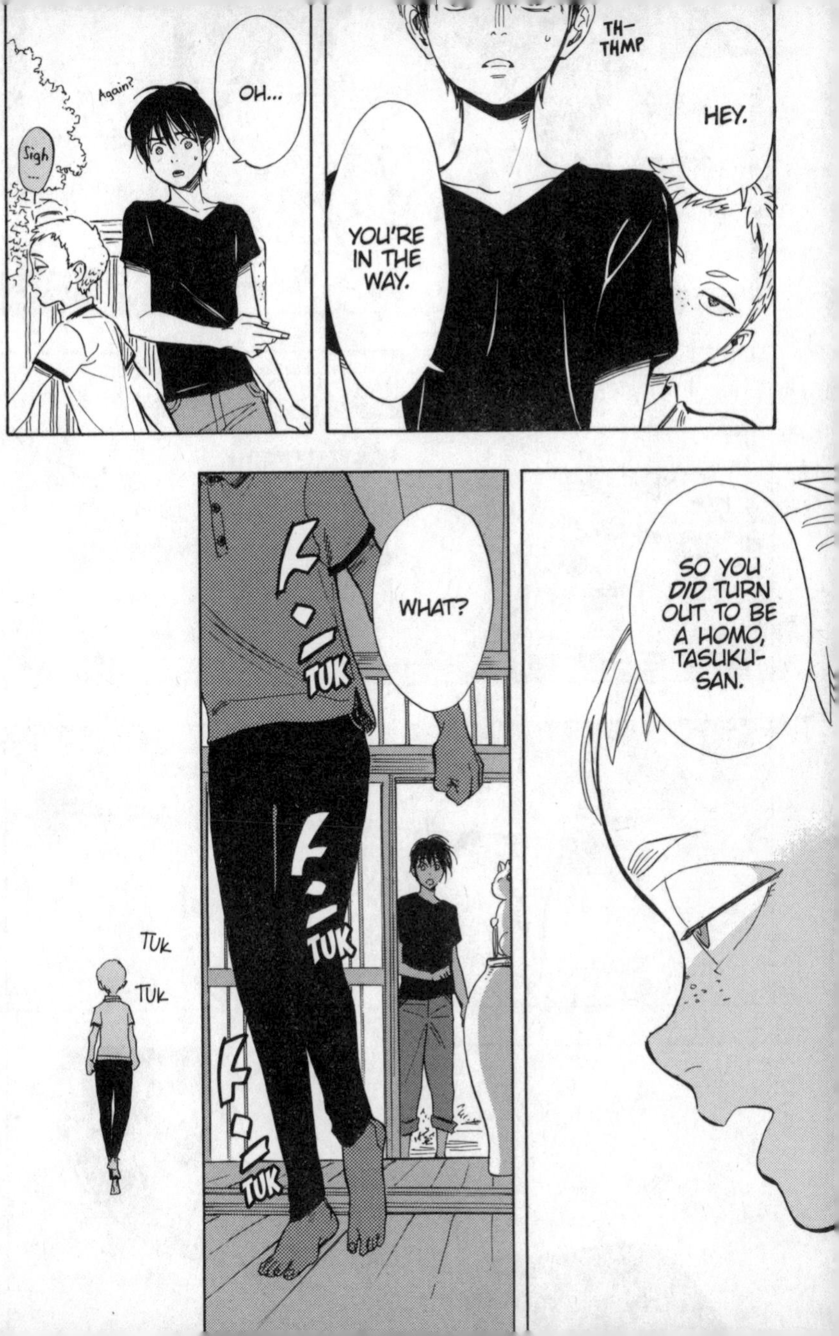
HEY.
TH-THMP
YOU'RE IN THE WAY.
OH...
Again?
Sigh...
SO YOU *DID* TURN OUT TO BE A HOMO, TASUKU-SAN.
WHAT?
TUK
TUK
TUK
TUK
TUK

[Research Assistance]

NPO Onomichi Akiya Saisei Project
Masako Toyota

Trois Couleurs Co., Ltd.
Hiroko Masahara
Koyuki Higashi

Kentaro Tsuru
Mizuki Kunigi

SHIMANAMI TASOGARE

Our Dreams at Dusk (1) end

SEVEN SEAS ENTERTAINM[...]

Our Dreams at Dusk

S H I M A N A M I **TASOGARE** — story and art by YUHKI KAMATANI — VOL. 1

TRANSLATION
Jocelyne Allen

ADAPTATION
Ysabet MacFarlane

LETTERING AND RETOUCH
Kaitlyn Wiley

COVER DESIGN
KC Fabellon

ORIGINAL EDITION DESIGNER
Hiroshi NIIGAMI (NARTI ; S)

PROOFREADER
Kurestin Armada
Danielle King

EDITOR
Jenn Grunigen

PRODUCTION MANAGER
Lissa Pattillo

EDITOR-IN-CHIEF
Adam Arnold

PUBLISHER
Jason DeAngelis

SHIMANAMI TASOGARE Vol. 1 by Yuhki KAMATANI
© 2015 Yuhki KAMATANI
All rights reserved.
Original Japanese edition published by SHOGAKUKAN.
English translation rights in the United States of America, Canada, and the
United Kingdom arranged with SHOGAKUKAN through Tuttle-Mori Agency, Inc.

Seven Seas press and purchase enquiries can be sent to Marketing Manager
Lianne Sentar at press@gomanga.com. Information regarding the distribution
and purchase of digital editions is available from Digital Manager CK Russell
at digital@gomanga.com.

Seven Seas and the Seven Seas logo are trademarks of
Seven Seas Entertainment. All rights reserved.

ISBN: 978-1-64275-060-7

Printed in Canada

First Printing: May 2019

FOLLOW US ONLINE: www[...]

READING DIRECTIONS

This book reads from *right to left*, Japanese style.
If this is your first time reading manga, you start
reading from the top right panel on each page and
take it from there. If you get lost, just follow the
numbered diagram here. It may seem backwards at
first, but you'll get the hang of it! Have fun!!

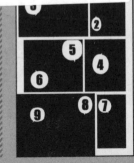